THE UNION *vs.* DR. MUDD

*GARRET=
ENJOY THIS STORY
OF THE NON
AUTORACING
MUDD!*

[signature] 21/100

UNIVERSITY PRESS OF FLORIDA

Florida A&M University, Tallahassee
Florida Atlantic University, Boca Raton
Florida Gulf Coast University, Ft. Myers
Florida International University, Miami
Florida State University, Tallahassee
New College of Florida, Sarasota
University of Central Florida, Orlando
University of Florida, Gainesville
University of North Florida, Jacksonville
University of South Florida, Tampa
University of West Florida, Pensacola

(Richard D. Mudd)

DR. SAMUEL A. MUDD

THE UNION
→ VS. ←
DR. MUDD

EXPANDED EDITION

🖋 **HAL HIGDON** 🖋

University Press of Florida
Gainesville/Tallahassee/Tampa/Boca Raton
Pensacola/Orlando/Miami/Jacksonville/Ft. Myers/Sarasota

Copyright 2008 by Hal Higdon
First cloth printing 1964 by Follet
First paperback printing 2008 by University Press of Florida
Printed in the United States of America on acid-free paper
All rights reserved

13 12 11 10 09 08   6 5 4 3 2 1

A record of cataloging-in-publication data is available from the
Library of Congress.
ISBN 978-0-8130-3267-2

The University Press of Florida is the scholarly publishing agency
for the State University System of Florida, comprising Florida
A&M University, Florida Atlantic University, Florida Gulf Coast
University, Florida International University, Florida State University, New College of Florida, University of Central Florida,
University of Florida, University of North Florida, University of
South Florida, and University of West Florida.

University Press of Florida
15 Northwest 15th Street
Gainesville, FL 32611-2079
http://www.upf.com

For Hig

CONTENTS

List of Illustrations	viii
Preface	ix
Introduction to Expanded Edition	xi

Part One. Thirteen Days in April

Chapter 1	3
Chapter 2	15
Chapter 3	26
Chapter 4	39
Chapter 5	57

Part Two. In the Footsteps of Poor Old Pilate

Chapter 6	67
Chapter 7	80
Chapter 8	94
Chapter 9	108
Chapter 10	127

Part Three. Somebody Had to Suffer

Chapter 11	139
Chapter 12	146
Chapter 13	156
Chapter 14	165
Chapter 15	175
Chapter 16	187
Chapter 17	195
Chapter 18	205
Epilogue	215
Conclusion to Expanded Edition: A Final Word	220
Original Bibliography	225
Updated Bibliography	227
Index	229

LIST OF ILLUSTRATIONS

Frontispiece (Dr. Samuel A. Mudd)   Facing title page
Plates   All plates follow page 112

The Lincoln Conspirators	1
Exterior of Mudd farmhouse	2
The Mudd guest room	3
Sarah Frances Dyer Mudd	4
The flight of John Wilkes Booth (map)	5
Gate leading to Mudd farmhouse	6
John Wilkes Booth	7
The monitor *Saugus*	8
Alleged conspirators being led to Old Capitol Prison	9
Judges at the Conspiracy Trial	10
Judge Advocate General Joseph Holt	11
Thomas Ewing, Jr.	12
Dr. Mudd—Sketch by Major General Lew Wallace	13
Accused prisoner, hooded and chained	14
Convicted conspirators being readied on the gallows	15
Conspirators hanged	16
Aerial view of Fort Jefferson	17
Colonel George St. Leger Grenfell	18
Dr. Mudd at Fort Jefferson	19
Bastion for state prisoners	20
Dr. Mudd's cell	21
View of Fort Jefferson parade field, showing lighthouse	22
Artist's conception of Dr. Mudd's attempt to escape	23
Moat of Fort Jefferson, showing sallyport	24

AUTHOR'S PREFACE

Perhaps more words have been written about the assassination of Abraham Lincoln than about any other incident in the Civil War. At least one widely read book, Jim Bishop's *The Day Lincoln Was Shot*, detailed the events of Lincoln's death. Dozens of volumes relating to John Wilkes Booth's infamous deed crowd library shelves. For the past ninety-nine years, scholars have picked over the events of the conspiracy plot until one would suspect that nothing is left untold. Yet thus far, one prominent person who figured in the nineteenth century's most famous crime has resisted definition. Millions know of Dr. Samuel A. Mudd, the doctor who set Booth's broken leg. Few know him well. And nobody has ever said with authority whether or not Mudd actually conspired with Booth and, most important, if the doctor deserved his fate. *The Union vs. Dr. Mudd* seeks to answer these questions.

In researching this book I have attempted to utilize all the skills of the scholar in uncovering pertinent information. Yet in writing it I have tried not to let the mechanics of scholarship interfere with the smooth flow of narrative. Thus I have incorporated the sources of materials within the text itself. I have done so deliberately to avoid the use of footnotes that often distract attention precisely when dramatic interest is mounting.

For those who want more information on Dr. Mudd and the Lincoln conspirators, I have provided a working bibliography at the back of the volume. This bibliography represents only the chief and the most important sources used in my studies. Any inquiry into the Lincoln conspiracy actually must begin with three basic volumes: Osborne H. Oldroyd's *The Assassination of Abraham*

A large share of the material on Booth and the conspiracy was gathered during my trip to Washington and in a study of Booth's escape route. After dealing through the mail for years with government organizations, I was pleasantly delighted with the politeness and courtesy of the staff of the National Archives. I met with equal courtesy at the Library of Congress, when I called there to examine Ewing's papers.

One of the best collections of Lincoln books was available, fortunately, at the University of Chicago library, not far from my home. I thank Sheldon Garber and Herman H. Fussler for providing access to the library's facilities and Nancy Bankier for assisting in many a search. Another debt of gratitude is due Richard E. Gosswiller, executive editor of *The Kiwanis Magazine*, especially for the title of this book, which he suggested.

I am indebted also to Carol Widrig and Marianne Burke for typing the manuscript, and to Ken Anderson, Arnold Leo, Lon Barton, and Esther Bourbules, for various kindnesses that made the completion of the manuscript possible. Finally, my thanks to my wife, Rose, and to my three children—Kevin, David, and Laura—for providing the special incentive to write a book.

INTRODUCTION

The tour boat skimmed across the waters of the Gulf of Mexico at a speed of 26 knots, nearly 30 miles per hour. At that speed, our trip would take just over two hours. We had left Key West earlier that morning, headed westward toward the Dry Tortugas, a collection of seven tiny coral islands so named in 1513 by Spanish explorer Ponce de León because of a large turtle (*tortugas*) population and lack of any drinkable water.

But turtles had not drawn me to the Dry Tortugas for what was my second visit. I wanted to see again Fort Jefferson, a mass of masonry, which first appeared on the horizon as a thin, brick red line, then began to dominate it as we drew nearer. The largest coastal fortress in the Western Hemisphere, Fort Jefferson is best remembered as an American Devil's Island, home after the Civil War for the victorious Union's most despised prisoners. This included Samuel A. Mudd, M.D., a doctor implicated in the conspiracy to assassinate President Abraham Lincoln. The Maryland doctor could not hide the fact that he knew assassin John Wilkes Booth but proclaimed his innocence of any crime. A vengeful federal government, specifically Secretary of War Edwin M. Stanton, refused to believe him. In a rush to justice, a military tribunal sentenced Dr. Mudd to life imprisonment, shipping him off the continent to Fort Jefferson to keep him out of reach of civilian lawyers trying to free him.

Fort Jefferson proved difficult to reach when I first saw it in 1963, while researching this book about its most famous prisoner. *The Union vs. Dr. Mudd* was my first book as a young author, and I wanted to absorb every last detail. This meant (my reportorial instincts told me) traveling to the Dry Tortugas to visit the fort, to walk its balustrades, to visit the clammy cell where Dr. Mudd had suffered.

So in 1963 I rented a car and drove from Miami to Key West expecting that I could find some way out to the fort by boat. But even though Fort Jefferson had been named a national monument in 1935, there was no easy way for historians, much less tourists, to access it. No catamarans bridged the distance at 26 knots. No guides from the National Park Service would be at the dock to greet me. It would take most of a day to get there, most of another day to get back. "Could I stay overnight?" I asked. Key West charter boat captains laughed when I even suggested it.

Not to be denied, but mostly as a symbolic gesture, I chartered a private plane to fly to the Dry Tortugas. With no place to land, we could do little but circle the fort two times, after which I told the pilot to return to Key West. Had I fulfilled my reportorial or historical obligations? Not too well, but a more serious visit to Fort Jefferson would have to await another age.

That age now has come. Although *The Union vs. Dr. Mudd* was a work of my past, and thirty-two more books on a variety of subjects followed, I still feel proud of that first book. When several years ago I learned that regularly scheduled ferries now allow easier access to Fort Jefferson, I vowed to visit.

Fort Jefferson might never match Yellowstone Park or Mount Vernon in number of visitors, but perhaps it need not. The mammoth brickwork merely needs to be itself: a military curiosity from which "a cannon ball never was fired in anger," so explained Jack Hackett, tour guide on the *Yankee Fleet*, which brought us from Key West. Indeed, our guide hinted, the fort owes much of its fame to the taciturn Maryland physician sent there in anger after President Lincoln's death, a death many believe he had nothing to do with.

Fort Jefferson was constructed beginning in 1846 to control traffic in the Florida Straits separating Key West and Cuba. After the Louisiana Purchase, the growing United States needed to protect its shipping routes between New Orleans and the Eastern seaboard. Occupying 12 of the 16 acres on Garden Key (Hackett informed our group of tourists), Fort Jefferson boasted 16 million bricks. Its gun ports could accommodate 450 straight-bore cannons capable of hurling iron balls three miles into the surrounding waters—or into the hull of an enemy ship. Merchant boats and vessels of war could moor beneath this protective umbrella confident that they could not be attacked. "Or so thought the fort's designers," Hackett suggested.

Alas, within a few decades after construction began, Fort Jefferson had become obsolete, a victim of improved technology. Warships with newly developed rifled cannons could sit safely beyond the three-mile umbrella and fire projectiles that could pierce the fort's walls and reduce it to rubble, as had been true during the siege of Fort Pulaski in 1862. A two-day bombardment with 5,300 shells reduced that fort at the mouth of the Savannah River to rubble. Although Union troops occupied Fort Jefferson at the beginning of the Civil War to prevent its falling into the hands of the Confederate Army, the fort and its defenders remained far removed from serious battles to the north.

Construction ceased by 1870, partly because of the fort's obsolescence, partly because yellow fever, endemic to the area, made living there risky. For most of the next century, Fort Jefferson remained largely inaccessible to tourists, who might have been attracted by its history or its wildlife. The Dry Tortugas islands were designated a wildlife refuge in 1908 to protect a sooty tern rookery from egg collectors, and Fort Jefferson became a national monument in 1935, but only a few government caretakers managed its vacant hulk.

In 1992, Fort Jefferson was granted status as a national park. Meanwhile, Dr. Mudd's heirs lobbied Congress to declare him innocent of complicity in the Lincoln assassination. The Mudd heirs' efforts proved only partly successful but attracted enough publicity to Fort Jefferson that in the year 2006, 64,122 tourists visited, according to park ranger Billy Strasser. Some came mainly to snorkel or fish, but others came to see what truly served as an architectural and historical wonder. Once there, they encountered the story of the Maryland doctor who had set the broken leg of John Wilkes Booth and nearly paid for it with his life.

Whether or not because of once having harbored Dr. Mudd and several other Lincoln conspirators, Fort Jefferson finally has emerged at the start of the twenty-first century as an intriguing tourist attraction. So finally did I find myself, accompanied by my wife, Rose, able to set foot on Garden Key and roam the vaulted chambers of Fort Jefferson, once prison for Dr. Mudd. In tour guide Jack Hackett we had more than an able leader. A whimsical man with a slouch hat, ruffled beard, and eyes that I know twinkled behind his sunglasses, he walked us through the fort, retelling its history from Ponce de León to present. He pointed out that the lower bricks were light red in color; the upper bricks, a darker red. "That's because the bricks first used were acquired from Southern states," explained Hackett. "Once the Civil War began, construction continued with bricks brought down from Danbury, Connecticut."

We climbed a circular stairway to a parapet overlooking a parade ground that could have swallowed a half dozen soccer fields. The parapet itself was six-tenths of a mile around, about a kilometer. I talked to several of the fort's rangers and learned some of them ran for recreation atop the parapet; five laps being the same distance as you would cover in a 5-K race. They knew my name, not merely as the young historian who had written about Dr. Mudd but as an author who later in life also wrote for *Runner's World*, my most successful work not historical but rather *Marathon: The Ultimate Training Guide*. I figure that more than a quarter million runners have used that book and my online programs to train for marathons. So do our lives suddenly shift in unusual directions. Ironically, that might describe what happened to the life of the physician who set the broken leg of John Wilkes Booth.

After a brief tour of the fort, we paused for a picnic lunch. Many from the tour boat then headed for the beach or to cross the short sand bridge to Bush Key to do some birding. Among the birds seen regularly at Fort Jefferson are black-bellied plovers, cormorants, sooty terns (which nest there in spring), brown noddies, and frigate birds. Of course, I had another mission. Warned of my coming, ranger Erin Kendrick had promised me a tour of Dr. Mudd's cell, that end of the island being temporarily off limits to most park visitors because of efforts to remove two fishing boats that recently had gone aground during a storm. As we passed beneath vaulted ceilings, I could not help but be reminded of Rome's Coliseum, which also had its dark side. Kendrick indicated one chamber, where they suspected Mudd might have been held early during his stay, then brought us to another identified by sign as "Dr. Mudd's cell."

"The evidence is clearer here," Kendrick explained, pointing to a bowl-like depression carved out of the concrete floor. "In his letters home, Dr. Mudd describes digging such a bowl to collect rain water for drinking."

I had read those same letters, collected by his daughter, Nettie Mudd, in a privately published book: *The Life of Dr. Samuel A. Mudd*. Writing home, Dr. Mudd described the yellow fever epidemic that hit the fort in 1867, causing 350 men (prisoners and jailers) to fall ill. Many died, including the fort's physician, Dr. James Smith. Dr. Mudd was pressed into service ministering to the ill. At that time, physicians believed yellow fever was spread through noxious fumes, such as those rising from the fort's rancid moat. We now know that the disease is spread through the bite of specific mosquitoes. Eliminate the mosquitoes, and you eliminate yellow fever, though to this day no cure exists for the disease.

Dr. Mudd's family used his humanitarian efforts during the yellow fever epidemic as reason to petition President Andrew Johnson for mercy. Coming from Tennessee, however, President Johnson feared appearing overly sympathetic to the defeated Confederacy. Johnson narrowly avoided impeachment by members in Congress who suspected him of complicity in the Lincoln assassination. President Johnson pardoned Dr. Samuel A. Mudd as one of his last acts in office on February 8, 1869.

Dr. Mudd returned home to Maryland. He would die in 1883 at age 49, never having quite overcome the suspicion that he knew John Wilkes Booth better than he wanted to admit. "His name was mud," seems to be an expression owed to Dr. Mudd, but lexicographical evidence suggests that the phrase dates back to 1840, or earlier.

It was during my discussions with the park rangers that I began to consider the fact that in the four decades since publication of *The Union vs. Dr. Mudd*, what we know about the man in that title has not changed perceptibly despite numerous attempts by book authors to spin the conspiracy in different directions. After shooting President Abraham Lincoln at Ford's Theatre in Washington on the night of April 14, 1865, assassin John Wilkes Booth leaped from Lincoln's box to the stage, breaking his leg. Booth limped out of the theatre and lunged onto a waiting horse, fleeing south through Maryland, hoping to escape to Richmond, Virginia, perhaps to be proclaimed a hero.

In the early hours of the next morning, Booth stopped at the farmhouse of the physician he apparently had met on at least two previous occasions. Dr. Mudd set Booth's broken leg, and the assassin continued his escape. But did Dr. Mudd know then of the actor's crime and, more important: did he conspire with Booth in planning it? Some historians insist he did; others disagree. "There will always be a question," conceded his great-grandson Thomas Boarman Mudd, when I talked with him recently.

That question is the one I sought to answer when I first set out to write this book, nearly a half century ago. Thanks to the University Press of Florida, publishers of this reprint edition, you can come to your own conclusion. Let me introduce you in the following pages to Dr. Samuel A. Mudd.

I. *Thirteen Days in April*

Chapter 1

IT WAS EARLY in the morning, Saturday, April 15, 1865. This most fateful day in the life of Dr. Samuel Alexander Mudd began at 4:00 A.M. with a pounding on the door of his farmhouse. Dr. Mudd, startled from his sleep, asked his wife to see who was knocking. "I'm not feeling too well," he grumbled.

"I would rather you go see for yourself," she said.

The pounding came a second time, and a third time. Dr. Mudd arose and, still in his night clothes, went out to the front door. "Who's there?" he called.

"We're on the way to Washington," came the muffled reply. "My partner had an accident. We've got to see the doctor."

Sam Mudd was a doctor by choice but a farmer by necessity. His father, Henry Lowe Mudd, a prominent landowner in the area around Bryantown, Maryland, had given Sam a 218-acre farm after his graduation from medical school. At first, the young physician had run the farm with the aid of eleven slaves. But after the Emancipation Proclamation in 1863, which freed the slaves in the secessionist states, Maryland, too, had outlawed slavery within her own boundaries. Now, in the days after the close of the Civil War, Sam Mudd's work force was reduced to two men: Frank Washington, a Negro, and John Best, an Englishman. Sam's medical practice had run down as he devoted his energies to the cultivation of his tobacco crop. To be awakened at four o'clock in the morning might be an ordinary occurrence for a doctor, but the thirty-one-year-old Sam Mudd was now principally a farmer.

"What sort of accident?" asked Mudd, opening the door.

"My friend was thrown from his horse," said the short man who was standing in the doorway. "He may have broken his leg."

3

That man, Dr. Mudd would later claim, called himself Henston. Mudd's wife remembered the name as Tyson. His real name was David E. Herold. He had dark hair and a smooth complexion. He was wearing a dark business suit. Mudd later said that the stranger who had called himself Henston seemed about seventeen or eighteen years old. David Herold actually was twenty-three.

Herold had tied his horse, a roan, to a tree. Nearby, the other stranger sat slumped on a bay horse, half-hidden in the early-morning darkness, his head bent forward, obviously in pain. He must have seemed a forbidding figure, since he was dressed all in black. His boots were spattered with mud. A hat pulled down over his forehead, a cloak thrown over his shoulders, and graying whiskers all but obscured his features. Dr. Sam Mudd, who later would be called upon to tell over and over again the details of this day, remembered that the second man had been called Tyser —or perhaps it had been Tyson, the name by which Mudd's wife knew Herold. To complicate matters further, Mrs. Mudd would remember this second man as Tyler. No matter. The dark figure on horseback was the twenty-six-year-old John Wilkes Booth: actor, lover, oil speculator, and, as of six hours before, assassin. Booth had just shot President Abraham Lincoln.

Mudd the farmer now acted as a physician. With Herold steadying Booth's horse, Dr. Mudd helped the actor down from the saddle. Booth winced as his left leg scraped the ground. "Lean on me," said Sam Mudd. He led the actor inside and eased him onto a sofa in the front room.

Herold remained outside, holding the horse's reins. "This horse won't stand without tying," he explained when Mudd returned. There followed one of those embarrassing moments of silence when everyone tries to think of a complicated solution to a simple problem.

"We'll put both horses in the stable," Mudd finally said. He whistled for Frank Washington, his farmhand, and the Negro came to lead the horses away.

Mudd and Herold moved into the house with Herold offering explanations. One of the horses had stumbled in a hole in the road, chattered Herold. The horse had fallen on his friend's left leg. He supposed the leg was broken. They had met a lady and a gentleman walking near Bryantown. They had inquired about a doctor. Then, a little farther up the road they had met a Negro. He had pointed the way to the Doctor's house.

If Mudd thought that that much traffic at this time of morning was unusual, he did not say so. He turned to the bearded man who was now lying on the sofa: "Does it hurt?"

Booth nodded.

"Show me where."

The actor pointed to the outside of his left leg, a few inches above the ankle.

Mudd only grunted. He disappeared into the bedroom and asked his wife to tear strips of cloth for bandages. Then he returned to the front room. Herold, talking again, said they were in a hurry. Perhaps if the Doctor could set the leg and fix a splint, they could be on their way. They would have another doctor examine the leg later. Booth slumped on the sofa, his face ashen.

"I can't work on him here," said Mudd, ignoring Herold's pleas. "We'll move him upstairs to the guest room, where he'll be more comfortable."

The guest room had two beds. Mudd and Herold lifted Booth to the bed near the wall. Mudd placed his hand on the long riding boot on Booth's left foot. As he gave a slight tug, Booth shouted in agony. "We'll have to cut the boot," said the doctor.

Dr. Mudd took a pair of scissors from his medical kit. Operating swiftly, he snipped the leather down the front and peeled the boot from the swollen foot. He carelessly tossed the boot under the bed.

Now Mudd discovered that Booth's leg was indeed broken. "There's a straight fracture of the fibula about two inches above the ankle," he announced to no one in particular.

Thirty miles to the north, in Washington, D.C., a group of doctors hovered around a patient in a much more serious condition. Surgeon General Joseph K. Barnes sat at the head of a bed in a rooming house across the street from Ford's Theater. On one side of the bed sat Dr. Robert K. Stone, Abraham Lincoln's personal physician. On the other side of the bed sat Dr. Charles Leale, twenty-three years old, who while attending a play at Ford's Theater had suddenly found himself a participant in a real-life drama. Now Leale held the hand of America's sixteenth President. Lincoln was slowly dying. His breaths came in rumbling gasps. His pulse flickered. A bullet had entered his head just below the left ear and had ground its way through bone and tissue to rest behind the President's right eye. That eye was now blackened. Lincoln had not seen his assailant. Nor had he regained consciousness since that moment six hours before when, during the third act of the play, *Our American Cousin*, a man dressed in black had quietly entered Lincoln's box and shot him in the head.

"Sic Semper Tyrannis," John Wilkes Booth spat out: "ever thus to tyrants," the motto of the State of Virginia. The brief epitaph went unheard by the audience, which was roaring with laughter at a funny line spoken by Harry Hawk, the only actor then standing on stage. But Major Henry Rathbone, a guest in the President's box, heard and understood. At the sound of the shot he leaped to his feet to struggle with Booth. Mrs. Lincoln, momentarily stunned by the sudden noise, did not realize her husband had been shot. Booth let his single-shot pistol drop to the floor, drew a knife, and slashed catlike at the major's arm. The major recoiled, then lunged again as the assailant climbed over the railing of the box. Booth started to drop to the stage eleven feet below. But in leaping, his spur hooked the flag hanging from the box. The flag ripped, and Booth fell like a sack of potatoes, landing off balance on his left leg. There was a sharp snap; a bone breaking. The audience did not immediately react. Many in their seats at first probably thought the man jumping out of the balcony box to be part of the play.

Within an instant Booth had risen, had half-run, half-hobbled across the stage past the startled Harry Hawk and out the back door to a waiting mount. Booth, after mortally wounding the President of the United States, had successfully escaped. But he had suffered a broken leg, which, before sunrise, would bring him in agony to the front door of Dr. Samuel A. Mudd's farmhouse. Mudd's farmhouse did not appear on Booth's planned escape route—at least, so it would seem. For more than six months, the Southern-sympathizing Booth had been planning, first, the abduction, and later, the assassination, of President Lincoln. At first he had plotted with others only to kidnap Lincoln and to spirit him to Richmond, Virginia, where he could be ransomed for much-needed Confederate troops. However, as the hopes of the Confederacy waned in early 1865, so did Booth's plans of abduction. After the second of April, no government remained to which Booth could present a captive President. Lincoln had visited Richmond on April 4, but as conqueror, not as kidnap victim. What had begun as a plot of redemption now became a plot of revenge. Booth and his fellow conspirators would now not only kill Lincoln, they would also strike down other Union leaders: Vice President Andrew Johnson, Secretary of State William H. Seward, and perhaps also General Ulysses S. Grant. Following this quick thrust at the heart of the United States government, Booth and his henchmen would flee south through Lower Maryland toward Port Tobacco, a Potomac River town. Booth had scouted this escape route thoroughly in the fall of 1864. With strong horses the conspirators could reach Port Tobacco before sunrise and be on their way across the river to friendly Rebel territory before Federal troops could awaken and establish road blocks. Booth guessed right in this instance. It would be many hours before the government would recover from the suddenness of the attack and send troops in pursuit of the assassin. However, much of Booth's well-knit plan came undone.

First, although newspapers announced his attendance, Grant decided not to go to the play with Lincoln. Lewis Paine, sent with Herold to Seward's home, succeeded only in severely wounding Seward. George Atzerodt, whose assignment was to kill Johnson, lost his nerve and, half-drunk, wandered out of town. Even though the conspirators scattered their shots wildly, the main target, the President, was hit. Booth faltered only in his attempt to escape. Instead of darting quickly toward the river, the injured man had to detour ten miles off his planned escape route to seek medical aid.

At almost the same time that Mudd was admitting his unexpected guests, a troop of Federal cavalry, headed by Lieutenant David D. Dana, younger brother of the Assistant Secretary of War, Charles A. Dana, galloped out of Washington. Dana's cavalry thundered across the Navy Yard bridge, the same span crossed earlier by Booth, and turned their horses in the direction of Piscataway, a village a dozen or so miles south of the capital. The young lieutenant had been ordered to patrol a triangular area including Piscataway, Accokeek, and Surrattsville. Mudd's farm did not lie within that triangle, but Dana later that day moved his troops on to Bryantown. At 4:44 A.M., on the morning of April 15, 1865, Secretary of War Edwin M. Stanton sent from Lincoln's sick room the first dispatch that actually acknowledged Booth as the assassin: "It is now ascertained with reasonable certainty that two assassins were engaged in the horrible crime, Wilkes Booth being the one that shot the President, the other a companion of his whose name is not known, but whose description is so clear that he can hardly escape."

The companion referred to in Stanton's dispatch was not, as one might imagine, David Herold. Stanton referred to Seward's assailant, whom he suspected to be John H. Surratt, but who actually was Lewis Paine. Herold was not yet known. At the precise moment that Stanton's dispatch clicked over telegraph wires throughout the country, Herold was on the second floor of Sam Mudd's house watching the doctor cut apart an old bandbox to make a splint for Booth's leg. Mudd finished his task and went downstairs.

By his own account, Dr. Mudd then worked in the yard with his two farmhands. According to his wife, he returned to bed. The detail is not important, but it is not the only inconsistency in the account given by the Mudds of that Saturday morning. By seven o'clock, breakfast sat steaming on the table and Dr. Mudd prepared to eat with his wife. According to the Mudds, they invited

Herold to join them. At breakfast, Herold talked continually despite his lack of sleep. He knew the region, having hunted in Lower Maryland many times. He mentioned many names—storeowner William Moore; E. D. R. Bean, who also kept a store in Bryantown; Len Roby, Rufus Roby, and Major James Thomas, Sr. He knew Parson Wilmer, who lived in a place called Piney Church. He said he and his companion would like to visit Wilmer. At one point Herold inquired the way from Mudd's place to Bryantown, although he had represented himself earlier in the morning as having come *from* Bryantown. But Mudd's suspicions apparently had not yet been roused. Eventually (so he would later claim) the specter of doubt would rise within his mind concerning the integrity of the two strangers. Meanwhile, the talk at breakfast became light.

"Are you a resident of this country?" asked Mrs. Mudd.

"No, ma'am," replied Herold, "but I have been frolicking around for five or six months."

"All play and no work makes Jack a bad boy."

"My father is dead, and I am ahead of the old lady."

After breakfast, Herold began to make new inquiries: "What is the distance to the river?"

"About eighteen or twenty miles," the doctor answered.

"We would like to go to Parson Wilmer's," Herold said again. "What is the nearest road we could take?"

Mudd moved outside with his guest and pointed in the direction of the Zekiah Swamp. There were two ways, he explained. One was by the public road leading by Beantown. The other led across the swamp, by which they could save a mile. The road through the swamp started directly opposite Mudd's house and followed a straight line. It was not a public way, but by taking down a fence they could get through. Mudd and Herold then went inside and up to Booth's room. The doctor quickly examined his patient and returned downstairs. Herold remained above to sleep.

Before Mudd left for the tobacco fields, where he would work until noon, Herold came downstairs. Would the Doctor loan them a razor? Perhaps his friend would feel better if he had the opportunity to shave. Mudd gave Herold a shaving kit. That afternoon Mudd would discover to his surprise that his patient's mustache had been shaved off. The beard, Dr. Mudd subsequently stated, was still intact.

Was it possible for Dr. Mudd *not* to become suspicious of such unusual events: strangers traveling at four in the morning; the sudden removal of a man's mustache, easily to be interpreted as an attempt at disguise? Perhaps Mudd had reasons to repress his suspicions, even to the point of concealing them from his wife. Or perhaps, in his country innocence, he truly suspected nothing at all.

Other motives might have caused Mudd to cloak his thoughts. Maryland, especially in the south, had been a slave state, and the doctor himself had been a slaveholder. The Federal government had moved rapidly, after the firing on Fort Sumter, to suppress secessionist sympathies, thereby instituting a semi-military rule that was not appreciated by the Marylanders. Lower Maryland—Union by name, but secessionist by inclination—had for four years been ridden with suspicious strangers, Confederate spies as well as Union counterspies. Things out of the ordinary had become quite the ordinary. If one harbored any suspicions, one soon learned to keep them to oneself.

Federal troops meanwhile began to close in on Booth. Lieutenant Dana arrived in Bryantown at about one o'clock the afternoon of the fifteenth, preceded by a guard of four men. News of the assassination, as well as the name of the assassin, spread through the village in a quarter of an hour.

Herold, perhaps anticipating pursuit, was anxious to leave. Could the Doctor fix crutches for his friend? With the assistance of the old Englishman, John Best, Mudd fashioned two crutches and ordered Frank Washington to take them upstairs. Herold had another request. Could the doctor find some sort of conveyance that his friend might ride in?

"I am going to Bryantown to get the mail and call on some sick," said Mudd. "If you will ride along with me, perhaps we can locate a carriage."

As the two were leaving on horseback, Mudd's wife asked if she might visit the sick man. "Yes, certainly," her husband replied. Mrs. Mudd placed cake, a few oranges, and a glass of wine on a tray and took it up to Booth's room. She found that he hadn't touched the breakfast tray she had sent up earlier. The actor's face was turned to the wall. Placing the tray on the table, she asked how he was feeling.

"My back hurts," Booth complained. "I must have wrenched it when the horse fell and broke my leg."

"Would you care for some cake and a little wine?"

"Do you have any brandy?"

"I can get you some good whiskey."

"No."

Mrs. Mudd began to withdraw. At the door she turned: "I guess you think I have very little hospitality. You have been sick all day, and I have not been up to see you." Booth did not reply. His face, she later said, remained turned to the wall throughout their conversation.

Dr. Mudd and Herold meanwhile talked with Mudd's father, who lived down the road. Henry Lowe Mudd owned several carriages, but only one could be used. No, you will not be able to borrow it, he said. He would need it to go to church the following day, Easter Sunday. Maybe Sam's friend would have better luck if he continued up the road to Bryantown.

Herold had no intention of going as far as Bryantown. Perhaps he realized that news of the assassination would by now be in town. They could not remain at the doctor's house much longer. Across the road from Mudd's farm, the thickly wooded Zekiah Swamp seemed to beckon. It was dark and largely untracked: an ideal hiding place. The Zekiah Swamp stretched all the way to the banks of the Potomac. From there, secessionist Virginia was within easy rowing distance.

Mudd arrived in Bryantown alone. Lieutenant Dana had by then established temporary headquarters at the local hotel. At some time between the hours of three and four o'clock, Dr. Mudd stopped at the general store of E. D. R. Bean and bought a few yards of calico. Bean, like everyone else in town, was talking about the assassination, but he believed that a man named Boyd (a renegade guerrilla known in the area) was the guilty one. "There's some very bad news, Sam," said Bean as the doctor entered his store.

"Yes," replied Mudd. "I am sorry to hear it."

There was considerable confusion in Bryantown over who had actually done the killing. There was doubt even in Washington. Though the well-known actor had been recognized by hundreds of the people in Ford's Theater who saw him leap from the President's box, the War Department had not acknowledged that Booth was the killer until far into the morning. Throughout the country the morning papers carried long stories on the assassination without a mention of Booth as the assassin. Thus the Boyd rumor would start. Some historians would later cite this as evidence that the War Department covered up for the President's killer. Whether true or not, by the end of the afternoon in Bryantown, Mudd knew that the name of Lincoln's assassin was Booth. Mudd returned home at a leisurely pace. At about five o'clock he stopped at the house of John Hardy, halfway between his own home and Bryantown, to inquire about some rail timber. Hardy greeted Mudd from outside his dwelling. Another man, Francis R. Farrell, was inside. Hardy talked with Mudd briefly and then yelled to Farrell: "The President has been assassinated!"

"Is that so?" said Farrell, coming out.

"Unfortunately so," said Mudd.

"Who did it?"

"A man named Booth."

Hardy asked the next question. "Sam, is that the same Booth that was down here last fall?"

"I don't know," replied Mudd. "There are three or four men by that name. I don't know which Booth was the assassin. If it was the same one who came here last fall, then I know him."

What Dr. Mudd meant was that he personally knew John Wilkes

Booth, but while some people in town named John Wilkes as the assassin, others pointed an accusing finger at the actor's equally famous brother, Edwin Booth. However, here was a surprising revelation. Dr. Mudd had previously met John Wilkes Booth. Why, then, had the doctor not recognized the man with the broken leg? Dr. Mudd's answer was simple: The injured stranger had a beard, whereas John Wilkes Booth never wore one. This was, indeed, a story to tax one's credence. How could an intelligent man, who was trained in the art of observation, be taken in by a false beard? Or, perhaps the false beard was Dr. Mudd's invention, for it seems equally unlikely that Booth would attempt such a disguise with a man whom he had met previously.

We can draw three portraits of Dr. Samuel A. Mudd at this point. One is Mudd, willing for some reason to help Booth, and who therefore journeys to town to scout the movements of Federal troops, aware that he harbors America's No. 1 fugitive from justice. Another is Mudd, the innocent and somewhat dull country doctor, who, having gone to town on business, returns home not knowing that the two strangers he had befriended might be dangerous. A third picture, somewhat fuzzier than the other two, is that of a pensive Mudd who learns in town of the terrible crime the two fugitives had committed and yet does not report them, but returns home slowly, trying to think out a plan of action. Perhaps he already feared that he might be caught in the toils, as it were, if he reported these men to the military.

But Booth would not stay much longer at Dr. Mudd's house. While Mudd was touring the stores of Bryantown, Herold had returned to the farmhouse. The front door was closed, so he tapped on the kitchen window. Mrs. Mudd and her servants were preparing Easter Sunday dinner. The doctor's wife let Herold in.

"Did you get a carriage?" she asked.

"No, ma'am," said Herold. "I decided to come back and try the horses."

Herold clomped upstairs to get Booth. The time had come to continue their escape, broken leg or not.

According to Mrs. Mudd, she was standing in the hall at the foot of the stairs when Herold helped Booth come down. Booth was using the crutch that Dr. Mudd had fashioned for him earlier in the day. At that point, the whiskers on his face slipped, and Mrs. Mudd realized that he was wearing a false beard.

Mrs. Mudd may have invented this episode to explain why she and her husband finally became suspicious of the two strangers. But if Booth actually was wearing false whiskers, the fact that Mrs. Mudd knew it lends further doubt to the idea that neither she nor her husband recognized Booth during his day at their home.

Mrs. Mudd later claimed that she did not comment on the false beard, but turned to Herold and said: "If you must go, do so. But if you want to, leave your friend here. We'll take care of him."

"If he suffers much we won't go far," said Herold. "I'll take him to my ladylove's not far from here."

They moved through the door. Herold boosted Booth onto the bay horse, then mounted the roan. Booth started down the road trying not to put too much weight on his left leg. Herold dallied briefly to thank Mrs. Mudd for her hospitality, then followed his friend down the path. Before he reached the road he encountered Dr. Mudd just returning from Bryantown. Herold, according to Dr. Mudd's later story, stopped to ask directions again, but Booth continued without a word. Herold pressed a roll of bills into the doctor's palm. The bills totaled twenty-five dollars—a generous fee for the time. Dr. Samuel A. Mudd described it later as "rather a trivial amount."

Chapter 2

WHEN JOHN WILKES BOOTH rode off toward Piney Church, it was the last time Dr. Mudd would see him alive. But the night before was not the first time the doctor had seen him. Despite Dr. Mudd's later claim that he did not recognize Booth the morning after the assassination, he had met the actor not once but *twice* before.

Their first meeting had taken place in November, 1864, at St. Mary's Roman Catholic Church, a handsome, red-brick structure that even today sits imposingly alone in an open meadow one mile south of Bryantown. Booth did not espouse Catholicism. He claimed to be Episcopalian, but was not above temporarily switching religions to obtain information. Already in this autumn of 1864, he was plotting to kidnap the President.

In August or September he had broached the idea to two former Confederate soldiers: Samuel Bland Arnold and Michael O'Laughlin. Plots to kidnap President Lincoln were not new. The previous year, a similar scheme had been presented to Confederate President Jefferson Davis. If Lincoln resists he might be hurt, Davis had reasoned. He might have wanted to see Lincoln captured; he did not want him killed. So Davis rejected the scheme, a fact that Northerners would later choose not to believe. Yet toward the end of the war, several groups apparently were plotting abduction. Rumors persisted in Maryland and Virginia that one night a carriage would rush down the roads and that in it would be the kidnaped Lincoln on the way to the Rebel capital.

Booth's plans, like those of others, depended on a surprise capture and a quick escape. Mrs. Lincoln enjoyed the theater. One night while she and her husband attended a play at either Grover's or Ford's theater, a gas valve would be closed in the basement.

The houselights would go off. Booth and his fellow conspirators would strike. After trussing up Lincoln, they would lower him from the Presidential box to the darkened stage. Quickly they would rush him to a carriage waiting in the alley. A whip would flick on a horse's flank, and the carriage would clatter across the Navy Yard bridge and on through Lower Maryland to a waiting barge on the Potomac River. Once in Virginia, Booth would be welcomed as a hero; the President would be ransomed for Confederate prisoners.

An alternate plan called for the capture of Lincoln while he was riding in the Presidential carriage. Booth's co-conspirators favored this plan; they considered the theater abduction both impractical and dangerous. But Booth evidently yearned to give his greatest performance on a stage.

It was not difficult to recruit men for the otherwise reprehensible crime of kidnaping. As conspirator John H. Surratt later put it: "Where is there a young man in the North with one spark of patriotism in his heart who would not have with enthusiastic ardor joined in any undertaking for the capture of Jefferson Davis?"

Late in the year 1864, actor John Wilkes Booth appeared in Lower Maryland to select an escape route, to buy swift horses, and perhaps to enlist the aid of local people sympathetic to the Confederate cause. He had a letter of introduction to a Dr. William Queen from a man in Montreal named Martin. Queen lived a few miles below Bryantown, about eight miles from the home of Dr. Mudd. Booth made at least two visits to Dr. Queen that fall, each time staying several nights.

The actor drained Dr. Queen's son-in-law, John C. Thompson, of information on the price of land, slipping in incidental questions on his main interest: the roads in Charles County. "Land varies in price from five dollars to fifty dollars an acre," Thompson explained. "Poor land is worth five dollars. Land with improvements or on the river might go for as high as fifty."

"Who around here has land to sell?" asked Booth.

"You might try Henry Mudd. He's an important landowner in these parts."

Henry Lowe Mudd was the father of Dr. Samuel A. Mudd. The next morning Booth, accompanying Thompson and Dr. Queen, met Samuel Mudd in front of St. Mary's Church at Bryantown. "Sam, I'd like you to meet John Wilkes Booth, the actor," said Thompson, casting the die that would eventually condemn Dr. Mudd.

Later, the doctor would describe this encounter in considerable detail: "Booth's visit in November, 1864, to Charles County, was for the purpose, as expressed by himself, to purchase land and horses; he was inquisitive concerning the political sentiments of the people, inquiring about the contraband trade that existed between the North and South, and wished to be informed about the roads bordering on the Potomac, which I declined doing. He spoke of his being an actor and having two other brothers, who also were actors. He spoke of Junius Brutus as being a good Republican. He said they were largely engaged in the oil business, and gave me a lengthy description of the theory of oil and the process of boring, etc. He said he had a younger brother in California. These and many minor matters spoken of caused me to suspect him to be a government detective."

John Wilkes Booth would later be called many names but not "Union spy."

Historian Osborn H. Oldroyd, writing in 1901 about those involved in the Lincoln conspiracy, considered Mudd to be inoffensive and respectable: "He was forty-five years of age, rather tall, and quite thin, with sharp features, a high, bald forehead, astute blue eyes, compressed pale lips, and sandy hair, whiskers, and mustache. He was known throughout the war as a strong sympathizer with the rebellion." Oldroyd was mistaken on Mudd's age—he was only thirty when he first met Booth—but he probably described the doctor's sympathies correctly.

Samuel Alexander Mudd was born December 20, 1833, the third son of Henry Lowe Mudd. "His name is mud" later became a term of derision which some lexicographers have (probably incorrectly) attempted to trace back to Sam Mudd's humiliation. At that time, however, the name Mudd stood high on the list of the most prominent families in Maryland—along with the Brents, the Merricks, the Plowdens, and the Jennifers. Sam's ancestor, Thomas Mudd, had arrived in Maryland from Bristow, England on August 14, 1665, at the age of eighteen. For his work in transporting himself and eight others into the colony, Lord Baltimore granted Thomas Mudd several large pieces of land, including one plot known as Boarman's Reserve, where Sam Mudd was born and where he grew up. Several of his present-day descendants still live there.

The picture of Sam as a child has been somewhat obscured by sentiment. "Even from his early years," wrote his daughter Nettie in 1906, "he was always thoughtful of others, always distinguished for his gentleness and kindness. When attending the public school, which he began to do when a little boy of seven years of age, such was his uniform courtesy and consideration for others that the companions of his early childhood remained his friends for life." Osborn H. Oldroyd, Jim Bishop, and other writers have referred less favorably to Mudd as "humorless," an evaluation that, whether deserved or not, has followed him through the years.

Sam remained in the public schools only two years, then his father hired a governess named Miss Peterson to tutor him and his sisters. At the age of fourteen he entered St. John's College in Frederick, Maryland. Two years later he enrolled at Georgetown College in Washington to complete his college training. His daughter tells us: "He was particularly interested in the study of languages and became proficient in Greek, Latin, and French; and was also a musician of recognized ability, performing with skill on the violin, piano, flute, and other instruments."

Sam Mudd had a childhood sweetheart, Sarah Frances Dyer, a girl he called by the nickname of Frank. While he went to St. John's College in Frederick, she attended Visitation Convent in the same city. Sarah Dyer was pretty, and practical. "Frank, are you going to marry me?" Sam asked her one evening.

"Yes," she replied. "When you have graduated in medicine, established a practice for yourself, and I have had my fun out, then I'll marry you."

Sam studied medicine and surgery at the University of Maryland, then known as Baltimore Medical College, and was graduated in March, 1856. He received a complimentary certificate of merit for his work at the University hospital. In her account, Nettie Mudd described her father's return from college: "Here on his father's estate may have been seen more than a hundred slaves, who made the evenings merry with song and with banjo and violin accompaniment. Scattered over various sections of the farm may also have been seen the 'quarters' of these humble colored folk, who were always treated with the kindest consideration by their master and mistress, and who would say of these white friends, after they had passed from earth, 'God bless my old Marse and Miss; I hope dey is in heaven.' Here my father began his public life as a practicing physician." On November 26, 1857, young Dr. Mudd was married to Sarah Frances Dyer at her family home.

Sam and his wife lived for two years at the Dyer estate. Jere Dyer, Mrs. Mudd's bachelor brother, resided with them. In November, 1858, the Mudds had their first child, a boy, whom they named Andrew Jerome. Then, in 1859, the young couple built their own home on the farm given to them by Sam's father. The next year, their second child was born. Lillian Augusta, known to everyone as Nettie, lived to the age of eighty, whereas her brother died when he was twenty-four years old.

The late 1850's and early 1860's were a troubled time for starting a family. The nation seemed to be on the brink of dissolution. John Brown's raid at Harpers Ferry to free the slaves, and his subsequent hanging, gave both secessionists and Unionists a symbol around which to rally. The economy of the Southern states had become inextricably attached to the utilization of slave labor. The Northern states, whether motivated by humanitarian or political reasons, sought to sever this umbilical cord.

Maryland stood on a teeter-totter between union and secession. Residents in the urbanized upper portions of Maryland linked arms with the North. Baltimore was strongly secessionst. Below Baltimore, green tobacco fields stretched to the sea, and the plantation owners, who needed slave labor, believed that the South was right. Sam's father was one of Maryland's most prominent slaveholders. The doctor himself owned eleven slaves. In the winter of 1861, Maryland Democrats demanded that the Union-sympathizing Governor Thomas B. Hicks call a special session of the legislature to discuss secession. He refused. When the legislature finally convened later in April (away from the capital and the danger from secessionist rabble-rousers in the gallery), only a vague statement of neutrality resulted. Maryland remained in the Union, held there by a thin thread of loyalty—and by the ominous presence of Federal troops. So delicate was the political situation in Baltimore that the newly elected Lincoln, on his way to Washington for the inauguration, moved undercover through town at night, wearing a soft hat instead of his identifying stovepipe top hat, a deception that infuriated the Marylanders when they heard of it. Word had reached the government that the President-elect would be mobbed and assassinated when he transferred to a Washington-bound train in Baltimore. Yet four years later, with the times no less settled and assassination threats again rampant, Lincoln went virtually unguarded to that evening performance at Ford's Theater.

In defending Dr. Mudd later, friends would point out that he had taken the oath of allegiance prescribed for voters, had supported a Union candidate in the 1864 election, and had regarded the war between the States as a failure. These may have been accurate representations of Mudd's views in 1864, but in 1862 he was definitely out of sympathy with the North. "The people of the North are puritanical, long-faced, or Methodistic and hypocritical," Mudd had written. "They deal in sympathetic language to hide their deception. Their actions are parasitical, covert, stealthy, cowardly. They are law-abiding so long as it bears them out in their selfish interests, and praisers and scatterers and followers of the Bible so long as it does not conflict with their passion. With these traits of character in your leading politicians and preachers, it is impossible that confidence can be inspired in the South."

Lincoln's Emancipation Proclamation of January 1, 1863, dealt a crushing blow to the Maryland planters. As it freed the slaves in the Confederate states, it also demoralized the slaves in Maryland. When, later, the state of Maryland, too, abolished slavery, the newly freed blackmen refused to work for "Old Marse and Miss," even for inflated wages. Dr. Samuel A. Mudd had to pay twice what he considered their rightful wage to maintain servants in his house and workers in his fields. He began to entertain the possibility of selling the farm and starting a medical practice in another location. At this point he met Booth.

Mudd's farm was in Charles County, five miles north of Bryantown and thirty miles south of Washington. It lay about a dozen miles off the most direct route south to the Potomac, but perhaps at this early date Booth's escape route had not yet been conceived. Dr. Mudd had met the visiting actor on a Sunday in November of 1864 at St. Mary's Church in Bryantown. Booth (the doctor would later claim) had represented himself as interested in buying land; Mudd had land to sell. Booth also wanted horses. Horses, however, were scarce in this late stage of the war, since many Maryland farmers had sold their spare horses to the government. "Do you know of anyone with a good riding horse for sale?" asked Booth.

"My next neighbor has one," Mudd replied.

That afternoon Booth accompanied Mudd home. What actually happened during this visit remains a mystery. Considering Mudd's anti-Northern sentiments, however, it is not inconceivable that the doctor talked with Booth about Southern hopes in the Civil War. Could it be that Booth at this time solicited Dr. Mudd's assistance in the abduction scheme? If so, Mudd never admitted to it. According to him, company was already in the living room with supper over when he arrived and asked his wife to meet the stranger. He introduced Booth, and they sat together talking until bedtime at about 9:30.

After breakfast Monday morning, Mudd took the bridle reins of his horse over his arm and walked with Booth across a field to George Gardiner's stables about a quarter-mile away. However, the actor returned alone for his overcoat, which he had left on the hall floor by the parlor. As he threw it over one shoulder, a letter dropped from a pocket. A few days later, Mrs. Mudd found the letter; it was obviously from a lady admirer. Her curiosity piqued, she read it closely enough to convince herself that "some poor man's home had been wrecked by the handsome face and wily ways of Booth." Since Booth did not return after she had discovered the letter, Mrs. Mudd said, she finally threw it into the fire.

Upon being introduced by Dr. Mudd to George Gardiner, Booth explained that he was interested in a horse to run in a light buggy. "I'm going to travel through the lower counties of Maryland to see if I can buy some land," Booth said.

"I've only got one buggy horse," replied Gardiner. "I can't spare him. But I do have a young mare."

"No."

"I have an old saddle horse. Maybe you'd rather have him."

Booth examined a one-eyed dark-bay horse and decided it would do. "I only want it for one year," he explained. After the sale of the horse, Booth and Mudd returned to the farmhouse. The next day Booth mounted his newly acquired saddle horse and rode off.

Several weeks later, Booth returned to Charles County on another "land-buying" expedition. This time apparently he did not see Mudd. He stayed again with Dr. Queen and talked to Dr. William T. Bowman about the purchase of property. When Bowman later told this to Mudd, the other seemed surprised. "Why, that fellow promised to buy mine," he said.

Mudd, as he eventually admitted, saw John Wilkes Booth once more before the assassination. Their second meeting occurred in Washington. According to Dr. Mudd, he visited that city on December 23, 1864, with Jeremiah T. Mudd, a relative. They planned to meet friends from Baltimore at the Pennsylvania House and escort them back to the doctor's home for the holidays. They left their horses at the Navy Yard, and walked into Washington late in the afternoon. After a restaurant meal, Mudd strolled past the

National Hotel, where Booth stayed when he was in Washington. Suddenly Mudd felt a hand on his shoulder. It was none other than Booth. He had been given the address of John H. Surratt, another man known to Mudd. Would the doctor make the introduction? How Booth associated the two Marylanders, we can only guess. We can also only speculate on the coincidence that Booth and Mudd should meet in a Washington crowded with Christmas shoppers.

John Harrison Surratt had resided with his mother, Mary Surratt, in a tavern about two-thirds of the way from Bryantown to Washington. Because, as Mudd later explained, it was the only tavern he cared to patronize along this route, he came to know Surratt. Surratt's occupation at that time was the running of Rebel dispatches between Richmond, Washington, and Canada. Even if Mudd was not aware of Surratt's underground activities, Booth, with his Confederate connections in Canada, probably knew of them. Why he should want or need Dr. Mudd to introduce him to the Rebel agent remains a question. Years later Surratt would hint that he had known Booth before Mudd ever introduced them.

In 1864, John Surratt had moved, with his mother, from the tavern in Surrattsville to Washington. She rented the tavern for five hundred dollars a year to a man named John Lloyd. Her new residence, part of her husband's estate, was located between Sixth and Seventh streets on H Street. She ran it as a boarding house. Booth suggested a walk in that direction; he promised not to detain the doctor more than five minutes. They had not gone far when Mudd observed Surratt walking up Seventh Street with another man. The latter was Louis Wiechmann, a government clerk who shared a room with Surratt at the boarding house.

"Surratt! Surratt!" called Dr. Mudd.

"John, someone's calling you," said Wiechmann.

Surratt turned to see Mudd approaching with Booth. The doctor made the introductions and, thinking his duty done, walked back with the others in the direction from which he had come. But in front of the National Hotel the eloquent Booth seized his arm.

"Come up to my room for a drink," he said. Surratt and Wiechmann accepted the invitation. Mudd went with them.

Booth had Room 84, a plushly furnished suite previously occupied by a congressman. He told his guests to be seated, rang the bell, and asked the servant to bring drinks and cigars. Mudd in the meantime motioned to Surratt. They moved into a passageway outside the room. Mudd apologized to Surratt for having introduced him to Booth. "He's a man I hardly know," he said. "I fear he may be a government detective."

Upon returning to the room, Surratt and Mudd took chairs around a center table. Booth and Wiechmann were seated on a sofa in one corner glancing over several Congressional documents. "I've just returned from the country," Booth said to Wiechmann "and I still haven't recovered from the fatigue. I've been thinking of buying Dr. Mudd's land."

"That's right," admitted Mudd.

"I got lost on my way back to Washington," Booth added, moving to a chair near Surratt. He pulled an old letter from his pocket and began to draw lines on it, presumably representing roads. He wanted to learn more about the back roads of Lower Maryland. Quickly and skillfully, he put his questions to Surratt. The information he gathered might profit a man who wanted to escape to Richmond.

After a quarter-hour in Booth's room, Mudd insisted that he must leave. The four left the hotel, and walked toward the Pennsylvania House, where Mudd's friends were waiting for him. Booth talked to Surratt; Mudd to Wiechmann.

"I suppose the war will end soon," commented Mudd. "The papers say that nine thousand prisoners have been taken from Hood's army. He's demoralized and falling back. His whole army may be captured and destroyed."

Wiechmann spoke with the expertise of his government clerkship: "The Commissary-General has requested provisions for only four thousand prisoners. I'm far from believing that the defeat of Hood is so disastrous."

"It is a blow from which the South will never be able to recover," replied Mudd. "The whole South lies at the mercy of Sherman."

The four parted company. The next day Mudd returned to his farm. He did not see Booth again for another four months. When Mudd opened his door early on the morning after the assassination, the actor was sitting heavily in his saddle, supposedly disguised, and with a broken leg. Dr. Mudd set the actor's broken bone, fashioned him a crutch, and saw him leave late that afternoon in the direction of Parson Wilmer's at Piney Church. Booth had no intention of going to Wilmer's; he disappeared instead into the bramble of trees and bush called the Zekiah Swamp less than one thousand yards behind Mudd's farm. Booth was gone, but he had cast a tragic shadow over the household of Dr. Samuel A. Mudd.

Unless Booth had already told him of the assassination of President Lincoln, Mudd probably first heard of it during his visit to Bryantown that afternoon. When he returned home, according to stories told later by both Mudd and his wife, he learned that the man with the broken leg had worn a false beard. The suspicions of the "humorless" doctor must then have been aroused. But darkness had fallen.

"I think I'll ride back into town and let the authorities know of this visit," he said.

His wife pleaded with him not to go. "Too many suspicious people have been prowling around here lately. I'm afraid to stay here alone. Please wait until morning."

Dr. Mudd decided to wait.

Chapter 3

OSCAR SWANN LIVED IN the Zekiah Swamp about two miles from Bryantown. Near nine o'clock on Saturday night, the fifteenth of April, the Negro Swann met two white men on horseback who were lost in the woods near his house. One he described later as a small man. The second he remembered as lame and carrying a crutch. The small man explained that his companion had broken his leg. They asked for whiskey. Swann gave them a drink and some bread. They offered him two dollars to take them to the house of a man named Burtle. Swann agreed, but when almost there the two strangers conferred and changed their minds. Would Swann take them instead to the house of Colonel Cox for five dollars more? Swann would, and they reached Cox's farm, a dozen miles away, at midnight. Cox came out with a candle. The two men got down from their horses. According to Swann, the others went into the house while he remained outside. Three or four hours later, the two men came out. Cox did not appear with them. The small man mounted his horse and began to ride off. His companion called sharply to him, declaring that he could not get on his horse without help. Swann and the small man boosted the lame man into the saddle. "I thought Cox was a man of Southern feeling," the latter grumbled. When Oscar Swann reached his cabin again the sun had almost risen.

Oscar Swann remembered little of the features of the lame stranger whom he had escorted across Zekiah Swamp the night after Lincoln's assassination. He recalled only the lameness and the crutch. But it was dark, and all white faces probably looked the same to him. However, other people have described Booth in glowing detail. A billiard room proprietor named John Deery stated: "He [Booth] was as handsome as a young god with his clear, pale, olive complexion, classically regular features and hair and mustache literally black as night." Actress Clara Morris said of Booth: "His coloring was unusual: the ivory pallor of his skin, the inky blackness of his densely thick hair, the heavy lids of his glowing eyes were all Oriental and they gave a touch of mystery to his face when it fell into gravity; but there was generally a flash of white teeth behind his silky mustache and a laugh in his eyes." Sir Charles Wyndham described the actor as follows: "Picture to yourself Adonis, with high forehead, ascetic face corrected by rather full lips, sweeping black hair, a figure of perfect youthful proportions and the most wonderful black eyes in the world."

Booth was only twenty-six years old when he conceived and hatched the plot to kill Abraham Lincoln. He had been born May 10, 1838, in Bel Air, Maryland, the ninth of ten children fathered in America by Junius Brutus Booth, the most famous player of his day. (Junius had sired two other children in England before coming to the United States.) There were four sons—two older than John Wilkes and one younger. Junius Brutus, Jr., and Edwin matched or exceeded their father's skill and fame. The youngest, Joseph, also went on the stage, but failed.

Historians have attempted to trace the suspected madness of John Wilkes Booth to his father, for Junius's fame rested as much on eccentricities as on talent. Once he had hurled himself from the deck of a riverboat. On another occasion he asked a clergyman to help him give public burial to a bushel of wild pigeons that had been shot as pests. At still another time he invited his acquaintances to attend the burial of a beloved friend at his country farm. Much to the irritation of the guests the "beloved friend" proved to be a horse. Junius drank with the fervor of an alcoholic. One evening his theatrical managers had to lock him in a hotel room to keep him sober for a performance. But when they returned he was blear-eyed drunk. He had bribed the bellboy to bring him mint juleps, which he had drunk through the keyhole by a long straw. Junius died in 1852, when Wilkes was only fourteen years old. The boy subsequently became very close to his mother. He used to say later that he failed to join the Confederate Army only because he promised her to stay out of the war.

John Wilkes Booth had the dash of his father. As a boy he used to hitch the family sleigh to the horses in July and clatter over rock-strewn country roads, the runners scraping sparks in his wake. He galloped through the woods around his Bel Air summer home on horseback, shouting defiant speeches and swinging a lance that had been given to his father by one of General Zachary Taylor's soldiers. The Booths lived in Baltimore during the winter. Across the street lived another boy, named Michael O'Laughlin, who was to die young because of his childhood playmate. Wilkes had other friends. He attended St. Timothy's Hall, an Episcopalian finishing school at Catonsville, along with a boy named Samuel Arnold, who later probably wished he had gone to school elsewhere. As an artillery cadet, Booth wore a steel-grey uniform and answered to the name of Billy Bowlegs, a celebrated Indian chief. His sister Asia, who married the well-known comedian John Sleeper Clark, remembers him as a plodding student who nevertheless retained information once he had absorbed it.

An apocryphal story exists about Booth's early school days. It probably was invented after the assassination, but it has become a part of the Booth folklore. A former classmate told of the students at St. Timothy's sitting around a campfire one night talking about their ambitions. Wilkes declared that he wanted to be admired by everyone.

"I want to do something," he said, "that will hand my name down to posterity, never to be forgotten, even after I've been dead a thousand years."

"How do you intend to achieve this fame you're always talking about?" asked one of his classmates.

"I'll tell you what I mean," Booth replied. "You've read about the Seven Wonders of the World? Take the Colossus of Rhodes, for example. Suppose that statue were now standing, and I should by some means throw it over? My name would go down to posterity."

"Suppose the falling statue took you down with it? What good would all your glory then do you?"

"I would die with the satisfaction of knowing I had done something no other man could ever do again."

Abraham Lincoln became Booth's Colossus of Rhodes, but first the young actor achieved a measure of fame on his own. So great were the theatrical accomplishments of his father and brothers, that the name Booth became a guarantee of box office success. When John Wilkes Booth stepped to the footlights at the age of seventeen, an eager and even sympathetic public awaited him. His brother Edwin had already captured the North; Junius Brutus, Jr., ruled supreme in the West. It was the South that John Wilkes would lay claim to—and claim it he did. Throughout his short but spectacular career, John Wilkes Booth received his greatest ovations in cities like Richmond, Atlanta, and New Orleans. "He was having a wrong tuition in the ardent South," admitted his sister, Asia, "where even his errors were extolled and his successes magnified. The people loved him; he had never known privation or want, was never out of an engagement, while Edwin had had the rough schooling of poverty." Many critics sneered at Wilkes as only a shadow of his father and brothers. They decried his movements, especially his leap onstage as Macbeth. "He's a better acrobat than an actor," they said.

Once Booth rehearsed a duel scene with a phlegmatic six-footer named McCollum. "Come on hard. Come on hot, old fellow. Harder! Faster!" Booth taunted him as their swords clashed.

McCollum became nervous. Forgetting that he had struck the planned number of headblows, he sliced down with his sword when Booth expected a thrust. Blood splashed across Booth's face, his eyebrow nearly cut through.

"Good God, what have I done?" McCollum cried in horror.

Booth brushed the blood from his eyes: "That's all right, old man. Never mind me. Only come on hard, for God's sake, and save the fight."

Sir Charles Wyndham remembered him as Hamlet: "Edwin's was a reflective Hamlet. As John Wilkes Booth played it, the

Danish prince was unmistakably mad throughout. Edwin's conception of the part was that of uneven and unbalanced genius, and wonderfully he portrayed it. But John Wilkes leaned toward the other view of the character, as was in keeping with his own bent of mind. His Hamlet was insane, and his interpretation was fiery, convincing and artistic."

"There is but one Hamlet to my mind," Wilkes himself said. "That's my brother Edwin. You see, between ourselves, he *is* Hamlet, melancholy and all." At the height of his career John Wilkes Booth earned twenty thousand dollars a year. But perhaps there was still within him a trace of jealousy. He would have to do something more sensational than act on stage to emerge from the shadows cast by his famous father and brothers.

"We regarded him as a good-hearted, harmless, though wild-brained boy," said Edwin of Wilkes. "We used to laugh at his patriotic froth whenever secession was discussed." In 1858, John Wilkes Booth left Richmond, where he had been appearing with a stock company, to join the hunt for the fiery abolitionist John Brown. Booth was present at Brown's hanging. The actor, however, thought Brown a hero. Asia said later that John Wilkes had felt a throb of anguish as he saw John Brown's eyes straining for those he vainly thought would come to his rescue. "He was a brave old man," thought Booth. "His heart must have broken when he felt himself deserted."

If John Wilkes Booth saw in Brown the touch of greatness, he saw in Lincoln the streak of the despot. "That sectional-candidate should never have been President," he wrote to Asia after Lincoln had been elected. "The votes were doubled to seat him. He was smuggled through Maryland to the White House. Maryland is true to the core—every mother's son. Look at the cannon on the heights in Baltimore. It needed just that to keep her [Maryland] quiet. This man's appearance, his pedigree, his coarse low jokes and anecdotes, his vulgar similes, and his frivolity are a disgrace to the seat he holds. Other brains rule the country. He is made the tool of the North, to crush out, or try to crush out, slavery, by robbery, rapine, slaughter, and bought armies. He is walking in the footprints of old John Brown, but no more fit to stand with that rugged old hero—Great God! no. John Brown was a man inspired, the grandest character of this century! He is Bonaparte in one great move, that is by overturning this blind Republic and making himself king."

In January of 1864, John Wilkes Booth traveled to Franklin, Pennsylvania, an oil boom town. His throat had troubled him, forcing temporary abandonment of his stage career. Accustomed to living like a prince, he saw in profits from oil an opportunity to maintain his standard of living. With him came John L. Ellsler, manager of the Cleveland Academy of Music, and Thomas Y. Meers, a gambler and former prizefighter. Forming the Dramatic Oil Company, these three speculators invested in land along the Alleghany River south of Franklin. Soon they brought in a well producing twenty-five barrels a day. Because this barely covered expenses, they decided to shoot the well with explosives to expand production. Instead they ruined the hole, and the well never produced another barrel of oil. Booth returned to Baltimore, his company having lost an estimated ten thousand dollars in the unsuccessful operations. Franklin residents later remembered Booth as a drinker and a brawler who flew into rages during political arguments.

Booth was soon to channel that rage in a fixed direction. At the end of the summer of 1864 he looked up Samuel Arnold, his former schoolmate, whom he had not seen for a dozen years. Arnold had served in the Confederate Army but had been mustered out after two years because of poor health. When Booth found him he was living with his mother on a farm near Hookstown, Maryland. While visiting his father in Baltimore, Arnold heard that Booth wished to see him at Barnum's Hotel.

"I hear you've been fighting for the South," Booth said when they met.

Then came a tap on the door. Booth rose and ushered in Michael O'Laughlin. O'Laughlin and Arnold had much in common, though they had never met each other. O'Laughlin, like Arnold, had known Booth as a boy. O'Laughlin, like Arnold, had served in the

Rebel Army. Booth called for wine, and the three men began to talk.

Abraham Lincoln was, of course, totally unaware of the plot being hatched against him. Even had he suspected, he probably would have shrugged it off as one of the hazards of his office. "I cannot possibly guard myself against all dangers," he once said, "unless I shut myself up in an iron box, in which condition I could scarcely perform the duties of a President."

At the inauguration in March of 1865, John Wilkes Booth, through the influence of the infatuated daughter of a Washington senator, sat on the speaker's platform within a few paces of Lincoln as the new President uttered the words: "With malice toward none, with charity for all." Had Booth been interested only in knocking over the Colossus of Rhodes, he might have performed that deed most spectacularly here. An assassination plot needs but one man. However, Booth had that day in Barnum's Hotel taken the first steps toward assembling a band of men whose prime purpose was, not assassination, but abduction.

Booth selected his band of conspirators carefully. Arnold and O'Laughlin, trained as soldiers, could ride and shoot. Lewis Paine Powell, another Rebel soldier best known by his middle name, had the brawn to carry out any order and would not ask why.

David E. Herold could not match Paine's body, but he had a cunning mind and, from frequent hunting trips, knew Lower Maryland extremely well. This chipmunk-faced boy, with only women in his family, worshiped Booth as if the other were his older brother. The actor would give him free tickets to the theater, invite him backstage, and feed his vanity by saying that he too might appear on the stage one day. Herold, however, was destined for backstage.

German-born George Atzerodt had piloted boats for the Rebel railroad from his home in Port Tobacco on the Potomac River. Atzerodt, like Paine, had been hired for his brawn—or, perhaps more accurately, his boat.

John H. Surratt had more experience in subterfuge than any

other member of the group—including Booth. He had served in the Confederate underground almost from the beginning of the rebellion, carrying messages and information between Richmond, Washington, and Montreal. Surratt knew every letter-stump and Confederate sympathizer along the underground railway he so frequently traveled. But Surratt did not take part in the final act of the conspiracy—nor did Arnold or O'Laughlin. Booth, Herold, Paine, and Atzerodt had to go it alone.

These seven men formed the main cast of conspirators in the plot that eventually evolved into the assassination of Lincoln. But three other persons would also find themselves accused of conspiracy. One was Mary Surratt, who owned the boarding house where for a time lived her son, John, and Paine and Atzerodt. In the last months of Lincoln's life, Booth had become a frequent visitor to the Surratt boarding house. Then there was Ned Spangler, a carpenter and stagehand at Ford's Theater, who had known and worked for Booth's family for years. The government would accuse him of helping Booth backstage on the night of the assassination. Last came Dr. Samuel A. Mudd, who according to those who many years later would rally to the defense of his memory, did nothing more than set a broken leg.

Mudd had introduced Surratt to Booth, supposedly warning him, however, to beware. "We met several times," Surratt said of Booth in a lecture at Rockville, Maryland, in 1871, "but as he seemed to be very reticent with regard to his purposes and very anxious to get all the information out of me he could, I refused to tell him anything at all."

Surratt, up to his neck in Rebel spy work, had good reason to be suspicious of Booth. Surratt finally confronted the actor: "It is useless for you, Mr. Booth, to seek any information from me at all. I know who you are and what are your intentions."

"I will make known my intentions to you," retorted Booth, "but first you must promise secrecy."

"I will do nothing of the kind," replied Surratt. "You know well I am a Southern man. If you cannot trust me, we will separate."

Booth now delivered a well-rehearsed speech, one that he had presented to Arnold and O'Laughlin several months earlier. He described the thousands of Confederate prisoners languishing in Northern prisons. The South, short on manpower, needed every soldier; but the North refused exchanges. "I have a proposition," whispered Booth, "which if carried out would bring about the desired exchange."

"What is your proposition?"

With the flair of a villain in a melodrama, Booth arose and looked under the bed, into the wardrobe, and even into the passageway. The walls, he explained, have ears. Then he told of his scheme: "I plan to kidnap President Lincoln and carry him off to Richmond."

Surratt, in his Rockville lecture, described his surprise: "To think of successfully seizing Mr. Lincoln in the capital of the United States, surrounded by thousands of his soldiers, and carrying him off to Richmond looked to me like a foolish idea. I told [Booth] as much. He went on to tell with what facility [Lincoln] could be seized, in and about Washington, as for example, in his various rides to and from the Soldier's Home, his summer residence. He entered into minute details of the proposed capture, and of the various parts to be performed by the actors in the performance. I was amazed—thunderstruck—and, in fact, I might also say, frightened at the unparalleled audacity of his scheme." Nonetheless, Surratt agreed to take part.

Booth had traveled north that fall in search of weapons and equipment to help further his plans. He had returned to Baltimore in November, to remain only a few days. Business called him south. "This business," wrote Arnold later, "consisted in the purchasing of horses and boats; if possible, also to ascertain the different crossings of the river and roads leading to them. The true motive of his visit was concealed from the inhabitants of that section under the cover that he desired to purchase lands for the purpose of settlement."

On this trip Booth first encountered Dr. Mudd. Since Booth was still actively recruiting conspirators, the question naturally arises if the actor approached Mudd about joining the conspiracy.

If so, did Mudd accept? There is no answer to this question. Arnold and Surratt, the only proven conspirators who survived to describe Booth's plottings, offered few clues. Neither ever mentioned Mudd as a co-conspirator. Yet, we cannot immediately assume that Mudd was innocent simply because they failed to incriminate him.

Booth returned to Baltimore in January to pick up a buggy and harness that Arnold had selected for him.

On January 18, 1865, the night came for action. Booth learned that Lincoln would attend Ford's Theater that evening to see Edwin Forrest play in *Jack Cade*. Two things went wrong: first, Arnold and O'Laughlin failed to appear; second, Lincoln failed to appear. The night was stormy, so the President had remained at home. Booth's finances had now become strained because of his inaction as a performer, and he had to visit New York in February to obtain additional funds. He returned to Washington about February twenty-fifth. On March fourth, he was present at the inauguration. On March fifteenth, the Lincolns attended, at Grover's Theater, a performance by the German Opera Company of *The Magic Flute*. Booth, believing that the President was ill with influenza, was not ready to act.

Apparently that same evening Booth called a meeting of the conspirators at Gautier's Restaurant on Pennsylvania Avenue. According to Thomas Miles, a Negro waiter, Booth arrived at about eleven o'clock and later was joined by *six* other gentlemen. Instead of entering the regular restaurant area they went to a private dining room.

Sam Arnold, in 1902, a few years before his death, wrote of this meeting: "Those present were the entire party or parties who were directly or indirectly connected in the affair, comprising in all seven persons, viz. John Wilkes Booth, John H. Surratt, Lewis Paine, George A. Atzerodt, David E. Herold, Michael O'Laughlin, and myself. This was the only assembling or meeting of the parties held either in the District of Columbia or any other place." Could Arnold have been mistaken about those "directly or indirectly" involved? Perhaps Booth kept secrets, though it is significant that neither Mudd, Spangler, nor Mrs. Surratt were present.

The air at Gautier's Restaurant was filled with smoke and argument. Surratt feared the government had learned of their plans. Double stockades were being erected at the bridge crossing the eastern branch of the river. Booth reiterated his plan to abduct the President from the theater. Arnold objected. The scheme was too impractical, he said. Booth threatened to shoot Arnold, then backed down. Too much to drink, he explained. Arnold, irritated by the constant delays, stated that unless the abduction occurred within the week he would quit, a promise he later fulfilled. Not until five o'clock in the morning did the seven men leave the restaurant.

Arnold and O'Laughlin remained in Washington awaiting action. Two days later, as they were on their way to lunch, they were stopped by Booth and Herold. Booth had news: "The President is going to visit the Soldier's Home. Be ready at two o'clock."

President Lincoln planned that day to attend the matinée of *Still Waters Run Deep*, scheduled for performance at the Soldier's Home on Seventh Avenue. The President would travel to the theater by carriage. "It was our intention to seize the carriage," said Surratt later, "and have one of our men mount the box and drive direct for southern Maryland via Benning bridge. We felt confident that all the cavalry in the city could never overhaul us. We were all mounted on swift horses besides having a thorough knowledge of the country, it being determined to abandon the carriage after passing city limits. Upon the suddenness of the blow and the celerity of our movements we depended for success. By the time the alarm would have been given and horses saddled we would have been on our way through southern Maryland toward the Potomac River."

This plan, more practical than Booth's kidnap scheme in the theater, might have worked. But when Booth and Surratt rode up to the carriage ready to pull pistols and clamber aboard they found a face other than that of the President staring out at them. At that moment Lincoln was reviewing the men of the 140th Indiana Regiment. These battle veterans had suddenly appeared in Washington with a captured Confederate flag to present to him. The President probably had enough Confederate flags, but he was too kind a man to disappoint his soldiers, and so he canceled his theater plans.

The conspirators, enraged, discouraged, certain that their plans had been discovered, rode off. Surratt left for Canada. Arnold and O'Laughlin returned to Baltimore, determined to have nothing more to do with Booth. Booth received a letter from Arnold in which the latter said that he was backing out of the plot. That letter eventually became a key piece of evidence implicating Arnold in the conspiracy. Booth failed to destroy the letter, as Arnold had requested, perhaps thinking he might someday be able to use it against the man who had deserted him.

Events now crowded one upon the other. On April third, Richmond fell. Lincoln visited that city the following day. On the ninth, the same day Lee surrendered to Grant at Appomattox, the President returned to Washington. Grant came to the capital on the thirteenth to make arrangements for the disbanding of his army. With him came Robert T. Lincoln, the President's son, a captain on Grant's staff. The President breakfasted with Robert on the morning of the fourteenth, then attended a cabinet meeting. Grant was present. Mrs. Lincoln had asked her husband to invite General and Mrs. Grant to Ford's Theater that evening to see Laura Keene play in *Our American Cousin*. The afternoon papers announced that Grant would accompany Lincoln; thus there might be a double dividend for an assassin. But the Grants decided instead to go to their home in Burlington, Vermont, to see their children. That afternoon the Lincolns went for a ride through the city by carriage. The President was cheerful. The end of the war had lifted a terrible burden from his shoulders. In the evening Lincoln talked with the Speaker of the House, Schuyler Colfax. At eight o'clock his wife opened his door to say that it was time to leave for the theater. They climbed into their carriage at the White House gate and ten minutes later stopped at the house of Senator Harris. The latter's daughter Clara and her fiancé, Major Henry R. Rathbone, would take the Grants' place. The theater party was late arriving at the theater. As Lincoln entered, the audience arose. He stopped at the door of his box and acknowledged their applause with a bow and a smile.

Many years later, in 1956, William Stump, a reporter representing the Baltimore *Sun*, visited the home of Samuel James Seymour, then ninety-five years old, who was the last person, still alive, to have been in Ford's Theater on the night of April 14, 1865. The *Sun*'s Sunday magazine, on the anniversary of Lincoln's birthday, printed the account of the interview. "I remember seeing the actors on the stage," Seymour recalled. "I remember seeing the President stand up and wave. I remember he was ugly. They say nobody in the audience saw him so maybe I didn't. I was little. I've heard so much I don't know. But I think I heard the shot and I think I saw Mr. Lincoln throw up his hands. They will say none saw him get shot though. 'Oh grandmother, the man [Booth] fell and hurt himself,' I said. I clung to her and then came the shouting and screaming. The next thing I remember we were outside and father was carrying me. I don't remember anything else except noise and the crowd."

Chapter 4

AT ABOUT FIFTEEN MINUTES after ten on Good Friday evening, a bullet fired from John Wilkes Booth's derringer pierced the brain of Abraham Lincoln. Lincoln lingered, then finally died at 7:22 on Holy Saturday morning. "Now he belongs to the ages," Secretary of War Edwin M. Stanton is reported to have said. At that moment Booth lay asleep in an upper room of the house of the luckless Dr. Mudd. The next day was Easter Sunday. Preachers throughout the land would speak of Abe Lincoln in their sermons. Some of Lincoln's enemies—and he perhaps had more than any other President—rejoiced at his death, making bitter jokes about whether or not Honest Abe would rise from the dead. They uttered such remarks in private—at least in the North. The mood of the Northern people was such that they would have avenged themselves quickly on any deprecators of their martyred President, for the North, which had won the war, was bitter indeed over the loss of their great leader. Their joy over the victory had been stolen from them, their anticipation of celebration abruptly extinguished. In Washington, government troops poured across the Navy Yard bridge to spread through Maryland in pursuit of the man who had slain their Commander-in-Chief.

One of Booth's pursuers was First Lieutenant Alexander Lovett of the Veteran's Reserve Corps. On Monday the seventeenth, Lovett received his orders from Major J. R. O'Beirne, provost marshal for the District of Columbia, and set off on the hunt for the killer. Lovett commanded nine mounted men. With him rode two special detectives from Major O'Beirne's office: Simon Gavacan and William Williams. Years later, Williams told a fanciful tale of their exit from the city, one that J. E. Buckingham, the doorman at Ford's Theater, published in 1894 in a volume of reminiscences.

"Captain Williams was guarding President Johnson," stated Buckingham. "About daylight the cavalry, under the command of Lieutenant Lovett, dashed up to the front of the hotel and Major O'Beirne commanded Captain Williams to take the cavalry and hunt for Booth.

" 'Where must I go?' asked the captain.

" 'How do I know,' replied the Major. 'Go and don't return to Washington until you find Booth; but mind—don't harm a hair on his head.'

"Mounting a magnificent charger, the captain clapped spurs and with a 'Come, boys!' the cavalry were soon going at a rapid speed toward the Eastern Branch Bridge, which was successfully crossed by the captain knocking the sentry down by running over him with his horse.

" 'There was no time to stand and explain to the sentry,' said the captain; 'time was precious.' "

Time had seemed equally precious to Booth three days earlier, but he had acted with more restraint. That Friday evening, Silas T. Cobb, a sergeant in the Massachusetts Heavy Artillery, was on guard at the Navy Yard bridge on the night of Lincoln's assassination. At about 10:40 a single horseman clattered onto the bridge approach. It was Booth. Cobb later recalled graphically the horseman and his horse: "He was mounted on a light-bay horse rather below medium size, dark legs, long mane. He was a very restive horse and looked as though he had been pushed on a short burst. He had a single bridle, black saddle, and English stirrups. The man who rode the horse was medium size, five feet seven-and-a-half or eight inches high as near as I can judge, neither slight made nor stout, but snug built and his motions indicated muscular power. He had a somewhat short black mustache in good trim and looking as though it had been recently colored. I noticed that his skin was white compared with the color of his mustache."

Booth's horse had indeed been pushed hard—at a gallop all the way from Ford's Theater. After the shot that had killed Lincoln, Booth had run unopposed, except for the brief grappling with Major Rathbone, out of the theater to where a stage boy named Peanuts John, asked to do so by Ned Spangler, was holding Booth's horse. Booth mounted, kicked the boy out of the way, then dashed off through the alley into the night just as his first pursuer, a member of the audience named Joseph B. Stewart, nearly reached his side.

Twenty minutes later Booth was at the Navy Yard bridge. "Halt, who goes there?" challenged Sergeant Cobb.

"Friend," said Booth.

"What's your name, friend?"

"Booth."

Booth dismounted, and said that he was headed home to Charles County. He lived in the country close to Beantown, he declared.

Cobb had never heard of Beantown. "Then you must never have been down in that country," countered Booth.

Cobb seemed reluctant to let the horseman pass. "Don't you know, my friend, that it is against the law to cross here after nine o'clock?"

"No," replied Booth. "I haven't been in town for some time, and that is new to me."

"I'll pass you, but I don't know if I ought to," said Cobb. Later, in the cold light of dawn, when he had to face the stares of his superiors, Cobb would wish that he had been more strict in following at least what he had represented to Booth as the letter of the law. Actually, the day before, sentries had been instructed to relax their rules. Booth undoubtedly knew this. The actor stoically walked his horse across the bridge and disappeared into the darkness. Fifteen minutes later, another horseman approached: David E. Herold.

"You can't pass," Cobb told him. "It is after nine, and it is against the rules."

"How long have these rules been out?" asked Herold.

"Ever since I've been here. Why weren't you out of the city before?"

"I stopped to see a woman on Capitol Hill and couldn't get off before now," Herold said, smiling. Cobb let him pass.

One more man rode to the bridge that night: John Fletcher, who earlier that morning had rented a horse to Herold. When Herold failed to return by dark, Fletcher reasoned that his horse had been stolen and so began to search for him. Herold, however, had had more important matters to worry about than the return of his rented horse. He had guided conspirator Lewis Paine to Secretary of State William H. Seward's house. As Herold waited outside, Paine gained entry by posing as a drug deliveryman. He then ran amuck through the house, stabbing anyone he encountered. The Secretary lay in bed with his neck encased in an iron brace, the result of a carriage accident earlier in the week. Only the brace saved him from a slit throat. When Herold, still waiting outside, heard the cries of "Murder!" he ran off in panic. Three days later, the police captured Paine at Mrs. Surratt's boarding house. Thrown from his horse and confused, he had been unable to find his way alone to the Navy Yard bridge.

Stableman John Fletcher did not continue to pursue Herold that night. Learning from Cobb that he would be unable to return after crossing the bridge, Fletcher retreated in disgust. He never saw his horse again.

Lieutenant Lovett continued where Fletcher had turned back. After crossing the eastern branch of the Potomac River, he and his small troop filed quietly into the Maryland hills. He passed the spot where, several days earlier, Polk Gardiner, riding to Washington in company with a friend, had seen two horsemen riding swiftly southward. Gardiner recalled the hour as between eleven and midnight. He saw the first horseman about three or four miles before reaching the capital. Like Sergeant Cobb, Gardiner remembered the man well: "He seemed to be a medium-sized man about five feet eight inches high and seemed to be dressed in black or dark clothes as far as I remember. He had a slouch hat on."

When Booth drew alongside Gardiner and his friend, Booth turned to them and asked: "Have you seen another horseman?"

"No, we haven't," Gardiner replied.

"Which way is the road to Upper Marlboro?" asked Booth. He had no intentions of going to Upper Marlboro, but apparently wanted to confuse his pursuers. The authorities accepted this misdirection when they questioned Polk Gardiner; but later, when Dr. Mudd spoke of Booth asking the way to Parson Wilmer's, they would brand the doctor a liar.

Booth sped off. A mile down the road Gardiner saw a second horseman. Herold, however, did not talk to Gardiner; instead he paused to ask questions of several government teamsters who were camped by the roadside. Polk Gardiner and his friend watched Herold rush off at a gallop. "Both those men are riding their horses to death to overtake each other," he said.

Lieutenant Lovett rode into Surrattsville Monday night. As early as the morning after the assassination, A. C. Richards, superintendent of the Washington police, had passed through Surrattsville and had stopped to question Lloyd, to whom John Surratt and his mother had rented their tavern. Richards wanted to know whether Booth or any other suspicious parties had spent the night there. The tavern keeper denied knowledge of any suspicious persons. "I call on God to witness the truth of my assertions," he said.

But subsequent events led the authorities to doubt that Lloyd had told the truth. Within hours after the assassination, the name of Surratt was linked to that of Booth. Police officers roused the sleepers at Mrs. Surratt's boarding house, and a boarder named Louis Wiechmann told a story about John Lloyd that seemed to implicate him deeply in the assassination plot.

Five to six weeks before the assassination, Surratt, Herold, and Atzerodt had come to Lloyd's house to deliver two carbines, ammunition, rope, and a monkey wrench. Lloyd had cached these items in the storeroom of the tavern. The day of the assassination, Mrs. Surratt and Wiechmann had brought a package from Washington that contained a spyglass belonging to Booth. According to Lloyd's later testimony, Mrs. Surratt had said: "I want you to have those 'shooting irons' ready. There will be parties here tonight who will call for them."

At midnight that night, Herold's shrill voice awakened Lloyd from a drunken sleep: "Lloyd, for God's sake, make haste and get those things!" Herold grabbed a bottle of whiskey as Lloyd stumbled into the storeroom. Lloyd brought the weapons out to Herold and discovered a second man sitting on a horse.

"I can't carry mine," said Booth. "I think my leg is broken."

Both men drank from the whiskey bottle, then reined their horses about. Herold paused and looked down at Lloyd. "I will tell you some news if you want to hear it."

"I am not particular," replied Lloyd dryly. "Use your own pleasure about telling it."

"I am pretty certain that we have assassinated the President and Secretary Seward!" The two horsemen vanished into the night.

When Lieutenant Lovett arrived in Surrattsville, he looked for Lloyd, but could not find him. Lloyd had left for Allen's Fresh to fetch his wife. Conveniently, she had been away for the week end. Lovett did meet two more special officers from Major O'Beirne's forces: Joshua Lloyd (no relation to John Lloyd) and George Cottingham. The lieutenant put them in charge of a guardhouse at the post office run by a man named Roby. As Lovett left the makeshift guardhouse to ride south, he said he hoped that he would soon arrest people to fill it. Guardhouses in and around Washington were rapidly being crowded as a result of the search for the conspirators, and Lovett would soon contribute his share of occupants. A few miles down the road at a village called T. B., Lieutenant Lovett met John Lloyd returning with his wife. Lovett arrested Lloyd and sent him under guard back to Roby's post office. He continued down the road toward Newportland.

Journalist George Alfred Townsend summarized the next leg of Lovett's journey for the readers of the New York *World*: "This little party, under the untiring Lovett, examined all the farmhouses below Washington, resorting to many shrewd expedients, and taking note of the great swamps to the east of Port Tobacco; they reached Newport at last and fastened tacit guilt upon many residents."

Lovett may have succeeded in fastening "tacit guilt," but he had temporarily lost Booth's trail. Booth had passed through T. B., then veered from the direct route south which was to have taken him to the Potomac. Studying Booth's tracks with the hindsight of history, it seems unlikely that this sudden swing eastward was planned. Had Booth continued to ride hard, he might have crossed the river by dawn. Before him in the early light of morning would lie Confederate Virginia. But now Booth's broken ankle began to throb and ache with a pain that even raw whiskey could not dull. In traveling at a leisurely pace, a rider hugs the side of his mount with his thighs, his weight distributed evenly across the saddle. Booth had been moving at a gallop, shifting his body weight into the stirrups and thus aggravating his leg. "I've got to find a doctor," Booth finally admitted to Herold.

From his trips into Charles County the previous fall, Booth knew of several doctors. Not all of them could be trusted to be discreet. Some lived in town, where Booth might be recognized. The Southern-sympathizing Dr. Queen, who several times had entertained Booth as his guest, lived too far away on the other side of Bryantown. However, one doctor known to Booth was relatively nearby on a lonely road at the edge of a swamp where a fugitive from justice might easily fade from sight. Booth and Herold turned their horses toward the farm of Dr. Mudd, and arrived there at four in the morning. Less than six hours had passed since Booth had shot the President.

Lieutenant Lovett rode with his tired men into Bryantown on Tuesday the eighteenth. Lieutenant Dana, in town since Saturday, had news. Two strangers had been in the vicinity over the week end. One had a broken leg, and a doctor named Mudd had set it for him. At this time no one in or out of Washington realized that Booth had broken his leg in the jump to the stage of Ford's Theater. Mudd would supply the first clue that the government was pursuing a crippled man.

Three days had now passed since two strangers had visited Mudd. They had arrived, and left, on Saturday, April 15. Mudd would later claim that he had wanted to go to the federal authorities on Saturday when he learned of the assassination and associated it with his guests' sudden departure. But it was already late in the evening, and Mrs. Mudd feared for her safety—her husband should wait until the next day. It is true that during the war both Union and Confederate spies used Maryland as their highway for travel south and north. Prowlers skulked constantly through the neighborhood. A month earlier, not far away, the notorious guerrilla Boyd, referred to earlier, had murdered an officer named Captain Watkins. Whether by design or not, Boyd became the alias used by Booth in almost every other house but that of Dr. Mudd. Only to Dr. Mudd did Booth and Herold call themselves Tyson and Tyler, which would later raise the question: Who invented these aliases, Booth or Mudd?

Other questions about Booth's stay at the house of Dr. Mudd are equally puzzling. Booth arrived at the doctor's house at four in the morning, a time when dark shadows and a high collar might at least temporarily have concealed his identity. But Booth was not reluctant to give his name to Sergeant Cobb at the bridge or to the drunken Lloyd. Why should he come masked to a house where he had previously visited as a guest? Why try to hide his face from a man who had met him not once but twice before and who, as a doctor trained in the art of examination, might be expected to pierce his disguise? Why did Booth not wear false whiskers at any other stop along his escape route? When these questions are posed, it becomes apparent that Dr. Mudd must indeed have known the identity of his injured guest. How could he help but think of John Wilkes Booth when that name was one of the subjects of the news in town? And, once put in mind of his acquaintance with the actor, how could he be taken in by Booth's flimsy disguise?

Even if we assume that Dr. Mudd knew the identity of Booth, we need not also assume that he was part of the conspiracy. The fact that Mudd's house did not appear on Booth's escape route seems to rule out any possibility of previous conspiratorial commitments on the part of Dr. Mudd. Booth apparently turned to the doctor in desperation—more from necessity than because of prior agreement. With the assumption, then, that Dr. Mudd recognized Booth when the actor arrived unexpectedly Saturday morning, we are left to ponder the doctor's subsequent role in the events of the next few days.

News of the assassination traveled slowly. Unless Booth or Herold confessed their crime to him, Mudd, on Saturday morning, could have had no knowledge of it. Dr. Mudd treated Booth's leg, as any doctor would have done. He tried to procure a carriage, but he seems not to have tried very hard. Herold accompanied Mudd on the way to Bryantown, then turned back, probably when he sighted Federal soldiers. If Mudd thought this behavior unusual, he gave no immediate indication. The doctor undoubtedly learned in Bryantown that John Wilkes Booth had killed Lincoln. Assuming that he had recognized Booth, Mudd must have realized that he had been placed in a highly compromising position. Should he inform the Federal troops? The Southerner in him must have rebelled against such a course of action. The troops might arrest him for housing the fugitives. He would have a hard time explaining away his two previous encounters with Booth. The troops would surely feel that the doctor's friendship with Booth meant that the doctor was in Booth's confidence. At this point, Mudd may have decided to let Booth and Herold go their way, hoping that their visit to him would not be exposed. Thus it could have come about that Dr. Mudd returned from Bryantown without mentioning the two mysterious strangers to the Federal troops. Later, family counsel may have convinced him that he had acted unwisely, for the splint on Booth's leg would have to be accounted for.

Dr. Mudd, as a physician, could respond positively to a broken leg, but he was otherwise a passive participant in the aftermath of Lincoln's assassination. The doctor found himself drawn along by events not of his making, and the suction of the whirlpool of fate would become stronger. It seems too harsh to charge that Dr. Mudd deliberately withheld information from the federal authorities that Saturday afternoon. He must have been in a state of confusion. After all, he had once befriended the assassin. As a Southern gentleman, the doctor would be influenced by this friendship, slender as it was. How could a man be expected to inform on an acquaintance who had come to him for help? However, Mudd must finally have appreciated the nature of the impossible position in which he had been placed. Furthermore, he may even have concluded that Booth was a madman—someone to be pitied although not to be trusted.

On Saturday evening, Dr. Mudd returned home from Bryantown, coincidentally, as his two visitors were leaving. It was then, if we accept the accounts by him and his wife, that he decided to tell his story to the federal authorities. If he had gone to the police at this point, he might have been spared his subsequent ordeal. But Mrs. Mudd did not want to be left alone that night—there had been too many strangers in the neighborhood.

Most historians have assumed that on the next day, which was Easter Sunday, Dr. Mudd attended St. Mary's Catholic Church near Bryantown. This raises the question: If Mudd was in the vicinity of Bryantown that day, why didn't he go directly to the authorities then? For this we do have an answer. Mudd originally met Booth at St. Mary's. Though the church was more than a half-dozen miles from his home, the doctor apparently attended Mass there regularly; eventually, he would be buried in its churchyard. However, a smaller Catholic church, St. Peter's, stood within a mile and a half of Mudd's farm. Mudd later testified that he attended Mass that day at Reeve's church. Perhaps this has befuddled historians. Reeve's church is actually St. Peter's Church, after Reeve, the man who owned the church land. The morning after Booth and Herold had visited his house, Sam Mudd thus attended mass at St. Peter's Church.

There he saw a second cousin, Dr. George D. Mudd, under whom Sam, as a medical intern, had once studied. They did not sit together during the service, but shortly after the congregation had dispersed, Sam rode up to his cousin's side. George lived in Bryantown and, as he later testified, had come into the neighborhood to have Easter dinner with his first cousin—Sam's father—Henry Lowe Mudd. As George and Sam Mudd rode slowly together over the mile and a half separating St. Peter's Church from Dr. Mudd's home, Sam told the tale of the two strangers. They had appeared on Saturday morning before daybreak. One had a broken leg. They seemed to be laboring under some excitement, more than could be explained by the injury. They had inquired the way to Parson Wilmer's. One had called for a razor and shaved himself. They had finally left his home and gone toward Bryantown.

According to Samuel Mudd, George reflected a while, apparently associating the two strangers with the assassins then being sought in the neighborhood. "I think you had better tell your story to the authorities," he advised Sam.

"I'm fearful for my life," said Sam. "They may have friends in the neighborhood who might try to kill me if I talked. It would look better if you had the authorities come to me."

George Mudd said he would be returning to Bryantown later that night: "I'll get in touch with them for you."

They were standing before the gate to Sam Mudd's farm when he made that promise. It was already about noon. George continued up the road a short way to the home of Henry Lowe Mudd. There the holiday meal was taken in a leisurely fashion. At last George Mudd arose from the table and declared that he must be getting back to Bryantown. On his way home, according to his own account, he stopped to call on a patient. He reached Bryantown after dark and decided to wait until the following morning to inform the authorities. Another day had been lost.

Monday morning George Mudd spoke to Lieutenant Dana. Dana likewise seemed to see no reason to move quickly. In the wake of the assassination many people had come forward with worthless information. Washington was already being deluged with crackpot leads. One letter-writer insisted that Booth was hiding in a Chicago house of ill fame; a medium in Detroit said that actors had hidden Booth in a hogshead under Ford's Theater. The announcement of a reward of $100,000 for the capture of Booth and his fellow assassins would lead to many false accusations. Perhaps Dana could not act at once because his men were busily running down false clues. But Lieutenant Lovett's arrival in town Tuesday quickly stirred him to action. Dana sent for

George Mudd. Lovett retired to a room with Mudd, and with the detectives, Williams and Gavacan, and Joshua Lloyd. For the second time George told the story of the two strangers. "Let's go talk to this Sam Mudd," said Lovett.

Dr. Mudd was working in the fields when the detectives arrived at his house late that afternoon and asked to see him. George Mudd remained outside until his cousin appeared. "The detectives want to know about those two strangers, Sam," he said. Sam grunted, then entered the house.

What went through Sam Mudd's mind at that moment? He probably went inside with the honest intention of helping the government. Even the fault-seeking government would later be unable to deny one important fact: Mudd, whether directly or indirectly, whether through his own desire or through the wishes of his family, had caused the authorities to appear; they did not come seeking him on the basis of any suspicion. However, he would have to relate an account that would negate his apparent complicity with the assassins. He could not long deny his acquaintance with Booth. Too many people remembered Booth's visit to Lower Maryland the previous fall. But he could deny having recognized Booth. During this first meeting with the detectives, as well as during a second meeting three days later, he told a story which he hoped would free him once and for all from implication in the conspiracy. But what he said seemed only to entrap him further. We can imagine the doctor's hesitant manner during his first meeting with the detectives. He probably faltered as he spoke, and tried to avoid contradictions in his story, hoping to convey an air of innocence. His words were reflected in the report which Lieutenant Lovett sent to his superiors several weeks later:

"When the doctor came in I questioned him about the two men that had stopped at his house on Saturday. He seemed to be somewhat excited and said that they were perfect strangers to him, that he had set one of their legs which had been broken by his horse falling on him and that was all he knew about that. He was then questioned in regard to the appearance of the men and did not give much satisfaction. He stated that the injured man was heavily armed with a pair of revolvers and seemed to be very much excited. Dr. Mudd seemed to be very much reserved and did not care to give much information."

The distortions of which Dr. Mudd was guilty were further distorted when Lovett's two detective-assistants, Gavacan and Williams, later insisted that the doctor had tried to deny the visit of the two strangers. The two detectives lied, for reasons we will examine below, but their statements were damaging for Samuel Mudd. Yet the doctor damaged himself more with his actual words than the two detectives did. Even though Lovett and the detectives seemed satisfied with the information they had obtained from Dr. Mudd, Lieutenant Lovett had actually become suspicious of Mudd. He later said: "I was then satisfied that it was Booth and Herold and made up my mind to arrest Dr. Mudd when the proper time came." Lovett and his companions further suspected that Mudd still knew the whereabouts of the fugitives. So they set a trap for him. Lovett hid several of his men in the surrounding thicket with instructions to follow Mudd should the doctor attempt to give further medical aid to Booth.

Herein, perhaps, lies the reason that Gavacan and Williams claimed that Mudd had denied the strangers' visit. With their minds riveted on the prospect of a share of the $100,000 reward money, the detectives did not immediately report to Washington about Booth's visit, nor about his broken leg. They did not want to split the reward with, or perhaps even lose it to, the other government representatives that would descend upon the area. Greed prevailed over common sense. The huge reward placed on Booth's head worked in the assassin's favor. Mudd could not lead the detectives to Booth because he had no idea where the actor might be. By the time the detectives realized this they would have to explain to their superiors why they had delayed three days before reporting Mudd's information. To lie about Mudd was easier than to confess that they had been greedy.

Meanwhile, Booth lay hidden by another Marylander. On Easter Sunday morning, Colonel Samuel Cox sent his son with a message to the house of Thomas A. Jones near the river: Come at once! Cox and Jones, though not related, had been raised together as children. Both had been slaveholders, but whereas Jones could count his slaves on the fingers of one hand, Cox had more than a hundred. Both sympathized with the South, Jones actively so. A hollow stump on Jones's farm had served as a Rebel post office. At dusk, boatsmen would cross from the opposite shore to leave and pick up packages and letters. So reliable was this service that Confederate cabinet members in Richmond would have the previous day's Washington papers on their desks each morning.

Jones saddled his horse and rode the four miles to the home of Colonel Cox. Cox met him at the gate and motioned him to walk away from the house. "Two men called at my house this morning before daybreak," said Cox in a guarded whisper. "I think one of them was Booth. Now, we want you to take charge of them, feed and care for them, and get them across the river as soon as you can. We must help them, as they are on our side."

Jones reflected. "I will see what I can do," he said, "but I must see these men first. Where are they?"

Cox explained that his overseer Franklin Robey had hidden them in a thick grove of pine. Soon Jones pushed his way through the brush and trees toward the hidden fugitives. As he drew near their hiding place he gave a signal. A young man stepped from a thicket: "Who are you? What do you want?"

"I come from Cox," said Jones.

"Follow me."

Thomas A. Jones trailed David Herold through the undergrowth to where a tired man covered with a blanket sat on the ground. Beside him lay a pistol. His slouch hat and his crutches lay by his side. Jones later said that he was exceedingly pale and that his features bore the traces of intense suffering. Jones stooped to talk to this man. He offered to bring food every day and at the earliest possible moment to see him across the river. Before he left, Jones reached down and shook the hand of the man he had promised to hide. The man spoke: "I killed President Lincoln. The

United States government will use every means in its power to capture me, but John Wilkes Booth will never be taken alive!"

The funeral service for Abraham Lincoln began at noon, Wednesday the nineteenth, in the East Room of the White House. The body was then transferred to a funeral car. At two o'clock the funeral procession moved slowly down Pennsylvania Avenue. Bells tolled. Cannon boomed off in the distance. When the car arrived at the eastern entrance to the Capitol, men carried the coffin into the rotunda and placed it on a catafalque. That same day Lieutenant Lovett left Bryantown and retraced his path to Surrattsville. Several of his detectives remained behind to observe the movements of Dr. Mudd. In the meantime, Lovett had questions to ask of tavern-keeper John Lloyd.

The nervous Lloyd seemed ready to talk. Since Monday he had been in the makeshift guardhouse at the town's post office. George Cottingham, one of the detectives left by Lovett to maintain the guardhouse, had during this time intimidated Lloyd by threatening to string him up by his thumbs. Lloyd finally admitted that Mrs. Surratt had been at the tavern the day of the assassination to leave a package for two men who would arrive that night. He blamed all his troubles on her.

"Why didn't you tell us this when we first asked you?" questioned the irritated Lovett.

"I was afraid some of their friends would shoot me," Lloyd defended himself.

"Did you know Booth and Herold? Had they ever been on your farm before?"

"I knew them," admitted Lloyd. "They have been at my house frequently."

Lloyd thus stepped up to his neck in the quagmire of the conspiracy. He had supplied the fleeing Booth and Herold with guns and ammunition. He knew they had killed the President and the Secretary of State. Knowing this, he had misled Federal troops when they came for information on the fugitives. He could clearly be prosecuted as an accessory after the fact. Yet Lloyd would never stand trial for his part in the conspiracy.

Meanwhile, the search for Booth had bogged down. A woman who lived alone a few miles from Port Tobacco reported a mysterious nighttime visitor. Each night for the past week a man had entered her cellar after she went to bed, and had remained until dawn. Could it be Booth? That night, government troops encircled her home. She had instructions to signal with a lamp as soon as her mysterious visitor appeared. At midnight, the light flickered in the window. The government troops advanced, only to find the cellar empty. "That's strange," said the woman. "I'm sure he was down there." Afterward, they discovered that she was insane; it had been another false lead.

In a moment of inspiration, Major O'Beirne, who had himself come by boat to the Maryland peninsula on Tuesday, disguised two of his men, Laverty and Hoey, as Booth and Herold. The two went from farm to farm asking for shelter and, in most cases, were immediately repulsed. But a man named Claggert told the two pseudo-fugitives to hide in the woods behind his house. Detectives immediately leaped upon Claggert, who protested that he meant only to hold the men so he could claim the reward. This government counterplot ended when Laverty nearly had his head shot off.

In some respects Lovett and his detectives, while visiting Dr. Mudd on Tuesday, had acted with equal ineffectiveness. They had proved as evasive with their questions as Mudd had been with his answers. "I did not mention Booth's name at all," admitted Lovett later. "It was not my business to tell him whom I was after." The detectives had also failed. They had not searched Mudd's house. Had they done so they would have discovered the clue that would have identified the two strangers as Booth and Herold. When Mudd set Booth's leg he had used a razor to slit and remove the boot. Working on his patient, he had thrust it into a corner. Later, a servant apparently swept the boot under the bed. There it lay forgotten until Lieutenant Lovett's second meeting with Mudd.

On Friday, April twenty-first, Lovett returned to Dr. Mudd's farm, this time accompanied by Colonel H. H. Wells. They told Mudd they planned to search his house. The doctor turned to his wife: "Go upstairs and bring down that boot."

She returned with a tall black riding boot and handed it to the officers. "Look at this, Colonel," said Lovett, pointing to an inscription on the inside of the boot. Wells, squinting, read the maker's name, the address of his place of business, and also, "*J. Wilkes*," with a dash after it.

"I think you had better come with us, Dr. Mudd," said the colonel.

In the carriage, riding to town, the officers showed Mudd a photograph and asked him if it resembled John Wilkes Booth. "I don't recognize that as the injured man," said Mudd, "but there is a resemblance around the eyes and hair."

At least one historian, Otto Eisenschiml, later would theorize that Colonel Wells showed Mudd a picture not of John Wilkes Booth, but of his brother, Edwin Booth. Edwin's picture was mistakenly being utilized by other detectives who were in pursuit of the assassin. Mudd also failed to identify a picture of Herold. This was hardly surprising. The photograph of Herold used on the reward posters showed him as a schoolboy standing beside a desk. The good farmer Mudd, however, proved more reliable when it came to describing Herold's horse. "That answers exactly to the description of the horse Herold stole in Washington," said Lovett.

Little doubt remained in the mind of anyone in the carriage that Booth and Herold had visited the doctor on Saturday. Nor did any doubt remain that Mudd was in trouble, for by this time he had created a fantastic story about his contacts with Booth. Dr. Mudd had claimed that he had not recognized Booth because the latter was wearing false whiskers. Mudd had lied by saying that he had not heard about the assassination until Sunday, April 16, but the detectives knew that he had been in Bryantown on Saturday when nearly everyone in town was talking about it. And, the doctor had claimed that he had met Booth only that one time when the actor was in Maryland on a land-buying expedition. By withholding the fact that he had also met Booth in Washington, Dr. Mudd had taken a dangerous step toward the gallows.

On the same day that Dr. Mudd was taken into custody, the body of Abraham Lincoln was moved from the Capitol rotunda, where it had lain in state three days. A carriage took it to the Baltimore & Ohio Railroad Station. Guards placed the body upon a funeral train to begin a winding, fifteen-hundred-mile journey to its final resting place in Springfield, Illinois. With the body went two officers, Major General David Hunter and Brigadier General Albion P. Howe, who would later figure prominently in Dr. Mudd's life. And deep in Zekiah Swamp, Booth and Herold, hidden by Cox and Jones, made plans to journey across the Potomac that night.

Chapter 5

IF JOHN WILKES BOOTH expected to be received as a hero in Virginia, he was disappointed. The Civil War had ended; few people had any interest in harboring suspicious strangers and thus aggravating the Union troops who were now controlling the state. While many Southerners would have applauded the kidnaping of Abraham Lincoln—had it been conducted with bravado—few applauded the assassination. There is valor in confronting an equal opponent with sabers drawn, with victory to the strongest. It is quite another matter to fall on a defenseless opponent and assassinate him. Booth had not killed; he had murdered. No Virginian could regard John Wilkes Booth as a hero.

Early the afternoon of Sunday the twenty-third of April, Elizabeth R. Quesenberry returned home to find her daughter talking to a stranger. "I wonder if you could furnish us with some sort of conveyance to take us up country," pleaded David E. Herold.

"Why can't you walk?" asked Mrs. Quesenberry.

"I can walk, but my brother sitting down by the river can't. His horse fell on him and broke his leg." Herold would repeat this story several times during the next few days. The brothers were named Boyd. They were Marylanders, escaped prisoners.

"Could you sell us a horse?" Herold finally asked Mrs. Quesenberry.

She stood firm: "If I were inclined to assist you I would give you a horse, but I'm not inclined to assist you. You must go away."

Herold tramped head down through the field to where Booth was waiting for him. After one day of hiding with Thomas A. Jones, the pair had attempted to cross the Potomac in a boat provided by Jones. They were swept upriver, however, a dozen miles out of their way at Avon Creek—still on the Maryland side of the river. In the morning Herold went to the house of Colonel J. J. Hughes and obtained food and information. Booth and Herold remained hidden all that day, Saturday, April twenty-second, then successfully crossed the river during the night. They left their boat in Gambo Creek.

Now they were in Virginia, yet still far from safety. When Federal troops later arrested Mrs. Quesenberry, she admitted that she had sent her brother after the two strangers with food. Herold later claimed they had then gone to a second house, where they gave a man a dollar for fourteen or fifteen biscuits and three slices of bacon. Finally, about an hour before sundown, Booth and Herold knocked on the door of William L. Bryant, a farmer. They offered him ten dollars if he would take them to the home of a Dr. R. H. Stewart.

"There are other doctors more convenient," Bryant said.

"Dr. Stewart was recommended to us," Herold insisted. Throughout the day, he would do most of the talking.

Later, Dr. Stewart seemed less than anxious to have the two strangers stay with him. "Dr. Mudd recommended we stop and see you," maintained Herold.

"I don't know any Dr. Mudd," retorted Dr. Stewart. Perhaps he suspected the identity of Booth and Herold, although eventually he would swear that he did not hear of the assassination until after their visit. The doctor previously had been arrested several times for his Southern sympathies. He had apparently had enough of military jails.

"The doctor and the well man talked," Bryant told authorities later. "I do not know what about, but I suppose about the other man's ankle. He had two crutches. I heard the doctor tell the well man that his brother could not stay there. He had no room for him. He had turned away some Maryland soldiers that day. After that I started for home, but the doctor helloed me to come back. I did so, but the doctor told me they could not stay there. The well man then asked me if I would take them over to a free fellow's named William Lucas which was about a quarter-mile around the road. I said I could do it."

Booth, reaching the home of the Negro, pulled a gun on Lucas's sick wife. "Get out of bed," he commanded her. "I'm sleeping here tonight." The next morning Booth gave Lucas twenty-five dollars to take them by cart to Port Conway on the Rappahannock River.

On Monday morning, April twenty-four, the eighteen-year-old Confederate Army lieutenant Willie S. Jett, bound for Bowling Green, left his brother-in-law's home, a half-dozen miles from Port Conway. Willie planned to see his girl friend in that town and then travel on to Richmond to obtain a parole from the provost marshal. He rode with two other friends who had fought by his side in Mosby's Command. As they came down the hill at Port Conway toward the ferry, Jett saw a wagon with two men in it standing at the wharf. One man suddenly jumped from the wagon, clutching at the same time at the inside of his coat—as though he carried a weapon in his pocket. The three Confederate soldiers rode by him onto the wharf. As they hailed the ferryboat, the strange man from the wagon followed them.

"Gentlemen, what command do you belong to?" asked David Herold.

"Mosby's Command," said Lieutenant Ruggles. Jett did not speak.

"If I am not too inquisitive, can I ask where you are going?"

Jett felt that the stranger was too inquisitive. His destination was his own business. He turned his back to the other. The stranger, however, wanted to talk. He began to speak of his wounded brother. They were Marylanders, he said, wounded at Fredericksburg.

Jett continued to gaze toward the ferry landing in Port Royal on the opposite side of the river. "Where was he wounded?"

"In the leg," said Herold.

Booth came hobbling onto the wharf. "Come, gentlemen," said Herold. "I suppose you are all going to the Southern army?"

None of the three replied.

"We're going ourselves," continued Herold, ignoring the rebuke. "We wish you would take us with you."

Herold, desperate, decided to play what he considered his ace. He motioned Jett to one side. "We are the assassinators of the President," he whispered.

Jett stared at him incredulously.

At four o'clock that same afternoon Lieutenant Colonel Everton J. Conger walked across Washington's Sixth Street wharf and onto the steamer *John S. Ide*. With him came Lieutenant L. B. Baker (the cousin of Secret Service chief Lafayette C. Baker), Lieutenant Edward Doherty, and twenty-six men of the Sixteenth New York Cavalry. Conger had a copy of a wire sent to the War Department by Major James R. O'Beirne. O'Beirne, after more than a week of futile efforts, had finally come upon one promising lead. A man named Henry Woodland, Thomas A. Jones's ex-slave, confessed to O'Beirne that over the week end Booth and Herold had crossed the Potomac into Virginia. O'Beirne tracked the fugitives across the river, then telegraphed to Washington for permission to continue on the trail. Permission was refused by the War Department. Historians Otto Eisenschiml and Theodore Roscoe have speculated that Secretary of War Stanton wanted Booth brought back dead rather than alive. Other theories revolve about the desire of the chief of the Secret Service, sensing the end of the hunt, to save for his cousin, Lieutenant L. B. Baker, a sizeable share of the $100,000 reward. A more charitable explanation might be that the government needed fresh troops for this all-important climax to the search. O'Beirne's men undoubtedly needed a rest.

Conger's force reached Bell Plaine at the bend in the Potomac on the twenty-fourth at ten o'clock in the evening. After disembarking from the steamer, they mounted and galloped off into the night. By four the next afternoon, Tuesday the twenty-fifth, the tired group of cavalrymen had reached Port Conway, on the Rappahannock, only twenty-four hours after Booth and Herold. "Rest here, men," Conger said. "We'll cross the river on the next ferry."

Conger dismounted. While his men refreshed themselves and fed their horses, he began to wander around the shacks near the wharf. He talked to a William Rollins. "Sure, I remember two strangers," said Rollins. "I was about to go out fishing yesterday when a young man came in and asked me for a drink of water. I handed it to him and he took it to his brother in the wagon."

Conger reached into his pocket. "Do these pictures look familiar?"

Rollins nodded.

The two men had not wanted to wait for the ferry, he told Conger. They had asked him to row them across the river and to escort them to Bowling Green. They had offered him ten dollars. Rollins had said no, he wanted to go fishing. He had promised that if the ferry had not appeared by the time he got back he would take them across himself. When Rollins had returned from fishing, he had seen three Confederate soldiers talking to the two strangers. The younger of the two, Herold, had come up to the house with one of the soldiers and had borrowed some ink. (As Jett later admitted, he and Herold were forging government paroles.) The two men had left with the three soldiers, Rollins said, and he had not seen them again.

Ferryman James Thornton, whom Conger also questioned, said that he, too, remembered five men passing over the day before.

The cavalrymen crossed the river at sundown and, with Rollins serving as a guide, reached Bowling Green by midnight. On their way to Bowling Green the troops had passed the farm of Richard H. Garrett. The previous day five men had arrived at Garrett's door. Willie Jett had never been introduced to Garrett before, but he had seen him on a few occasions and knew him as a Southern sympathizer. Jett tipped his hat and dismounted. "Here is a wounded Confederate soldier that we want you to take care of for a day or so," said Jett. "Can you do it?"

"Yes," said Garrett, "certainly I will."

Jett helped Booth from his saddle, then remounted to ride on to Bowling Green that same night. "We will see you again," said Jett as he went off, although he later told Federal troops he had had no intention of returning. He had no use for fugitive assassins.

Booth and Herold slept overnight in the Garrett house, but the next afternoon they panicked when they heard Colonel Conger's troops sweeping by. They hurried to the woods and did not reappear until after supper. The Garretts were disturbed by this strange behavior.

"Why are you hiding yourselves now that the war is over?" asked Jack Garrett, the owner's son.

"I don't care to meet any Federal soldiers," Booth replied.

Garrett grew suspicious. He left the house and rode to a neighboring farm where he inquired about the Federal troops now in the neighborhood. They were pursuing two men, he was told. "Two men?" asked Garrett. "What do they look like?" The descriptions he received impressed him. The men being pursued were obviously the two at his father's house.

"What have you done?" Garrett asked bluntly of the fugitives when he returned.

"We got into a little brush over in Maryland," said Booth. "But it's all over."

"We can't have you here. I don't want you to bring any trouble to my father."

Booth, offering Garrett $150 for his horse, promised to leave in the morning. Garrett refused the offer but agreed for ten dollars to take Booth and Herold in the morning to Guinea Station eighteen miles away. Booth said he had heard that a Maryland regiment that had not yet disbanded was quartered there. He asked if he could sleep outside rather than in the house. Garrett led Booth and Herold to a tobacco barn, where the furniture of neighbors who feared theft by soldiers had been stored. With his two guests inside, Jack Garrett locked the door, then he and his younger brother, both armed, went to a nearby shed to keep watch.

Less than a dozen miles down the road, two hands jerked Willie Jett out of bed shortly after midnight. Lieutenant Colonel Conger had finally tracked him to a room in a Bowling Green hotel that was owned by the father of Jett's girl friend. "Where are the two men who came with you across the river?" Conger asked.

Jett pulled on his clothes. "I know who you want," he said. "I'll tell you where they can be found."

The cavalrymen wearily remounted—they had been in the saddle thirty-two hours, with little rest—and returned along the road over where they had just come. They were now heading for Garrett's barn.

The ferryman James Thornton would never forget the three boatloads of passengers he had ferried across the Rappahannock River on three successive days in April, 1865. First, on Monday, came Booth and Herold in company with three Confederate soldiers. They had to wait a long time on the Port Conway side of the river. When Thornton finally bumped his ferryboat against the wharf he noticed the five men talking among themselves and also to William Rollins. They had little to say to Thornton, but then, he was colored. Casting off, the ferryman asked Booth to get down from his horse as it was against the rules for anyone to ride a horse on the boat. Booth snarled a refusal. Thornton grudgingly allowed him to stay mounted. He remembered that the members of the party whispered among themselves all the way across.

The next day, Tuesday, the cavalry came. They wanted to know about the men who had passed the day before. Thornton said that because of a heavy wind he had made but one trip across the river that day. The only passengers were three men with horses and two men who had been brought to the river's edge in a spring wagon. He understood that they wanted to go to Bowling Green. The officers asked Thornton to come along as a guide, but he asked to be excused, pleading an injured finger. The entire group—twenty-six cavalrymen, three officers, Rollins, and all their horses—crowded onto the ferry. "The ferry will sink!" warned Thornton. One of the officers ordered the enlisted men to bail if the ferry shipped water.

The morning of the third day, Wednesday the twenty-sixth, an officer rode into Port Royal and awoke ferryman Thornton. "Be ready to take an important party across the river," the officer said. Soon the same group of cavalrymen that had crossed going south the afternoon before moved slowly onto the wharf, escorting an old ambulance wagon. Several curious people peeked into the back of the wagon and saw a pair of feet protruding from under a blanket. "Get back there!" ordered the soldiers. In a short time every inhabitant of Port Royal knew that the mysterious body under the blanket was the assassin of the President. Thornton was never paid by the troops for their rides; he went to his deathbed with the United States government owing him his little fees, which might have been a relatively important sum for him.

For drama and violence, Booth's last moments on earth matched anything in his stage career. Led by Willie Jett, Conger's troops arrived at the Garrett house in the black hours before dawn. They surrounded the barn where Booth and Herold had hidden. "Surrender!" the soldiers demanded. Booth yelled back a curt No! But soon David Herold stumbled out alone. The soldiers then set fire to the barn to force the other out. Suddenly, a shot echoed over the roar of the flames. Booth had vowed that he would never be taken alive, but today nobody knows whether he killed himself or was shot by the trooper Boston Corbett, who claimed the honor (and a share of the reward money).

They dragged Booth, who, though shot, was still alive, from the flaming barn and pulled him to the porch of the Garrett house. Later, at least one Northern doctor wrote a letter to a newspaper maintaining that, from a medical point of view, Booth's last moments surely must have been spent in agony. This did little to satisfy the vengeful Northerners, who had hoped that Lincoln's assassin would be brought back alive to endure the humiliation of public trial and death on the gallows. They had been cheated of full revenge, for Booth had died in obscurity on Garrett's porch.

Now no archfiend remained to swing by his neck in payment for Lincoln's murder. With Booth gone, all eyes turned to eight persons being held in Old Capitol Prison. Included among this number was the Maryland doctor who had set an assassin's broken leg.

II. *In the Footsteps of Poor Old Pilate*

Chapter 6

THE MORNING AFTER the assassination, actor Junius Brutus Booth, Jr., walked leisurely downstairs to the lobby of Cincinnati's Burnett House, where he had spent the night. He ordered breakfast in the hotel's restaurant and ate it calmly, unaware that outside on the streets, mobs were ripping down the posters that advertised his appearance scheduled for that evening. Nor did he suspect that his younger brother at about that same hour was sleeping fitfully in the home of a Maryland doctor. Junius finished his breakfast and prepared to take a stroll.

"I think it would be best for you not to go out into the streets," the clerk advised him. The clerk was Emil Benier, who would later describe the day's events to historian Osborn H. Oldroyd.

Junius Booth looked at the clerk in amazement. "What do you mean?"

"Haven't you heard the news?"

"I have not."

"Your brother killed the President."

Junius stood frozen, unable to speak. The clerk suggested that he retire to his room. Accompanied by several theater friends who had been standing in the lobby, John Wilkes Booth's brother slowly ascended the staircase.

No sooner had he disappeared than a mob stormed the front door of Burnett House. Benier later estimated their number as five hundred. "Where is he?" a voice demanded. The mob roared when told that the assassin's brother had already left the hotel. They rushed from the lobby, hoping to corner the actor somewhere else.

"They would have hanged him in a minute if they could have

laid hands upon him, so great was their rage," reported Benier. "After leaving they returned almost immediately, but by this time we had removed Booth from his room to that of a friend. The mob watched the house so closely that it was four or five days before he had a chance to leave. We finally smuggled him away, however."

The fury of the populace exploded in other cities as well. Three days after the mob scene in Cincinnati, Colonel Ingraham in the provost marshal's office of Washington, D.C., ordered several suspects sent under guard to Old Capitol Prison. The men had been captured in Prince George County, Maryland. One of them was John Lloyd, the tavern keeper with whom Booth had stored the guns which the assassins picked up when they were a third of the way between Ford's Theater and Mudd's farm. To avoid attention, the guards marched their captives through back streets. Still, a large crowd gathered and began to follow. The crowd increased at each corner. Rumors spread: *"They've captured Booth and Surratt!"*

By the time the prisoners had passed the Baltimore Depot, the whispered rumors had become enraged shouts: "Hang them!" "Kill them!" Someone picked up a rock. Soon stones showered upon the prisoners. Enough bounced off the heads of the guards to prod them to do their duty. They wheeled and pointed their bayonets at the crowd. Finally, the guards got their badly bruised captives to Old Capitol Prison.

Meanwhile, Federal troops roaming the Maryland countryside did little to endear themselves to the local populace. In Port Tobacco they used the tombstones at St. Ignatius Church for target practice. A company of soldiers marched onto the farm of Dr. Samuel A. Mudd and set up camp. They burned fences, destroyed wheat and tobacco, and ripped boards off the corncrib. The corn tumbled onto the ground, and the soldiers' horses trampled it underfoot. The men broke into the meathouse and took whatever they pleased. A few days after their arrival, Mrs. Mudd's sister-in-law came by for garden seeds. Mrs. Mudd tied the seeds into packages and placed them in a basket. When the two women left the house there were no soldiers nearby. However, when they reached the garden, soldiers swarmed from the woods. "What do you have in that basket?" demanded an officer.

"Seeds," said the frightened Mrs. Mudd.

She unwrapped the packages and showed the seeds to the officer. He seemed crestfallen. "I thought you were carrying food to Booth," he said. A few days later, word came of Booth's death in Virginia. The troops packed their tents and returned to Washington. Behind them they left a farm in ruins. There was neither owner nor farmhands to supervise repairs.

During the first few days after Lieutenant Lovett and Colonel Wells escorted Dr. Mudd to Bryantown, he had not been treated as a criminal. The colonel permitted him to spend Friday and Saturday nights at home. On Sunday Dr. Mudd went to church, as he did every Sunday. He also walked in the swamp with the soldiers in an unsuccessful attempt to retrace Booth's flight. The next morning, April the twenty-fourth, an officer and three soldiers arrived at the Mudd house, with two farmhands from Henry Lowe Mudd's farm in custody. They asked Dr. Mudd and one of his farmhands to come with them. A soldier saddled the doctor's horse, and the nine men left for Washington. As they departed, Mrs. Mudd began to weep. An officer turned in his saddle. "Don't grieve and fret," he said. "I'll see that your husband soon returns to you." Dr. Mudd would soon learn that not all United States Army officers were so considerate.

Dr. Mudd rode away, perhaps little realizing the seriousness of the charges which would later be raised against him. He may have believed (or may have been *led* to believe) that his role in Washington was to testify against the two men who had come to his door. Others who directly or indirectly had aided Booth, many of whom had no connection or sympathy with him or his crime, also went to jail at this time. By the end of April, a total of two hundred people—mostly Marylanders—had been arrested. This number included Willie Jett and John Lloyd, both of whom had known Booth, had known of his crime, and had helped him. Yet these men would never appear in court except as witnesses for the prosecution. Also arrested was the older Garrett, who denied having had Booth in his house. In prison, too, were Colonel Samuel Cox and Thomas A. Jones. These two had hidden Booth for a week, but they would return to their homes without having had to face trial. If the government had been seriously interested in prosecuting accessories after the fact, it could have had them by the dozen.

The dragnet reached out. The number of those arrested included four mysterious men in female attire who were discovered in Washington a few days after the assassination. History has yet to explain their role in Lincoln's death. The dragnet caught Louis Wiechmann. It caught John T. Ford, whose only apparent crime was owning a theater at the wrong time. It caught the comedian John S. Clarke, Booth's brother-in-law. It caught Junius Brutus Booth, Jr., probably safer in jail now than out of it. It even brought in Edwin Booth.

Edwin Booth's implication was ironic. Edwin was as loyal to the Union as his brother Wilkes was disloyal. Because of Edwin's great dramatic accomplishments the name Booth could have gone down in history without any assistance from his infamous brother. A month earlier (according to a newspaper account of the time) Edwin was waiting in Trenton, New Jersey, to board a train to Washington. As the train stood on the tracks, a number of passengers chatted in the station's refreshment saloon. Then, with a toot of its whistle, the train began to move. The crowd, rushing from the saloon onto the platform, scrambled hastily for the doors of the moving train. Suddenly, one man's foot slipped. He pitched forward, off balance, toward the rolling wheels. If a hand had not at that moment shot from the crowd to halt his fall, he might have been crushed beneath the train.

The person who almost fell was Robert Lincoln, son of the President. The hand that saved him from death was that of Edwin Booth. When Robert Lincoln's superior officer, Ulysses S. Grant, heard of the incident, he wrote a letter to Edwin Booth, thanking him, and adding that he would gladly serve him if he could. Edwin Booth replied to Grant that his only desire was to play before him in Richmond after the fall of the Rebel capital.

The loyal and the disloyal at first received equal treatment under the law. But the same dragnet that snared Edwin Booth, John Ford, and four men in women's clothing also brought in Samuel Arnold, Michael O'Laughlin, George Atzerodt, and Lewis Paine. Not all those who occupied cells in Old Capitol Prison were without guilt, and those who had caused them to be placed there did not necessarily operate from motives of revenge.

And so Dr. Mudd sat in his cell and stared at bare walls and iron bars. He had not yet lost hope. "I am very well," he wrote his wife from prison the Saturday after he left home. "Hope you and the children are enjoying a like blessing. Try and get someone to plant our crop. It is very uncertain what time I shall be released from here. Hire hands at the prices they demand. Urge them on all you can and make them work. I am truly in hopes my stay here will be short when I can return again to your fond embrace and our little children."

If one man could be blamed for Mudd's ordeals—both present and future—that man was the Secretary of War, the Honorable Edwin McMasters Stanton. This able but fiercely partisan Cabinet officer probably felt little animosity for Dr. Mudd as an individual. Mudd seems instead to have represented in Stanton's eyes all who had surreptitiously aided the Confederate cause. So large a number could not conveniently be brought to trial, but one man, Mudd, could stand in their place. Similarly, Mary Surratt probably represented all Confederate women who had conspired against the government and then depended on their womanhood to escape justice. Dr. Mudd and Mrs. Surratt may have stood trial at least in part for the sins of others—as symbols. A more unfortunate choice of symbols could not have been made.

Stanton seems to have been motivated by a desire to bring the conspirators to instant justice; if they were bruised in the process, that could not be helped. Indeed, Edwin M. Stanton remains one of the least understood figures of the Civil War. A tireless administrator, he operated the War Department with quick (if not always quiet) efficiency. His dispatch, in less than seven days, of twenty-three thousand men to support General Rosecrans at Chattanooga has been described by historians as spectacular. No one has ever doubted his love for the Union, but entire volumes have been written attempting to implicate the controversial Secretary almost as deeply as Booth in the conspiracy to destroy Lincoln.

Brevet Colonel Horace Porter, Grant's aide-de-camp, who appeared briefly at the trial of the conspirators, subsequently described Stanton (in his book on Grant's campaigns): "The Secretary had a wide reputation for extreme brusqueness in his intercourse even with his friends, and seemed determined, as an officer once expressed it, to administer discipline totally regardless of previous acquaintance. A Frenchman once said that during the Revolution, while the guillotine was at work, he never heard the name of Robespierre that he did not take off his hat to see whether his head was still on his shoulders; some of our officers were similarly inclined when they heard the name of Stanton." The Secretary acted the part of an antagonist to Lincoln in the Cabinet and behaved even more antagonistically when he was in the Cabinet of Andrew Johnson. He scoffed at Lincoln's reconstruction plans. Yet Porter stated that Stanton frequently broke down after Lincoln's death and wept bitterly at the very mention of the President's name.

Edwin M. Stanton, born in Steubenville, Ohio, in 1814, left school at thirteen when his father died. He worked in a local bookstore, and continued his studies part time. He became a lawyer, moved to Pittsburgh in 1847, and came to Washington in 1856 to devote himself to cases before the Supreme Court. As a government lawyer two years later, he battled, with typical Stantonian ferocity, a group of Californians who defended land claims that dated back to that state's Mexican government. Stanton reportedly saved the United States 150 million dollars. Under President Buchanan he served briefly as Attorney-General. He later helped Simon Cameron, the Secretary of War in Lincoln's Cabinet, to draft a report recommending the arming of slaves. That report displeased Lincoln. It caused Cameron to be dismissed, but Stanton was appointed to his post. The new Secretary severely censored the press and perhaps too freely exercised his power of arrest, yet few could deny his accomplishments in speeding the conclusion of the war.

Stanton, a thick-set man of medium height, had a massive head and a heavy neck. His nose was broad, his eyes were large, and his mouth was wide and stern. Beneath it grew a mammoth black beard, which he perfumed. Horace Porter once confessed: "I never see the impress of his unrelenting features upon a one-dollar treasury note without feeling a chill run down my back."

After the assassination, Stanton once again demonstrated his efficiency. Under his guidance the government trapped all of Booth's accomplices except Surratt. They arrested Michael O'Laughlin in Baltimore on Monday, the morning of the seventeenth. Besides being known as a friend of the assassin, O'Laughlin resembled a suspicious-looking character who before the assassination had been reported skulking around Stanton's house. In Booth's trunk, less than twenty-four hours after Lincoln's death, the police found a letter from a man who signed himself "Sam." "Do not act rashly or in haste," Sam had written, suggesting also that Booth advise Richmond of "the plan." As authorities soon discovered, the letter was written in the dainty hand of Samuel Bland Arnold, a man easy to locate. Arnold had been employed for two weeks as a clerk at Fort Monroe, where Jefferson Davis would later be imprisoned. Like O'Laughlin, Arnold was arrested on Monday. That same night, soldiers marched to the home of the missing John H. Surratt. As they prepared to take his mother (Mary) and his sister (Anna) into custody, there was a knock at the door. A man covered with mud, with a torn sleeve for a hat, and with a pickaxe on one shoulder, was on the doorstep. "I'm supposed to dig a drain for Mrs. Surratt tomorrow," he drawled. Mrs. Surratt screamed she had never seen the man before. But the man standing there was Lewis Paine, who had assaulted Secretary Seward. After being thrown from his horse and thus missing the planned rendezvous with Booth and Herold at the Navy Yard bridge, Paine had wandered through Washington for three days. Now hunger had brought him to the one house in town where he might get food, but which was most likely to be under surveillance by the authorities.

On the Saturday Lincoln died, the commander of the monitor *Saugus* received an order to move to the middle of the Potomac River opposite the Navy Yard and to await there the capture of the President's assassin—dead or alive. Tuesday, the *Saugus* welcomed its first guest—Lewis Paine. He was thrown below in irons. The following day, officers dragged Sam Arnold aboard and confined him in a narrow, iron-walled cubicle that was normally used as a water closet. Arnold, never a man to mince words in detailing his agonies, later reported his treatment during those first few days of imprisonment: "The irons were so tightly fitting that the blood could not circulate and my hands were fearfully swollen, the outward skin changing its appearance to a mixture of black, red, and purple color. This fact was reported to Captain Muroc, who kindly had them changed for a pair that fitted easier placed upon me. The heat was intense. The atmosphere breathed was obtained through a register as it was puffed up by fans used for this purpose, it more frequently happening than otherwise that the machine was not at work, which caused a suffocating sensation to creep over me. To sleep was an impossibility on account of the extreme pain accruing from the torturous irons used."

On Thursday, the War Department printed its posters offering a total of $100,000 reward money. "The murderer of our late beloved President, Abraham Lincoln," the poster said, "is still at large. $50,000 reward will be paid by this department for his apprehension." Also offered was twenty-five thousand for John H. Surratt and twenty-five thousand for David Herold. Seventy-five thousand dollars eventually was paid out. Of this sum, $15,000 went to E. J. Conger, the officer in charge of the troops that had captured Booth. Boston Corbett, the sergeant who claimed he had shot Booth, received only $1,653.85, the same as did each of the other enlisted men in the pursuit party. After his capture Lewis Paine was adjudged worth only $5000. Since he had stumbled guilelessly into the arms of the law, the relatively small sum seems justified. But no reward would be paid to the captors of John H.

Surratt a year and a half later. His value had by then declined like the stock of a bankrupt company—or more aptly, like Confederate money.

Those who tracked down George Atzerodt, however, received a full twenty-five thousand dollars, though the German's picture and identity had not appeared on the reward poster. A detail of soldiers cornered Atzerodt at four P.M. the Thursday after the assassination at the home of his cousin Richter, twenty-two miles north of Washington. Both Atzerodt and his cousin were soon in irons on board the *Saugus*. After three days the government ordered Atzerodt transferred to the monitor *Montauk* in order to separate the two relatives. That same Sunday, Paine, already manacled, had a ball and chain fastened to each ankle. On Monday the twenty-fourth, Ned Spangler joined the prisoners aboard the monitors. The government by then had apparently decided that the lowly stagehand had assisted Booth in his run from the theater. Several people backstage were willing to testify that Spangler had struck a man who had identified Booth. "Don't say which way he went," Spangler was said to have muttered as Booth made his escape. Finally, on Thursday at 1:45 in the morning, David E. Herold and John Wilkes Booth arrived on board the *Montauk*. Herold was thrown in a hold and kept under guard. The dead Booth was placed on the monitor's deck, where he lay wrapped in an army blanket.

Booth's body remained on the *Montauk* deck throughout Thursday morning, a makeshift canvas tent shielding it from the warm sun and from the eyes of the curious who thronged to the edge of the river. One by one those who had known Booth—a dentist who had filled his teeth, a doctor who had operated on him, theatrical people, a woman friend who reportedly snipped a lock from his hair—trooped on board the iron monitor to identify the body.

Thursday afternoon, members of the *Montauk's* crew, under the supervision of Secret Service chief Lafayette Baker, lowered Booth's body and an enormous ball and chain into a boat. This was to delude the crowds on the bank into believing that the body would be buried at sea. Baker later said that the special detail had rowed downstream to Geeseborough Point (a marsh where the army dumped dead mules), had waited there throughout the early evening, then had finally delivered the body at the landing of Washington Arsenal. This arsenal, built in 1803, served during the Civil War as a depot for army supplies, for it was strategically situated at the junction of the Potomac and Anacostia rivers. Baker's rowboat pulled up to the arsenal landing at midnight. Considering later events, the Secret Service chief and other government officials seem to have had a fixation on that hour as the time everything involving the conspirators must take place. Baker's picturesque route may or may not be accurate, but the body did lie buried in an unmarked trench on the arsenal grounds for nearly four years. "While the most notable of the gang of assassins has got a quick dispatch," editorialized the New York *Times*, "there are yet left scores of his confederates, scarcely less guilty, against whom the vengeance of the law will be meted out in a less summary form."

The previous Sunday, Secretary Stanton had ordered that all prisoners on board the monitors be hooded "for better security of conversation." The order seemed unusual, since the prisoners were already in solitary confinement. The press later reported that the hoods had been placed on the prisoners to prevent them from committing suicide: Lewis Paine was said to have tried to crack his skull by bashing it against the iron walls of his cubicle. Arnold, however, considered the hoods merely another torture device of the authorities. "This covering for the head was made of canvas," he agonized, "which covered the entire head and face, dropping down in front to the lower portion of the chest, with cords attached, which were tied around the neck and body in such manner that to remove it was a mortal impossibility. No doubt Stanton wished one to accustom oneself to the death cap before one's execution."

The hoods remained on the prisoners day and night. They could not wash. The hoods were not even removed for meals. Soldiers had to help the prisoners with their food. Thus the suspected conspirators remained aboard the monitors through the first week in May. Rumors circulated through Old Capitol Prison that the government planned to sink the prison ships with all prisoners on board.

When he had arrived under guard in Washington on Monday the twenty-fourth, Dr. Mudd was not taken immediately aboard the monitors. Instead he was sent to Old Capitol Prison. He remained there at least until Saturday, when he wrote his wife a letter anticipating an early release. The evidence implicating Dr. Mudd in the conspiracy did not seem overwhelming at that moment. He had met Booth the previous fall, but so had many other Marylanders. The escaping assassin had come to his door in the middle of the night. With a broken leg the actor had to go somewhere for medical aid, and Mudd was simply a doctor of whom Booth knew. No one could expect a doctor to turn away an injured man. It could be proved that Mudd's farmhouse was actually far from the best route that would normally be chosen by a fleeing assassin on the way South. Mudd could not have known of Lincoln's assassination the very night it had occurred; that is, unless Booth had told him. The doctor's implication seemed accidental—until a man named Wiechmann began to tell a strange story.

Louis J. Wiechmann, as described by historian Osborn H. Oldroyd, was "a dapper man with wavy hair and a prim mustache." Time has the ability to alter public opinion, and history would brand Wiechmann, because of his supposed prevarications, as the archvillain of the Lincoln conspiracy trial. He had been born in Baltimore and at the time of the trial was twenty-three years old. After the excitement caused by the assassination had diminished, he changed the spelling of his name from Wiechmann to *Weichmann*, since that was the way the reporters who had covered the trial spelled it. In 1859, his father had sent him to St. Charles College in Howard County, Maryland, to begin studies for the Catholic priesthood. There he first met John Surratt. Both young men left the school in 1862. Wiechmann had then sought to enter a seminary in Philadelphia, but failed to gain admittance. In September of 1863, he obtained a position as a teacher at a school in Pikesville, Maryland. He was there two months. He then went to another school in Little Texas, Maryland. That school burned down in December. Soon after, he arrived in Washington to teach at St. Mathew's Institute, but he was there less than a year. Some historians hint that Wiechmann was discharged for homosexual tendencies, an attempt to read a homosexual pattern into the conspiracy plot; but there is little more to this than speculation.

In January of 1864, Wiechmann obtained a position in the War Department as a clerk at eighty dollars a month. He had visited his friend John Surratt in Surrattsville the previous spring and while there had seen Herold in the company of several musicians, but did not meet him. When Surratt's mother rented her tavern and opened a boarding house in Washington, Wiechmann became his old friend's roommate. Surratt later would claim that Wiechmann not only gave him confidential War Department information, but also knew of Booth's plans. But Booth supposedly would not allow Wiechmann to join the plot because the young clerk could neither ride well nor shoot.

As the Lincoln assassination investigation continued, Louis J. Wiechmann gave evidence that compromised the innocence of Dr. Samuel A. Mudd. A short time before the trial of the conspirators began, he had returned to Washington after aiding federal detectives in an almost successful attempt to track John Surratt to Canada. As Surratt's roommate, Wiechmann was deeply implicated. He probably realized that he could best save his own neck by convincing the government that he was more useful as a witness than as a defendant. We can speculate that, at one time or another, the officials at Old Capitol Prison must have paraded their band of suspects before the eyes of Wiechmann. "Have you ever seen this Dr. Mudd before?" they would have asked.

"Yes," Wiechmann could have replied after some studied hesitation. "I remember once meeting him on the streets of Washington—in the company of John Wilkes Booth."

The prison officials undoubtedly looked at Mudd and nodded,

for the cast of characters in the trial of the conspirators was now complete.

Perhaps Mudd, too, would have fared better had he talked as volubly about Booth as Wiechmann did about all the conspirators. Mudd's self-respect, however, had not yet been drained from him. Thus the doctor was to suffer heavily, while men such as Wiechmann were never punished.

Chapter 7

IN EARLY MAY, 1865, the chief of the Secret Service, Lafayette Baker, entered a room in the penitentiary located on the grounds of Washington Arsenal. Immediately behind him, like ducklings trailing their mother, came four officers. Baker and his assistants would remain on duty continuously throughout May and June, and into July. The second night after their arrival, they went—at midnight—to a wharf on the river's edge, the same wharf to which Booth's body had been delivered a few weeks earlier. A company of infantry marched behind them. Brevet Major General John F. Hartranft, detailed by Secretary Stanton to supervise prison and prisoners during the coming trial, peered into the darkness. Soon a gunboat steamed into view, docked, and seven faceless figures stumbled, chains clattering, onto the wharf. Soon newspaper readers throughout the country would be familiar with their names: Herold, Paine, Atzerodt, Arnold, O'Laughlin, Spangler, and Mudd. The hooded conspirators marched between two lines of armed soldiers into the prison. Mrs. Surratt was brought later in a closed carriage.

These unfortunate eight would soon become the most heavily guarded prisoners in the world. Judge R. A. Watts of Adrian, Michigan, then a young officer attached to General Hartranft's staff, recalled the security preparations. "The next morning," wrote Judge Watts a half-century later in the *Michigan History Magazine*, "a brigade of infantry, a battery of artillery, and a battalion of cavalry reported to General Hartranft and went into camp just outside the arsenal grounds. During the day one of the regiments marched inside the enclosure and stacked arms." A high board fence surrounded the grounds. A heavy guard surrounded the fence. The three-story brick prison deep within the grounds was surrounded by a thick brick wall about twenty-five feet high. Each morning a new regiment of infantry marched into the arsenal grounds; the other regiment marched out. "The same regiment never returned," said Watts, "nor did the same soldier ever stand guard twice on the same spot. When all the regiments of the brigade had been used as guards, another brigade took its place, and thus many regiments were used during the two months time."

The conspirators were scattered throughout the prison in solitary cells. Each man's cell was flanked on both sides by empty cells to prevent any possible communication by means of tapping on its walls. Beside each cell two armed soldiers stood guard night and day. A company of infantry watched the main door leading into the tiers. "The company of soldiers was relieved each morning," Judge Watts wrote, "others always taking their place and as in the case of the outside guard, the same men never returned a second time and no soldier ever stood guard at the same post twice nor more than two hours." Such fussing over guards might have served a better purpose had it been done at Ford's Theater on a certain Friday night a month earlier.

The security measures seemed severe, but the crime had been severe. Samuel Arnold remembered vividly the next scene. His story, *Defense and Prison Experiences of a Lincoln Conspirator*, was published privately in book form after his death. "I had been but a few days incarcerated at this place," wrote Arnold, "when I was aroused at midnight in my cell by Major General Hartranft, holding in his hand a lantern and some papers, which was seen after the removal of the hood from my head. He asked me if I could read, to which I replied in the affirmative. He then placed in my hand a paper containing the charge and specifications against me and others, which I perused in that silent midnight hour by the dim glimmer of a lantern, after which, the hood being replaced upon my head, he retired, leaving me to ponder over the charge, alone in my solitude."

Arnold and the other seven prisoners had been charged with

"maliciously, unlawfully, and traitorously" conspiring with John Wilkes Booth, John H. Surratt, and numerous members of the Confederate government (including Jefferson Davis and Clement C. Clay) to kill and murder Abraham Lincoln "within the Military Department of Washington aforesaid" as well as to attempt, also "maliciously, unlawfully, and traitorously," the murder of Ulysses S. Grant, William H. Seward, and Andrew Johnson. Since eight persons were to be tried simultaneously, the charge had to be omnibus. The accusation was therefore inaccurate for most of the prisoners. Sam Arnold continued: "The next morning I was removed from my cell and conveyed up several flights of stairs and seated upon a bench, when the hood was removed and I found myself in the presence of a number of the marshalled heroes of the United States, decked in their glittering uniforms, and on either side, victims like unto myself, weighted down by chains and irons. The Court of Military Inquisition was convened."

The decision to try eight civilians in a military court has been severely criticized in historical and judicial circles. None of the conspirators—certainly not Mrs. Surratt—had ever served in the army or navy of the United States. Paine, Arnold, and O'Laughlin had at one time, however, fought in the Confederate Army. Trial of civilians by military tribunals in war areas had been sanctioned by President Lincoln and Congress—but the war had ended. Also, the civil courts in Washington had never ceased to function. Civilians had committed the crime, true; but then they had committed it against the President, technically Commander-in-Chief of the United States Armed Forces. President Johnson's Cabinet debated whether the trial should be military or civil. Gideon Welles, the Secretary of the Navy, a calming voice in times of crisis, favored a civil trial. So did Secretary of the Treasury Hugh McCulloch. Attorney-General James Speed was at first uncertain, but Secretary Stanton argued vehemently for the military trial. "The proof is clear and positive as to their guilt," he said.

Of course, guilt or innocence should not even have entered into the discussion. But perhaps Stanton feared the infiltration of Southern-sympathizers on a civil jury. The public seemed to demand swift justice, untempered with mercy, and civil law, with its provisions for continuances and appeals, might provide justice that was deliberate rather than swift.

Attorney-General Speed finally advised the President to appoint a military commission. Fifteen years later in the face of severe criticism Speed would still cling to his view: "The military commission which tried the assassins of the President was carefully selected. It was composed of men taught by experience and habit to maintain coolness and equanimity in the midst of the most exciting scenes. If it was possible at that period and at that place to have secured a fair trial, the method adopted was the most certain to secure it."

When on the first day of the trial, Friday, May 9, 1865, guards yanked the hoods from the heads of the conspirators, Mudd and the others faced nine stern-looking men: Hunter, Wallace, Foster, Kautz, Howe, Comstock, Porter, Clendenin, and Harris. These nine had been chosen to be both judge and jury to the accused.

The highest ranking officer, and therefore president of the commission, Major General David Hunter, was a handsome but belligerent West Pointer from Washington, whose grandfather had been one of the signers of the Declaration of Independence. Between his enlistments in the army Hunter had settled in Chicago and, as a friend of fellow Illinoisan Abraham Lincoln, had in 1861 accompanied the new President on his inaugural trip to Washington. Four years later, he accompanied the President's remains back to Springfield. Between these two journeys Hunter had commanded the White House guard, had been severely wounded at the Battle of Bull Run, had burned Virginia Military Academy, had ordered the freeing of slaves in the area under his command (an order Lincoln had annulled), and had advised the recruiting of Negro regiments. The Southern states branded him a criminal, ordering his execution if captured. If this death sentence disturbed General Hunter, he let no hint of his feelings appear during the trial. Reporters described him as sitting through many sessions with his eyes closed, but then the press itself would soon be wearied by the testimony.

To the right of the sixty-two-year-old Hunter sat a man twenty-four years his junior. This officer played only a slightly less significant role in the trial than Hunter. Yet his fame rests more solidly in another area. People today remember Major General Lew Wallace as the author of the biblical novel *Ben Hur* (*A Tale of the Christ*), written in 1880. Because of his role in the conspiracy trial, however, many in 1865 accused him of harboring un-Christian ideals. Wallace had grown up in Brookville, Indiana, where he reportedly evinced more interest in drawing pictures and in playing truant than in studying. (He would devote a good portion of his time during the long trial to the making of pencil sketches of the prisoners.) Wallace studied law in the offices of his father (once governor of Indiana), fought in the Mexican War, gained election to the state senate, and at the outbreak of the Civil War, formed a regiment to join the Union Army. One member of this volunteer regiment (and now a fellow judge) was Brigadier General Robert S. Foster, about whom John Lloyd told a shocking story.

At the trial of John H. Surratt, which took place several years after the group conspiracy-trial, innkeeper Lloyd declared that he had been interrogated by an officer while in prison in 1865. He recalled that other prisoners had mentioned that the officer's name was Colonel Foster. Foster had wanted information, but Lloyd had insisted he had already told everything to Colonel Wells.

"Do you know what you are guilty of?" the officer had roared at Lloyd.

"Under the circumstances, I do not," Lloyd had replied.

"You are guilty as an accessory to a crime the punishment of which is *death!*"

Lloyd, however, would not face death. Nor would any of the several dozen Marylanders and Virginians who might logically have been charged as accessories after the fact. For John Lloyd was too important a part of the government's case against Mary Surratt: He would testify that Mrs. Surratt had visited his inn in

IN THE FOOTSTEPS OF POOR OLD PILATE 85

Surrattsville the afternoon of the assassination to leave a package for Booth. (Louis Wiechmann, who accompanied Mrs. Surratt that day, corroborated Lloyd's testimony.) But while giving this evidence at the group conspiracy-trial, Lloyd thought he noticed that one of the judges resembled the officer who had interrogated him in jail. Was the "Colonel Foster" of Old Capitol Prison the Brigadier General Robert S. Foster of the conspiracy trial? Lloyd's truthfulness has often been challenged by historians, some of whom claim that Booth and Herold never even stopped at Surrattsville and that they escaped instead through Upper Marlboro. If Lloyd was mistaken about Foster, it is understandable, for during the trial it was often difficult to distinguish the judiciary from the prosecution.

Brevet Major General August V. Kautz sat to the left of Hunter. A straight-shouldered man of thirty-seven, Kautz had come to America with his parents from Baden, Germany. He, too, had been at West Point. In June of 1863, Kautz had commanded one of the cavalry brigades near Monticello, Kentucky, that chased and captured Colonel John Morgan and his raiders. Near the end of the war, Kautz had entered Richmond victoriously at the head of a Negro division.

Gray-bearded Brigadier General Albion P. Howe came from Maine. He had taught mathematics at West Point. He had commanded the battery of troops that moved swiftly to Harper's Ferry to restore peace after John Brown's raid. While doing so, he may have rubbed shoulders with a young actor named Booth who had rushed from a stage engagement in Richmond to witness Brown's execution. At the time of the trial, Howe was in command of a large military depot in Washington. He stood, as a member of the guard of honor, by President Lincoln's remains in the White House, then, along with Hunter, rode the funeral train to Springfield.

Brevet Brigadier General Cyrus B. Comstock served only one day on the military commission before he was excused. Brevet Colonel Horace Porter went with him.

The reason why Porter and Comstock were excused is not known.

Porter's daughter and biographer, Elsie Porter Mende, claimed that the defense objected to her father because he was aide-de-camp to Grant, a man the conspirators had allegedly tried to kill. But the defense had not even been appointed on the first day of the trial when Porter was retired. If there had been defense counsel they might have done better by sending several others packing along with him. Actually, the defense had no say in the matter at any time. Perhaps Porter himself asked to be excused and thus avoided a disagreeable task. To replace him and Comstock, the government the next day appointed Brevet Colonel Charles S. Tompkins and Brevet Brigadier General James A. Ekin. They, as well as Lieutenant Colonel David R. Clendenin, are remembered for little more than the fact they cast their votes at the close of the trial.

One last member of the court remains: Brigadier General T. M. Harris. In 1892 Harris wrote a book on the assassination and the trial. The study has provided historians with little insight on the hearings (Harris merely rehashed already-published evidence), but it has provided much insight on amateur phrenologist T. M. Harris. Harris believed that a man's character could be read by the bumps on his head, and so he analyzed Dr. Samuel A. Mudd as follows: "He might just as well have admitted his complicity in the conspiracy. Mudd's expression of countenance was that of a hypocrite. He had the bump of secretiveness largely developed, and it would have taken months of acquaintanceship to have removed the unfavorable impression made by first scanning of the man. He had the appearance of a natural born liar and deceiver."

Thus fortified, the military commission met.

The trial was held on the third floor of the old penitentiary building on the grounds of Washington Arsenal. The temporary courtroom was about forty-five feet long and thirty feet wide. The walls of the room had recently been cleaned and whitewashed. Cocoa matting covered the floor. All the furniture in the room was new. Gas lights had been provided for evening sessions.

The nine military judges appeared, dressed in full uniform.

IN THE FOOTSTEPS OF POOR OLD PILATE

They sat around a large table on the north side of the room along with the Judge Advocate General and his staff. Before them, between two of three posts supporting the ceiling, stood the witness stand. Behind it, on the south side of the room, was a table for the newspaper reporters. Counsel for the prisoners also sat at this table, or at one of two tables near their clients. Behind the reporters' table, and filling all unoccupied space, sat those spectators with sufficient influence to gain admittance.

The eight prisoners entered the courtroom through a large door in the west wall. They sat along this wall on a raised platform with a railing separating them from the rest of the courtroom and from their lawyers. Occasionally, the overflow of spectators would crowd in front of the prisoners, blocking their view of the court. With the exception of Mrs. Surratt, who always sat apart from the others at a table in the southwest corner of the room, the prisoners would appear in different seats in the dock. But always, between each of them stood a guard in the light-blue uniform of the Veteran Reserve Corps.

Each of the male prisoners but one wore stiff shackles on their wrists joined by ten-inch iron bars. Thus they could not move one arm without moving the other. For some reason Dr. Mudd was burdened only with ordinary manacles. Chained to each prisoner's leg was an iron ball, estimated by reporters as weighing fifty pounds. Since the guards carried these balls when the prisoners had to move about, it would appear that the weights were a greater strain on the guards than on the prisoners.

Mrs. Surratt at first appeared in irons. After reports of her treatment appeared in the press, her chains were quietly removed. But the men wore their chains during the entire trial. After the first day, they did not appear in court wearing their hoods, but only in the last few weeks of the trial would the government cease using the hoods when the prisoners returned to their cells. This trial marked the first time since 1696 that a prisoner in an English-speaking court had been tried in irons. The theory of "innocent until proven guilty" seemed hardly to apply here.

The burden of proving the "guilty" guilty fell to a trio of government lawyers led by a man Sam Arnold described as looking like some grim statue carved in stone. On the night of the assassination, Judge Advocate General Joseph Holt was speaking at a dinner in Charleston, South Carolina. His speech could well have served as keynote address for the trial of the conspirators. The Judge spoke with eloquence: "In these events, so entrancing for us all, and in those which must rapidly follow, may be found proof, well-nigh conclusive, that the Republic which was born on the fourth day of July, 1776, was born not for death, but for immortality, and that though its bosom may be scarred by the poniards of conspirators, and though its blood may be required to flow on many fields, yet that neither the swords nor the bayonets of traitors can ever reach the seat of its great and exhaustless life."

Holt once had been a newspaper editor in Louisville, and he had also been a lawyer in Mississippi. President Buchanan appointed him, first, Postmaster General, and later, Secretary of War. In September of 1862 President Lincoln made him Judge Advocate General of the Army. Holt had organized the Bureau of Military Justice, which reached out in time of war for suspicious persons not otherwise subject to military trial. Gideon Welles said he fully expected Holt to "hang the murderers before Lincoln was buried."

Aiding Holt were two assistant judge advocates. John A. Bingham's main function was to cross-examine the defense witnesses. This he did with the fury of a famished wolf. Later he achieved an even more dubious honor as the congressman who managed the impeachment trial of President Andrew Johnson. Judge Watts, a silent observer at the conspiracy trial, remembered Bingham well: "When referring to the rebellion or any of its leaders, especially Mr. Davis, his invective burned and seared like a hot iron, but when he touched upon the great and lovable qualities of the martyred Lincoln, his lips would quiver with emotion and his voice became as tender and reverent as if he were repeating the Lord's prayer."

Henry L. Burnett, Holt's other assistant (some would say, henchman) concerned himself mainly with the preparation of evidence. He rarely spoke in court, although he had a considerable knowledge of military justice. His two preceding military trials had involved, first, an Indiana lawyer named Lambdin P. Milligan, sentenced to death by hanging in Indianapolis, and second, the British soldier-of-fortune Colonel George St. Leger Grenfell, sentenced to death by hanging in Cincinnati. Neither man would hang; both would later figure in the life of Dr. Samuel A. Mudd.

The court convened briefly the first day without the presence of reporters and without the presence of lawyers for the accused. The next morning, following instructions to "bathe" the prisoners, the guards dunked them in ice water. They also gave them clean clothes.

On the second day of the trial, May the tenth (John Wilkes Booth's twenty-seventh birthday if he had lived), the charges and specifications were again read to the accused. "Not guilty," they pleaded. The accused were asked if they objected to any member of the commission. "No, I do not," each prudently replied. The court then decided on the rules under which it would operate: Sessions would begin at 10:00 A.M. with a one-hour recess at 1:00 P.M. A copy of the testimony would be provided for the press. The argument on any objection would be limited to five minutes for each side. Counsel for the prisoners would immediately furnish the Judge Advocate General with a list of the witnesses required for the defense, whose attendance would be procured in the usual manner. But the prisoners did not yet have counsel.

The newspapers the next day announced that Dr. Samuel A. Mudd had picked as his attorney Robert J. Brent, a Maryland congressman. Mudd may have wanted Brent, but Brent did not want Mudd, and he refused the appointment. Two other lawyers, James E. Morgan and Henry A. Clark, also declined to assist Mudd. The defense of a Lincoln conspirator apparently had no appeal to them; certainly it could be no stepping stone to fame. These initial refusals, however, turned out to be the Maryland doctor's first stroke of luck since Booth had knocked on his door nearly a month ago. Mudd eventually obtained Thomas Ewing, Jr., who, besides being the most capable of the defense attorneys, brought with him an air of prestige that even the gold-braided military judges could not ignore.

Though only thirty-five years old at the time of the trial, Thomas Ewing, Jr. had already established himself as a distinguished statesman and soldier. His father, Thomas Ewing, had served as United States Senator from Ohio, Secretary of the Treasury under President Harrison, and Secretary of the Interior under President Taylor. While still in his teens, Thomas Ewing, Jr., became one of President Taylor's private secretaries. After graduating from Cincinnati Law School, Ewing moved to Kansas and in January, 1861, became the first chief justice of that new state's Supreme Court. He entered the army a year later, and immediately set about ousting the guerrilla bands from the Kansas-Missouri border. Later he fought a defensive battle which probably saved St. Louis from capture by Confederate troops. To him went much of the credit for keeping Missouri in the Union. Ewing rose in rank to major general before, near the end of the war, he resigned to resume his law practice. The two stars and epaulets he had once worn had no place now on his civilian shoulders, but the military judges facing him probably remembered that he had earned them. They would treat the young lawyer with a certain respect not granted the other members of the defense, most of whom they suspected of Southern sympathies. The fact that Ewing's brother, Hugh, was also a general and that his brother-in-law was General William Tecumseh Sherman, could not impair his prestige in the eyes of the court. Mudd named Ewing as his attorney when the court met for its third session on Thursday, May eleventh. He also named Frederick Stone of Maryland.

Mary Surratt asked to have Frederick Aiken and John W. Clampitt as her attorneys. The next day Stone stated that he would also appear for David Herold; Ewing accepted Sam Arnold as an additional client; Walter S. Cox took Michael O'Laughlin; and William E. Doster became counsel for Paine and Atzerodt. Not until Monday the fifteenth would the unlucky (and probably innocent) stagehand, Ned Spangler, obtain an attorney. Ewing finally agreed to accept the burden of the Spangler defense in addition to that of Arnold and Mudd. As time would prove, Thomas Ewing, Jr. would do better than any of the other attorneys in protecting his clients, but success in the Lincoln conspiracy trial would be only relative.

One more lawyer was introduced for the defense, a man who stood higher than even Thomas Ewing, Jr. in reputation—if not in the esteem of the court. Reverdy Johnson, at that time one of the federal senators from Maryland, had been President Zachary Taylor's Attorney-General. Though he had battled secession in his home state, the military court probably remembered him more for his anti-abolitionist role in the famous Dred Scott decision of the Supreme Court. So when his name was offered on the twelfth as counsel for Mrs. Surratt, General Hunter reached for a note which had been passed to him earlier. "The admission of Reverdy Johnson before this court is objected to on the ground that he does not recognize the moral obligation of an oath that is designed as a test of loyalty," read Hunter tonelessly. The courtroom gasped in surprise.

Reverdy Johnson arose and took a step forward: "May I ask who the member of the court is that makes that objection?"

"Yes, sir," thundered Hunter. "It is General Harris, and if he had not made it, I should have made it myself."

Hunter and Harris based their objection on a letter Reverdy Johnson had sent to his constituents the year before, which advised them that the oath then required of voters in Maryland was unconstitutional. Johnson was acknowledged as one of the nation's leading experts on constitutional law, but at this time many people considered any criticism of government policy to be treason. (Perhaps Harris disapproved of the bumps on Johnson's head.) The court may have anticipated Reverdy Johnson's presence, because, two days earlier, they had read into their rules of procedure a requirement that all counsel must file evidence of having taken the oath then prescribed by act of Congress. But Johnson himself was a member of Congress. He remonstrated: "I have taken the oath in the Senate of the United States—the very oath that you are administering; I have taken it in the Circuit Court of the

United States; I have taken it in the Supreme Court of the United States; and I am a practitioner in all the courts of the United States in nearly all the states; and it would be a little singular if one who has a right to appear before the supreme judicial tribunal of the land, and who had a right to appear before one of the legislative departments of the government whose law creates armies, and creates judges *and* courts-martial, should not have a right to appear before a court-martial. I have said all that I propose to say."

Johnson did not have to say more. He had knocked at least one prop from under this assemblage of military men appointed to be judges. Lew Wallace finally admitted: "It is certainly within the knowledge of every member of this commission that the honorable gentleman had often taken that oath now dispensed with." Reverdy Johnson was accepted, but his usefulness had diminished. At least, so he thought. He appeared only once more, although he worked throughout the trial as adviser behind the scenes. When at the end of the trial he drafted a challenge to the court's jurisdiction over civilians, he let someone else read it to the judges.

If the military treated the conspirators brusquely in the third-floor courtroom, they treated them brutally in the prison cells below. When Dr. Mudd and the other prisoners were returned to their cells after the first day's hearings, they discovered that the latest model in hoods had arrived, one of an even more torturous and painful pattern. "It fitted the head tightly," wrote Arnold later, "containing cotton pads which were placed directly over the eyes and ears, having the tendency to push the eyeballs far back in their sockets, one small aperture allowed about the nose through which to breathe, and one by which food could be served to the mouth, thence extending with lap ears on either side of the chin, to which were attached eyelets and cords, also the same extending from the crown of the head backward to the neck. These cords were drawn as tight as the jailor in charge could pull them, causing the most excruciating pain and suffering, and then tied in such a manner around about the neck that it was impossible to remove them."

At the opening of the trial, Ewing visited Sam Arnold in his cell; he had not yet decided whether to accept his case. Before Ewing arrived, the jailers temporarily freed the prisoner of his hood and threw it into a corner. "What is that?" asked Ewing when he observed the strange article.

"A torture device invented by the Secretary of War," replied Arnold.

Ewing bent to examine the hood and, according to Arnold, made some uncomplimentary remarks about Stanton. "I hope that when you defend me," said the prisoner, "you tell the world of the treatment we are getting here."

"The less you say about that the better," advised Ewing. "You have a damned hard court to try you, and as for Judge Holt, he is a god-damned murderer."

Arnold, when he tried to defend himself before posterity some thirty-nine years later, may or may not have accurately reported Ewing's sentiment. But after his meeting with Ewing, Arnold's hopes of obtaining justice faded. "Hope died within my heart at his utterances," he said. "From that hour I endeavored to nerve myself to meet my fate, fully expecting to meet with death."

Correspondent George Alfred Townsend, writing for the New York *World*, came to approximately the same conclusion. In describing the prisoners to his readers, after he and other reporters finally were admitted to the courtroom, Townsend related a rather grim anecdote about a boy at school who is asked a familiar question about the Constitution of the United States: "What rights do accused persons enjoy?"

"Death by hanging," answered the boy.

Townsend added: "The boy would have been correct had the question applied to accused persons before a court-martial."

Chapter 8

"WILL YOU STATE WHEN you first made your acquaintance with Dr. Mudd?" The Judge Advocate directed his question to the witness, Louis Wiechmann.

"It was on or about the fifteenth of January, 1865."

"State under what circumstances."

"I was passing down Seventh Street with Surratt," said the witness, "and when nearly opposite Old Fellow's Hall someone called out, 'Surratt, Surratt!' On looking around, Surratt recognized an old acquaintance of his of Charles County, Maryland. He introduced Dr. Mudd to me and Dr. Mudd introduced Mr. Booth, who was in company with him, to both of us. They were coming up Seventh Street and we were coming down."

General Hunter leaned forward in his chair and shot a question at the witness: "Did you mean *J. Wilkes* Booth?"

"Yes, sir," said Wiechmann. "J. Wilkes Booth."

The conspiracy trial had just begun, and one falsehood in the story which Dr. Mudd had told to the federal authorities was already exposed: Mudd had not met Booth on only one occasion. Wiechmann's testimony, however, contained a small error. The date of the doctor's meeting in Washington with Booth was December, 1864—not January, 1865. This later provided Dr. Mudd's defense team with its only opportunity to discredit Wiechmann's statements.

On Friday, May twelfth, the court had sat in secret session to hear testimony linking the assassins with Jefferson Davis's Confederate government—testimony which at a calmer time would have been adjudged worthless. At the next session, Saturday the thirteenth of May, newspaper reporters finally gained admittance, by pass and under strict guard, to the third-floor courtroom with its brightly uniformed judges and its manacled prisoners. It was also on that day that the government presented Louis Wiechmann, its most important witness in the case against the Maryland doctor.

The government did not attack Dr. Mudd immediately. The first target was George A. Atzerodt, the Port Tobacco boatman who had been assigned the task of killing Vice President Johnson. Thereafter little order was maintained in presenting witnesses. First Atzerodt, then Mudd, then Mrs. Surratt, then O'Laughlin would be attacked. After that the prosecution would suddenly shift back to Atzerodt. Not only did reporters and spectators become confused, but often the prosecution itself had difficulty in keeping track of the vast number of witnesses (483 were subpoenaed in all) that, like ants at a picnic, trooped in and out through the courtroom door. "So great was the number of witnesses to be examined," wrote court recorder Benn Pitman three decades later in describing the trial for his fellow phonographers, "that the majority were brought to the stand without Judge Advocates seeming to recollect the precise facts to which the witness was to testify. Many questions were asked and only drew forth unimportant or irrelevant matter and frequently it was only toward the close of the examination that the special facts for which the witness was called were evolved."

But on this first day of open testimony, the prosecution had not yet lost its way. John Lee, a Washington policeman, marched to the witness stand to tell of raiding and searching George Atzerodt's room at Kirkwood House the night after the assassination. Lee exhibited his haul, which included: Booth's bankbook, a loaded revolver, three boxes of cartridges, a large bowie knife, and a toothbrush. Robert R. Jones, the clerk at Kirkwood House, then showed the court a hotel register with Atzerodt's name on it. The reason these two witnesses had been called seemed precise and clear: Andrew Johnson stayed at the Kirkwood House; Booth had sent Atzerodt there to kill him.

Then Louis J. Wiechmann, War Department clerk and roommate of John H. Surratt, took the witness chair. Dr. Mudd, resting his arms on the table before him in order to lighten the weight of the handcuffs on his wrists, stared straight ahead. The correspondent for the New York *Times* described the doctor as looking "calm, collected, and attentive." But Mudd had good reason to fear Wiechmann. Throughout his imprisonment, the doctor had clung tenaciously to his statement that he had had only one encounter with Booth. How else could he satisfactorily explain his inability to recognize the injured assassin on the fateful Saturday? Only three persons could rebut the doctor's claim that he had met Booth but once. Booth was dead. Surratt was hiding in Canada. And the last of the three was sitting now in the witness chair.

"Where did you go then?" asked Judge Holt, picking up the thread of narrative as Wiechmann finished telling of his meeting with Mudd and Booth on the streets of Washington.

"He invited us to his room in the National Hotel," replied the witness.

"Who?"

"Booth," answered Wiechmann. "He ordered us to be seated and ordered cigars and wine to the room for four, and Dr. Mudd then went out to the passage and called Booth out and had a private conversation with him. Booth and the doctor then came in and called Surratt out, leaving me alone."

"How long?"

"Fifteen or twenty minutes."

Wiechmann had remained sitting on a lounge near the window; thus he could relate to the court nothing about the hallway conversation. The three had finally returned, and Mudd had moved over to apologize to the clerk for the private conversation. "Booth is interested in buying some of my land," Mudd had said. Booth had also apologized, offering the same reason for the huddle in the hall. In a statement following the trial, Mudd admitted he had had a short conversation in the passageway with Surratt. He had wanted to warn the Rebel courier against Booth, whom he suspected of being a government spy. According to Mudd, Booth had never talked in the passageway and the conversation had lasted only a few minutes, not fifteen or twenty.

IN THE FOOTSTEPS OF POOR OLD PILATE 97

But Wiechmann, not Mudd, now was on the stand. The War Department clerk told how Surratt, Booth, and Mudd had moved to a table in the center of the room to talk in a whisper. "Did you see any manuscripts of any sort on the table?" asked Judge Holt.

"No," answered Wiechmann. "Booth at one time cut the back of an envelope and made marks on it with a pencil."

"Was he writing on it?"

"I should not consider it writing, but marks alone."

"Did you see the marks?"

"No, sir. I just saw the motion of the pencil."

Louis Wiechmann's testimony concerning the conference of Mudd, Booth, and Surratt at the National Hotel seemed ominous indeed for the Maryland doctor. This was true even though defense lawyers would accurately classify it as merely circumstantial evidence. The three could have been planning an assassination in the passageway, or they could have been discussing the price of farmland. Booth's cryptic pencil marks on the back of the envelope could have detailed an escape route, they could have represented farm boundaries and roads, or they could have been marks in a game of ticktacktoe. But even if the defense could have erased from the impressionable minds of the military commission the undertones of conspiracy in Wiechmann's testimony, the defense could not deny the fact that Mudd had lied about the number of times he had met Booth.

Holt continued to draw details from Wiechmann on the comings and goings of Paine, Atzerodt, and Booth at Mrs. Surratt's boarding house. The clerk had never seen Mudd there. He admitted driving the accused woman, Mrs. Surratt, to Surrattsville twice: three days prior to, and on the day of, the assassination. Reverdy Johnson cross-examined Wiechmann on behalf of Mrs. Surratt, then arose and left the courtroom, never to appear again officially during the trial.

Thomas Ewing then laid the groundwork by which to devalue Wiechmann's statements about Dr. Mudd. He bore down first on the one fact in the clerk's testimony which his client apparently had informed him could be proved false. "What time was it you said Dr. Mudd introduced Booth to yourself and Surratt?" asked Ewing.

"It was the fifteenth of January, I think," replied Wiechmann.

"Have you no means of fixing the exact date?" asked Ewing, jumping on this brief indecision of the witness.

"Yes, sir," Wiechmann replied. "The register at the Pennsylvania House could be had. Dr. Mudd had his room there at the time." The register at the Pennsylvania House would indeed be fetched, but at this point Ewing made certain he nailed the witness down.

"Are you sure it was before the first of February?"

"Yes, sir," answered Wiechmann. "I am sure."

"Are you sure it was after the first of January?"

"Yes."

The many historians who would later spring to the defense of Mary Surratt have often condemned Louis J. Wiechmann as a liar. Wiechmann, after the trial, never gave up his efforts to mitigate the part his evidence had played in the trial. However, though Wiechmann's testimony had weighed heavily against him, Dr. Mudd apparently bore little malice against the War Department clerk. "Wiechmann seemed, whilst on the stand, to be disposed to give what he believed a truthful statement," Mudd later wrote. If Wiechmann had erred on the witness stand, at least Dr. Mudd seemed willing to concede that it might have been due to a memory fogged by the passage of five months' time. The defense, the prosecution, and history might quibble over the details of Mudd's meeting with Booth, but one fact could not readily be denied: there had been that meeting.

The trial progressed, and Dr. Mudd, staring at the procession of witnesses, pondered his fate. At the same time, the men of the press stared at him and painted their word-portraits. "Dr. Mudd has a New England and not a Maryland face," George Alfred Townsend informed the readers of the New York *World*. "He compares to those on his left as Hyperion to a squatter." "Last on the bench was Dr. Mudd," wrote Ben Perley Poore, "whose ankles and wrists were joined by chains and anklets instead of the unyielding bars which joined the bracelets and anklets of the others." Townsend said: "He had a sort of homebred intelligence in his face, and socially is as far above his fellows as Goliath of Gath above the rest of the Philistines." The readers of the New York *Times* read: "Here is a man apparently about forty-one or forty-two years old." "He was about sixty years of age," reminisced Poore, "with a blonde complexion, reddish face, and blue eyes." (Neither reporter came close: Mudd was thirty-one.) "His high, oval head is bald very far up," wrote Townsend, "but not benevolently so, and it is covered with light, red hair, so thin as to contrast indifferently with the denseness of his beard and goatee." "He does not seem to be distressed," added the *Times* correspondent, "but is interested in the trial." Townsend said: "His nose would be insignificant but for its sharpness, and at the nostrils it is swelling and high spirited. His eyes impinge upon his brows, and they are shining and rather dark, while the brows themselves are so scantily clothed with hair that they seem quite naked." The *Times* correspondent continued: "He is dressed genteely in black and wears slippers." "Mudd is neatly dressed in a grass-green duster and white bosom and collar," wrote Townsend (apparently on another day). "He keeps his feet upon the rail before him in true republican style and rolls a morsel of tobacco under his tongue." "This man is Dr. Mudd," summarized the New York *Times* reporter, "against whom it was at first supposed but little if anything of guilt could be shown, but against whom now the testimony thus far seems fearfully pointing." Townsend concurred: "The military commission works as if it were delegated not to try, but to convict, and Dr. Mudd, if he be innocent, is in only less danger than if he were guilty."

On the morning of the sixteenth of May, at the end of the trial's first week, the military commission traveled to Ford's Theater. Judge Holt had suggested the visit. He wanted the court to view first-hand the scene where the crime of the century had taken place. Word spread. By 9:30 A.M. when the members of the court arrived in their carriages, a large crowd had gathered, eager to see the celebrities. Hunter, Wallace, Harris, Judge Holt, and the others pushed inside. The court reporters, the newspapermen, and two or three senators also strutted through the arched doorways. Soldiers barred the crowd. Thus the first sightseeing tour of Ford's Theater began.

The commission stood grimly in the box where Abraham Lincoln had laughed at the play. They stared down across the empty stage at the area of shadows into which the murderer had fled. Then the commission members turned and walked noiselessly back to their carriages.

On the witness stand that day was Lieutenant Alexander Lovett.

Judge Holt asked about Lovett's interview with Mudd which had taken place the Tuesday after the assassination: "State what questions were addressed to him by you and other members of your party and what was said."

"We first asked him whether there had been any strangers at the house," Lovett testified. "He said there had. At first he did not seem to care about giving us any satisfaction. Then he went on and stated that on Saturday morning, at daybreak, two strangers came to his place. One came to the door and the other sat on his horse."

In examining Lovett and the other detectives who had first questioned Mudd, Judge Holt dwelled on the doctor's apparent evasiveness. Holt continued: "How long did he say they remained there?"

"He said they remained a short time. This was the first conversation I had with him."

"You stated that Dr. Mudd said they were there a short time? Do you mean they went away in the course of the morning?"

"That is what I understood then."

"Did he state to you whether at that time or before, he had heard anything in regard to the assassination of the President?"

"He said that he heard it Sunday at church."

The Judge Advocate continued to draw from Lovett the details of that first interview. Mudd told Lovett that one of the men had come with a broken leg, which the doctor set. This same man had called for a razor and water to shave off his mustache. One of the detectives said that sounded suspicious. Mudd replied: "Yes, it looked suspicious." The injured man had also had a long pair of whiskers. The two strangers had left in the direction of the swamp. Mudd described them and their horses to Lovett. "I was entirely satisfied," the Lieutenant told Holt, "that these parties were Booth and Herold."

"Will you state whether you had a subsequent interview with Dr. Mudd?" continued Judge Holt.

"Yes, sir."

"How long after the first one?"

"At the first one I had my mind made up to arrest him when the proper time came. The second interview occurred on Friday the twenty-first. We went back for the purpose of arresting him."

"State what he then said in regard to these men."

"When he found we were going to search the house, he said something to his wife, and then she brought down a boot and handed it to me. He said he had to cut it off in order to set the man's leg. I turned the boot down and saw some writing on the inside: 'J. Wilkes.' I called his attention to it. He said he had not taken notice of that before."

A soldier moved to a table at the front of the court. He carried a large boot with a slit down one side. He presented it to General Hunter. Hunter examined the boot and handed it to Wallace. As the boot passed from major general to brigadier general to colonel the testimony continued. When Holt had finished with the witness, Ewing began the cross-examination:

"When you asked the doctor how long those two men had stayed he said they had not stayed long?"

"At our first interview he told me they stayed but a short time," said Lovett, "and afterwards his wife told me that they stayed until three or four o'clock on Saturday afternoon."

"You need not state to the court what his wife said!" Ewing fired back.

When Mudd's other attorney, Frederick Stone, cross-examined the same witness he stumbled just as badly. It is a rule among lawyers never to present a question to a witness unless his reply is known in advance. Nevertheless, Stone asked: "You say that Dr. Mudd seemed to be very much alarmed?"

"Yes," replied Lovett. "He turned very pale in the face and blue about the lips—like a man who is frightened after recollection of something he had done."

Judge Advocate General Joseph Holt must have silently chuckled at the manner in which the defense attorneys were providing him with his best ammunition. "You stated that Dr. Mudd appeared very much frightened," said Holt in re-examining the witness. "Did you address any threat to him?"

"No, sir," replied Lovett. "I was in civilian clothes at the time."

"His alarm, then, was not in consequence of anything you had said or done."

"No, sir. He seemed very much concerned when I turned the boot inside out. Some of the men present then said that the name of 'Booth' had been scratched out, but I suggested that it had not been written."

"Will you state what was his manner. Was it frank or evasive?"

"Very evasive. He seemed to be very reserved."

It was Dr. Mudd's nature to be reserved. But the court was not interested in analyzing Mudd's character or dwelling on psychological insights—other than those indicated by the bumps on his head. Even more damning testimony came from the next witness, Joshua Lloyd, one of the detectives who had accompanied Lovett to Mudd's farm that first Tuesday after the assassination.

"Did you in the course of your pursuit go to the house of the prisoner, Dr. Samuel Mudd?" Holt asked Joshua Lloyd.

"Yes, sir."

"On what date did you go there?"

"On Monday, April eighteenth," replied Lloyd. He was somewhat mistaken. The day was Tuesday, not Monday. (When Benn Pitman's government-approved and government-edited edition of the trial record was published, this minor misstatement had quietly been corrected.) Holt wanted to know what questions Joshua Lloyd had asked Dr. Mudd.

"I asked him if he knew that the President had been assassi-

nated," the witness answered. "He replied that he did. I then asked him if he had seen any parties looking like assassins pass that way and he said he had not."
"That was the first interview?"
"Yes, sir."
Detectives Williams and Gavacan agreed with Joshua Lloyd that Mudd had denied the visit of the two strangers. Lovett, however, did not remember it that way, and Ewing, in presenting his defense, would provide solid reasons to show that Dr. Mudd would never have made such a denial. Meanwhile, Colonel Wells gave his version of Mudd's story. Ewing cross-examined him: "At the time that Mudd gave you this information did you see anything that was extraordinary?"
"He did not seem willing to answer a direct question and I saw that unless I did ask direct questions all important facts were omitted by him."
"Was he alarmed?"
"He was much excited."
Wells later answered a question with a statement that summarized the prosecution's case against Mudd: "I said to him that he was concealing the facts, and that I did not know whether he understood that was the strongest evidence that could be produced of his guilt at that time and might endanger his safety."
It would indeed endanger Dr. Mudd's safety. When the judges of the conspiracy trial met in secret session, one point weighed most heavily in their minds: Mudd appeared reluctant to give information. Wells, however, scored one more point against the young doctor before he left the witness chair. Holt re-examined him: "Will you state at what time Dr. Mudd professed to have recognized Booth as the man he had been introduced to?"
"During their stay at his home," answered Wells.
"So you understood him to admit that he recognized him before he left."
"Yes, his expression was he did not know him at first, but on reflection he recollected him."
Colonel Wells, who had practiced law in Detroit before entering

the army during the war, undoubtedly realized the implications of his testimony—and so did Mudd. Reporters described the doctor as "wincing" and "disturbed." The correspondent for the New York *Times* said of Wells: "His testimony was clear and comprehensive and fixed the guilt of Dr. Mudd as an accomplice of Booth beyond a doubt."

Thus far the prosecution had proved—at least until the defense could prove otherwise—that Dr. Samuel A. Mudd had met John Wilkes Booth at least *twice* prior to the assassination (once at church, once in Washington), and that he had been evasive when questioned by the detectives pursuing the assassin. The prosecution also had called witnesses who had seen Dr. Mudd in Bryantown on Saturday. There he could have learned not only of the assassination but also the name of the assassin. This would refute his statement that he had not heard of Lincoln's death until church on Sunday. Ewing would later try to counter this damning evidence, but he would not succeed.

Now suddenly the testimony turned in another direction. On the eighteenth of May, the government ushered Marylander Daniel J. Thomas into the courtroom. Dr. Mudd must have looked in puzzlement at the witness, wondering why this man should have been brought to testify. He soon discovered why. Holt's questions thrust quickly: "State whether or not you are acquainted with the prisoner at the bar, Dr. Mudd."

"I am, sir."

"State whether or not some weeks before the assassination of the President you saw him and had a conversation with him."

"Yes, sir."

"Where did it occur?"

"At Mr. Downey's."

"In that conversation did he speak of the President of the United States?" Judge Holt had led his witness down a carefully prepared road. Thomas replied:

"He said that the President of the United States was an abolitionist and that the whole Cabinet was such, and that the South would not be subjugated under abolition doctrine. He said that the whole Cabinet would be killed within six or seven weeks, and every Union man in Baltimore. He made a remark to me that I was no better than they were."

The defense would later have some interesting statements to make about Daniel J. Thomas. They would, in fact, bring no less than sixteen witnesses to the stand in an attempt to destroy his credibility in the eyes of the military commission. But for the present, Thomas's testimony prevailed. The reporter from the New York *Times* commented for his morning edition: "Dr. Mudd's status was more clearly defined today, and when it was proved he said, some two months ago, that in six or seven weeks the President and his Cabinet would be killed, the prisoner was much amused and treated the matter as though what he had said to the witness was a mere joke; and such his counsel attempted to prove it to be. As the case progresses this prisoner comes out prominently, and it would now appear that he was, though removed from active participation in the recent conclaves of the plotters, one of the principal actors in the bloody drama."

Bit by bit the evidence mounted against Samuel Mudd. "State who visited him," asked Holt a week later of Mary Simms, a former slave of Dr. Mudd.

"A man by the name of Surratt visited him," she replied. "And a man named Walter Bowie."

"Who called this man Surratt?"

"Dr. Sam Mudd. And Dr. Sam Mudd's wife called him Surratt."

"State the appearance of the man Surratt."

"He was young looking, rather slim, neither very tall nor short. His hair was rather light, at least not black." It was a fair description of John Surratt—or of any one of a thousand other men. However, Surratt (according to Wiechmann, who should have known) was six feet tall and was therefore better than average in height.

A strange story soon emerged about a group of men dressed in gray coats trimmed with yellow who, the previous summer, had hidden in the swamp behind Dr. Mudd's house. In addition to Surratt there was Captain White from Tennessee, Captain Perry,

Andrew Gwynn, Benjamin Gwynn, and George Gwynn. Dr. Mudd made Mary Simms carry food to them. The servants carried bedclothes out into the woods. Surratt had been a regular visitor. He began to appear once every week or two in the winter. He used to go to Virginia and come back, and to Washington and back, and every time he brought the news. Mary Simms did not remember the month when Surratt last came, but apples and peaches were then ripe. The defense would offer interesting testimony in rebuttal, but for the present the prosecution drew forth other telling details.

Holt questioned the brother of Mary Simms, Elzee Eglent, about Dr. Mudd. "Did he say anything to you, before you left him, about sending you to Richmond?"

"Yes, sir," replied Elzee. "He told me the morning he shot me that he had a place in Richmond for me."

Ewing jumped up: "I object to that question and the answer!"

"The object of the question is to show disloyalty," Holt dryly said. The objection was overruled. Mudd had, indeed, in a moment of anger the year before, fired a shotgun and hit the leg of his disobedient slave. If Mudd could shoot a slave for some minor wrong, would he help shoot a President, too?

The prosecution rested its omnibus case on May twenty-fifth, reserving the right to introduce additional testimony later. One witness they called after the defense had begun was a Presbyterian minister named William A. Evans. He thought he had seen Dr. Mudd going into the Surratt boarding house in March. Another late witness was Marcus P. Norton of Troy, New York, a man who had stayed two months at the National Hotel in early 1865. He thought he recognized Mudd as the man who on March third had burst into his room by mistake, searching for Booth. The testimony of neither witness would prove conclusive. In fact, their appearance did much to discredit the prosecution's case. Anna Surratt and Honora Fitzpatrick (the latter a boarder at Mrs. Surratt's house), both denied, as had Wiechmann, having ever seen Mudd at Mrs. Surratt's. Evans himself rather compromised his story when he said: "I have been so confused since the death of President Lincoln that I really at times am bordering on insanity almost." As for Norton's claim, the defense would later prove, by consulting Dr. Mudd's patients, that the doctor could not possibly have been in Washington on or around March third.

But the testimony of Evans and Norton came as icing on a cake that had already been baked. The correspondent for the New York *Times* summarized the case against Dr. Mudd at this point: "As early as November last, he is shown to have been in the confidence of Booth. He has a suspicious meeting with Surratt and Booth at the National Hotel in January. He introduces Booth to Surratt. Booth visits him at his room in the Pennsylvania House. The assassins fly to his house direct after committing the murder. He dresses Booth's wound and assists the escape of the latter and Herold, and when called upon by the officers three days afterward denies that he knows either of the criminals. When arrested on the Friday following, he prevaricates, lies outright, and finally admits he knew Booth. He says he first heard of the assassination at church on Sunday after it was committed; and yet it is shown by abundant proof that he was in Bryantown on the day preceding, Saturday, at an hour when the populace was all excitement, the town guarded by and full of soldiers, and every man, woman, and child in the place had not only heard of the murder, but knew the name of the assassin. Dr. Mudd is doubtless guilty, but with what degree of punishment he will be adjudged remains with the commission to determine."

The *Times* correspondent's reasoning appears cloudy. For example, no evidence had been introduced to show that Booth visited Mudd in his room at the Pennsylvania Hotel. But perhaps this summary by a supposedly unbiased observer gives insight into the method in which the tumblers clicked into place within the minds of those whose duty it was to distinguish innocence from guilt.

If Hunter, Wallace, Harris, and the other officers of the commission had immediately retired to their secret chamber for deliberation and judgment, Dr. Samuel A. Mudd would have been surely and promptly led to the gallows with the words, "Guilty as charged," ringing in his ears. But the defense was yet to have its day.

Chapter 9

EACH MORNING DURING THE TRIAL, chief court-reporter Benn Pitman rode from his office to the arsenal grounds in a special military carriage. Two cavalrymen rode behind him on horseback, swords swinging from their hips and loaded Winchester rifles resting across their pommels. This solicitous treatment had been designed not for Benn Pitman, but rather to protect the record of the previous day's hearings, which accompanied him in the carriage. Six reporters, with Pitman in charge, worked every day of the trial to record every word spoken in the whitewashed room on the penitentiary's third floor. Following the day's hearing, Pitman would return to his offices and, with the assistance of two army privates, make two copies of the day's proceedings. The original script remained as the court record, one of Pitman's copies was given to the War Department and the other was retained by Pitman himself. Each morning the court read and corrected the previous day's testimony. By the end of the trial, this testimony covered 4300 pages, making a pile of manuscript more than twenty-six inches high. The arguments presented by the defense and by the prosecution added another seven hundred pages. Eventually Benn Pitman, with his wife's help, sifted this mass of statements, misstatements, and denials for printing as a reasonably compact, fine-type, 422-page, War Department approved, official edition of the court record.

Other editions also appeared. Journalist Ben Perley Poore supervised the production of a three-volume work presenting the complete testimony. Many of the books in this set were destroyed in a warehouse fire shortly after their publication; today the third volume is extremely rare. T. B. Peterson & Brothers printed an unexpurgated edition of the record which appeared day by day in the Philadelphia *Inquirer*. The Peterson edition is smaller than Poore's or Pitman's—so small one almost needs a magnifying glass to read it. The Pitman edition, however, contains an index, which has endeared it to scholars.

The citizen of 1865 did not depend on book publishers for news of the desperate eight who were accused of having conspired to kill the President. The Lincoln conspiracy trial, as the American press saw it, was one of the biggest news stories of all time. The public could follow the trial proceedings day by day in their favorite newspaper.

During the early weeks of May, the reporters assigned to this trial-of-the-century wrote paragraph after paragraph about the prisoners sitting in the dock, describing their appearances, how they reacted to testimony against them, the chances of their being acquitted—or hanged. But as the trial continued into June, as the summer heat of Washington turned the jammed courtroom into an oven, and as the evidence and counter-evidence became less and less dramatic and more and more repetitive, papers like the New York *Times* seemed to regret their decision to print the complete testimony each day. News of "That Interminable Trial" (as the *Times* headline-writers soon dubbed it) shifted from column one, page one, to the inside pages, and the correspondent who had been supplying the paper with daily dispatches no longer worried about the appearances and the reactions of the prisoners. Instead, his brief stories speculated on how soon the trial would end. On the twenty-fourth of June this string of heads appeared on a column in the New York *Times*:

The Trial of the Assassins
ANOTHER LONG, DULL, DISMAL
DOLEFUL DAY'S DOINGS.

PROTRACTION PROTRACTED AND
PATIENCE TIRED OUT.

THE OLD, OLD STORY, OVER
AND OVER AGAIN.

A FAINT GLIMMER OF SOMETHING
NEW FROM CANADA.
THE GLIMMER GOES OUT IN GLOOMY
GOOD FOR NOTHINGNESS.

And while the staff of the *Times* amused themselves writing headlines, while General Hunter dozed, while General Wallace passed the time sketching pictures, while General Harris studied cranium bumps, Thomas Ewing, Jr., fought for his client. If he bored reporters by presenting sixteen witnesses to testify on a single subject, perhaps he could be excused: A man's life depended on Ewing's skill as attorney.

Ewing aimed his sharpest volley—sixteen rebutting witnesses—at prosecution witness Daniel J. Thomas. In one sense Thomas offered Ewing his biggest challenge. Thomas had accused Dr. Mudd of predicting in advance a large-scale assassination plot. If Thomas was a reliable witness, Mudd was lost, for Thomas had seemingly proved that the Maryland doctor knew of Booth's assassination plan six to seven weeks before its execution at Ford's Theater. But whether the prosecution fully realized it or not, their star witness was very vulnerable. On the twenty-sixth of May, Mudd's defense team called to the stand Dr. John C. Thomas, a physician from Woodville, Maryland.

Frederick Stone opened the examination: "State whether you are a brother of the D. Thomas who has been examined here as a witness."

"I am," replied the doctor.

"State whether your brother made any communication to you on the subject of a conversation with Dr. Mudd in relation to the assassination of the President."

"The conversation that passed was at my house on Sunday morning. He came there to Woodville to church. I asked him the news. He was just from Bryantown the day before and he was full of news. He was speaking of the arrest of Dr. Mudd and the finding of a boot at his house, and during the conversation repeated a remark that Dr. Mudd had made some months before."

"State whether he had ever mentioned that conversation to you before that time," Stone said.

"No, never before that time."

The prosecution probably nodded at this revelation. So Thomas had waited until after Mudd's arrest; what does that prove? But the time of Thomas's conversation was only incidental to the next point. Stone said: "State whether you have, or not, attended your brother professionally."

"I have in some serious attacks," admitted Dr. Thomas. "He had a very serious paralysis attack with paralysis of the body. He was for some time laboring under considerable nervous depression and was mentally affected by it so that his mind was not exactly right for a long time."

Stone confidently put his next request to the witness: "State whether your brother's mind is now sound at all times."

"I am under the impression that it is not at all times."

With that statement the value of Daniel Thomas as a key witness for the prosecution disintegrated. One by one the neighbors of Thomas appeared to call him a known liar whom they would not believe on oath. William J. Watson stated that Thomas had asked him for a certificate which would say that Thomas's share of the reward money should be $10,000 for providing incriminating evidence against Dr. Mudd. Watson had known that Thomas could not have had such evidence. "Let's say it should be $20,000," said a friend of Watson's in jest. "No, sir," Thomas had replied in all seriousness. "I would not have either of you gentlemen swear falsely though by your doing so it would give me $20,000."

Daniel Thomas would not get even $10,000. The prosecution probably wished they had never brought him to the stand. They also probably regretted, to a lesser extent, the presence of the Reverend William A. Evans and of Marcus P. Norton, whose integrity as witnesses was also severely undermined by an alert defense. "It appears to be established sufficiently that Thomas is entirely unreliable," wrote the New York *Times* correspondent on June seventh. (It was a rare admission on the part of the *Times* that the case against Dr. Mudd was not airtight.) "Mr. Norton is evidently mistaken in his identity of Mudd as the man he saw seeking Booth, and the statement of Reverend Mr. Evans, an erratic individual who testified yesterday to seeing Mudd enter the house of Mrs. Surratt on a given day, is also worthless and discredited by all who heard him testify. The rejection of the evidence of these three, Thomas, Norton, and Evans, we regard as certain. But the case against Mudd is not thereby weakened materially, inasmuch as the prosecution does not absolutely depend on any fact that these witnesses testify to."

In addition to disproving what Thomas, Norton, and Evans had said, the defense also exposed the evidence of the Negro servants, particularly that of Mary Simms (who had said that Mudd had secreted Rebel agents, including Ben Gwynn and John Surratt, in the swamps during the previous summer). To do this, the defense first called on Jere Dyer, Dr. Mudd's brother-in-law. "State whether you were at Dr. Mudd's house or in the neighborhood with Ben Gwynn in the summer of 1861," began Ewing.

"I was, in September, 1861," replied Dyer.

"How long were you at the house?"

"We were in the neighborhood about a week."

"What were you doing?"

"We were knocking about in the bushes and pines," said Dyer. "There was a report that everybody was to be arrested. They were arresting a great many men in that neighborhood. Mr. Gwynn came down and said they had been to the house to arrest us. I also received notice that I was to be arrested. I came to Dr. Mudd's and stayed about there, sleeping in the pines between his house and mine several nights."

"Where did you get your bed clothing?" asked Ewing.

"At Dr. Mudd's house."

"Where did you get your meals?"

"When we were near his house, Dr. Mudd brought the meals," replied Dyer. "He would sometimes bring down a basket with bread, meat, whiskey, and such—and the girl, Mary Simms, sometimes brought coffee."

Ewing next sought to establish that Dyer was speaking about

1. (*Library of Congress*)

The Lincoln Conspirators as they appeared in contemporary accounts. Dr. Samuel A. Mudd's picture was not included, for reasons unknown. "Payne" was actually Lewis Paine Powell.

2. (Richard D. Mudd)

3. (Richard D. Mudd)

4. (Richard D. Mudd)

The home of Dr. Mudd. The porch was added sometime after 1915.

The Mudd guestroom. John Wilkes Booth rested overnight, on the bed at the right, before continuing his escape.

Dr. Mudd's wife, Sarah Frances Dyer Mudd, as she appeared in her later years.

The flight of JOHN WILKES BOOTH

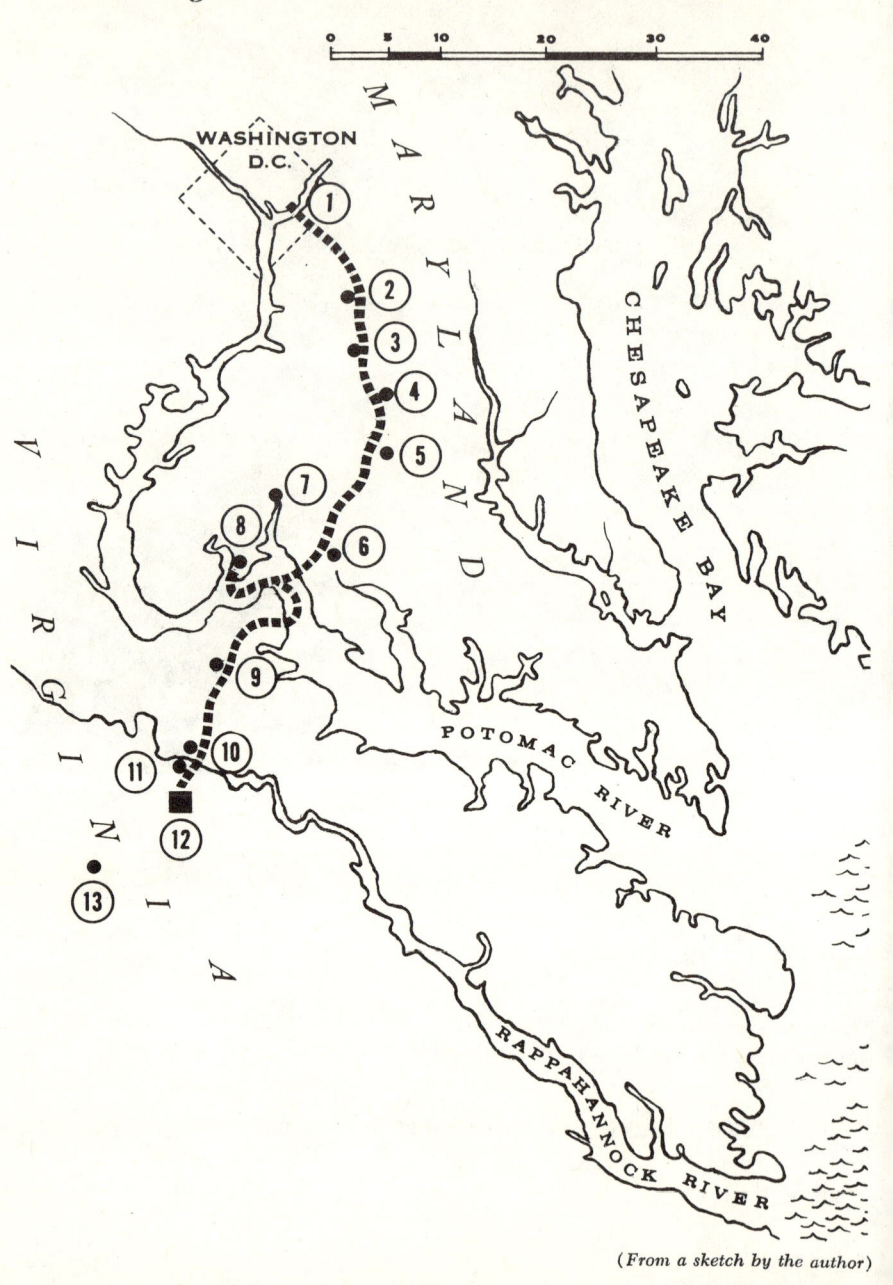

(From a sketch by the author)

1. Navy Yard bridge
2. Surrattsville
3. T.B.
4. Dr. Mudd's farm
5. Bryantown
6. Col. Cox's house
7. Port Tobacco
8. Col. Hughes's house
9. Lucas's cabin
10. Port Conway.
11. Port Royal
12. Garrett's farm
13. Bowling Green

6.
7. (Richard D. Mudd)

5. After assassinating President Lincoln on April 14, 1865, John Wilkes Booth fled from Ford's Theater. He crossed the Navy Yard bridge and was soon in the Maryland countryside, where he was joined by David E. Herold. Together they reached Virginia. Federal troops hunted them down. On April 26, at Richard Garrett's farm, the two men were surrounded in a tobacco barn. After the barn was set afire Herold was taken alive. Booth was wounded and died on the porch of the farmhouse.

6. John Wilkes Booth, from a contemporary engraving.

7. Gate leading from the main road to Dr. Mudd's farm, from a contemporary photograph.

8. (*National Archives*)

8. The monitor *Saugus*, one of the ships in which those suspected of taking part in the Lincoln Conspiracy were temporarily imprisoned.

9. This engraving, which appeared in *Harper's Weekly* in 1865, shows fifteen suspected conspirators being led from a wharf on the Potomac to Old Capitol Prison in Washington. Of the many people arrested by the Secret Service and military authorities, eight were finally brought to trial. Mrs. Surratt is the second figure from the right.

9.

(Culver)

10. (*Library of Congress*)

11. (*Library of Congress*) 12. (*Library of Congress*)

10. The court-martial, known as the Conspiracy Trial, was conducted by a military commission, the judges and advocates of which were: (from left to right) Col. David R. Clendenin; Col. Charles S. Tompkins; Gen. Thomas M. Harris; Gen. Albion P. Howe; Gen. James A. Ekin; Gen. Lew Wallace; Gen. David Hunter; Gen. August V. Kautz; Gen. Robert S. Foster; Hon. John A. Bingham and Col. Henry L. Burnett; and Hon. Joseph Holt.

11. Advocate-General Joseph Holt.

12. Dr. Mudd's attorney, Thomas Ewing, Jr., in his uniform as a major general in the Union army.

13. Drawing of Dr. Mudd made by General Lew Wallace during the Conspiracy Trial.

13.

14.   (*Culver*)

14. Although the accused conspirators were kept in strict isolation, this drawing was conceived for *Harper's Weekly* and was published with the following caption: "Lewis Paine, the assassin of Mr. Seward, awaiting his trial in the penitentiary at Washington, guarded by a sentry of the 2nd Reserve Corps."

15. Mrs. Surratt, Lewis Paine, George Atzerodt, and David Herold were convicted of having conspired with Booth to murder President Lincoln, General Grant, Secretary of State Seward, and Vice President Johnson, and were sentenced to death by hanging.

16. The death sentence is carried out. Dr. Mudd, Samuel Arnold, Ned Spangler, and Michael O'Laughlin, convicted of the same charge as those hanged, were sentenced to imprisonment at Fort Jefferson.

15. (Culver)

16. (Culver)

17.   (*United States Department of the Interior*)

17. Aerial view of Fort Jefferson, on the Dry Tortugas at the tip of the Florida Keys. Construction was begun in 1846, and though unfinished, the fort was manned during the Civil War to prevent capture by Southern forces.

18. Colonel George St. Leger Grenfell, at the age of twenty-eight, from a sketch made in Paris in 1836 by E. Naquier.

19. Dr. Mudd in the carpenter's shop of the fort.

20. The bastion in which Dr. Mudd was imprisoned. The casemates on the ground floor, to the right of the coconut palms, mark his quarters.

18. *(G. R. Greene)*    19. *(United States Department of the Interior)*

20.   *(Today's Health)*

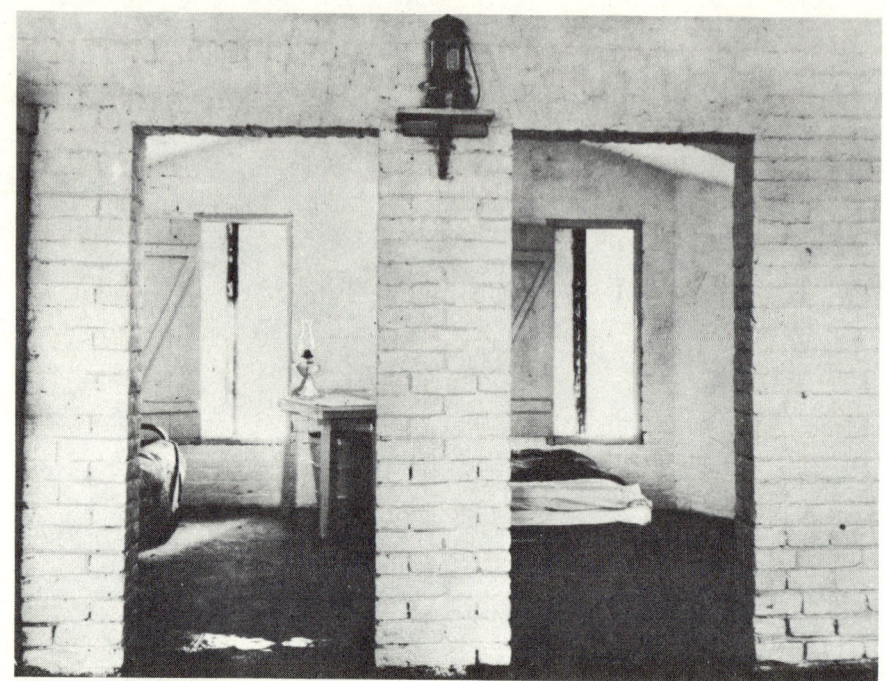

21. (*Today's Health*)

22. (*United States Department of the Interior*)

23.   (*Culver*)

21. Dr. Mudd's cell.

22. The lighthouse and part of the parade grounds. Prisoners and disobedient guards were beaten here and forced to carry cannon balls around the grounds.

23. Dr. Mudd's attempt to escape, as depicted by *Harper's Weekly* with the following explanation: "When Dr. Mudd, one of the conspirators to assassinate President Lincoln, was carried to the Dry Tortugas, he gave the Government officers due notice that he should escape if possible. He was allowed great liberties, and on the twenty-fifth of September, 1865 he made an attempt to escape by concealing himself in a cannon on the steamer *Thomas A. Scott*. . . . Information was immediately given, and after a careful search, Lieutenant Arthur G. Tappan discovered the doctor in the position indicated by our artist, who was one of the passengers on the steamer." Actually, Dr. Mudd was hidden, by a member of the *Scott's* crew, under the planks of a lower deck.

24. (*United States Department of the Interior*)

24. Sallyport of Fort Jefferson. In the summer of 1867, yellow fever raged inside the fort, and Dr. Mudd distinguished himself by his dedicated service during the panic. In October, 1959, President Dwight D. Eisenhower authorized the placing of a bronze plaque in the fort, commemorating Dr. Mudd's heroism.

the same episode as that which Mary Simms had related earlier. Ewing asked: "Were apples and peaches ripe about that time?"

"It was about peach season."

Ben Gwynn followed Dyer to the stand to insist that only he, Dyer, and his brother (Andrew Gwynn), had hidden in the swamp. It had been 1861, not 1864 as Mary Simms had claimed. Several Negroes swore they would not believe Mary Simms, not even under oath. No, they had not seen John Surratt around Dr. Mudd's place that summer or any other summer. But the prosecution, in cross-examining witnesses, had a distinct advantage over the defense. "Have you been loyal during the rebellion?" Judge Holt barked at Jere Dyer.

"I do not know that I have been guilty of any act against the government," said Dyer, hedging just enough to give Holt the opening he desired.

"I speak of your sentiments," snapped the Judge Advocate. "Have you during this rebellion desired to see the government succeed in putting it down?"

"I never wanted two governments," said Dyer, hedging again. More artful dodgers in the twentieth century would learn the value of the Fifth Amendment in fending off similar questions.

"The question is a direct and plain one. I desire you to answer."

"I can only answer that by saying I never wanted this government broken up. I would rather have seen one government."

"Will you please answer the question directly, *yes* or *no!*"

"As I hardly understand your question, I think I have desired the government to succeed."

"You say you have committed no overt act of disloyalty?"

"Not that I am aware of."

Judge Holt turned from the witness. The high-ranking army officers sitting at the judge's table, and perhaps frowning, had spent four years pointing their bayonets at men like Jere Dyer. The officers did not need eyeglasses to see Holt's point.

Ewing called Negro Charles Bloyce to the stand. "Do you know the prisoner, Dr. Samuel A. Mudd?" asked Ewing.

"Yes, sir."

"Have you ever seen Ben Gwynn or Andrew Gwynn?"

"Yes, sir; about four years ago when the war first commenced."

"Did you see either of them at Dr. Mudd's house last year?"

"No, sir."

"Did you see or hear anything of Watt Bowie, John H. Surratt, Captain White of Tennessee, Lieutenant Perry, or John Wilkes Booth?"

"No, sir."

"Neither saw nor heard of any of them about Dr. Mudd's house last year?"

"No, sir."

"Did you know of any Confederate officers or men in uniform being there last year?"

"No, sir."

"Do you know Mary Simms?"

"Yes, sir."

"Do you know what the colored folks about there think of her as a truth teller?"

"The folks there said she was not much of a truth teller, that she told such lies they could not believe her."

"What did they think about Milo Simms?"

"They thought the same about him. I used to think myself that he was a liar, because he used to tell me lies sometimes."

"What was Dr. Mudd's character as a master of his servants?"

"I would call him a first-rate man," said Bloyce humbly. "I never heard of him whipping or saying anything to them."

When Bingham rose to cross-examine, he had one point to make and he made it well: "Did you ever hear anything about his shooting any of his servants?"

"I did hear that," admitted Bloyce.

"You thought that was first-rate fun?"

"I don't know about that," said Bloyce. The courtroom rocked with laughter.

This provided the trial with one of its few light moments. It was about this time that the New York *Times* correspondent wrote: "The evidence has grown uninteresting and the management of the defense has become quite farcical." He probably underestimated the defense—perhaps not in the hopeless cases of Paine and Herold, but certainly in the case of Dr. Mudd. Although Holt and Bingham railed against the questionable loyalty of Mudd's friends, although they ridiculed with some effect the testimony of defense witnesses, they did not combat their opponent successfully on strictly legal grounds. Wielding cold logic like a sculptor might wield a fine chisel, Ewing chipped away at the prosecution's case against his client. He had punctured the testimony of Thomas, Evans, and Norton. He had cast doubt on the testimony of the four servants who insisted Mudd had hidden Rebels in the swamp during the previous summer. However, the testimony by Wiechmann (that Mudd had met Booth and Surratt in Washington in January), presented a serious challenge to Ewing. The defense attorney handled it with his usual skill. To begin with, Ewing called Samuel McAllister to the stand. "What is your occupation?" asked Ewing's associate, Stone.

"I am clerk in Pennsylvania House, Washington."

"Have you the register of that house with you?"

"I have," said McAllister, indicating a large book before him.

"State whether the name of Dr. S. A. Mudd appears on that register as having been entered in the month of January, 1865."

"I have examined the month carefully and the name does not appear."

Stone quickly drew from the witness the date of Mudd's last registration at the hotel: the twenty-third of December. "What is the rule of the house in regard to guests registering their names?"

"I object to that question," said Bingham.

"Objection overruled," decided the court. It was one of the few "victories" for the defense.

McAllister continued: "All persons stopping at the hotel are required to register their names. Often people come in and take meals. They do not register their names, but no person stops in the house overnight without being required to register."

The defense did not press its point further. Louis Wiechmann had stated emphatically that the date of his introduction to Dr.

Mudd was the fifteenth of January. "I am sure," he had said. Yet the defense had just demonstrated that Dr. Mudd might not have been at the hotel on that date—*ergo*, Wiechmann could have lied. Of course, Mudd *had* stopped at the hotel three weeks earlier than Wiechmann's date, and had indeed met Booth and Surratt, much as Wiechmann had indicated. The defense, undoubtedly aware of this, did not dwell much longer on Wiechmann's testimony. The prosecution apparently had no more to say. It remained for the court itself to score a somewhat significant point. General Hunter leaned down over his desk and pointed his finger at the Pennsylvania House clerk: "Do you know whether Dr. Mudd might have been under an assumed name?"

"I could not tell anything about that," answered McAllister.

"Are you acquainted with the person registered as Mudd?"

"No, sir."

Even though the defense had not completely refuted the charges of conspiracy on the part of Dr. Mudd, they had at least cast a shadow of reasonable doubt on those charges. But would the rule of reasonable doubt apply? R. A. Watts, the judge from Adrian, Michigan who witnessed the trial as an army officer on General Hartranft's staff, seemed to think not. "To those who listened as spectators," Judge Watts later wrote, "this rule of reasonable doubt had but little if any place in this trial. It seemed to be only a question of probabilities. Neither the members of the commission nor the people of the North were in a frame of mind to entertain or even tolerate any technical rules."

Yet Dr. Mudd's part in the conspiracy plot seemed far from clear. His house was not situated near a route which would be used by fleeing assassins or abductors who were intent on getting as far south as possible, as quickly as possible. Jere Dyer, Mudd's brother-in-law, testified that Dr. Mudd did not live on any of the direct roads leading from Washington to the Potomac. "A person leaving Washington intending to strike the Potomac above Pope's Creek or Upper Cedar Point Neck," said Dyer, "would go out of his way seven or eight miles to pass Dr. Mudd's. A person starting

IN THE FOOTSTEPS OF POOR OLD PILATE 117

from here to strike the Potomac at Port Tobacco, would be nearest Dr. Mudd's at Troy, where the main road crosses. That is seven or eight miles from Dr. Mudd's, and by the nearest road it would be ten or twelve miles." Therefore, so the defense pleaded, Mudd's house could not logically have been included in the original conspiracy plans. If Booth had gone out of his way to stop at Mudd's house, it must have been due to unforeseen circumstances, rather than to design.

But if Mudd had no hand in the assassination, why had he hesitated? Why had he lied when the detectives came to call? With the manhunt on since the early hours of Saturday morning, why had he waited until Tuesday to tell his story? Therein lay the crux of the case against Sam Mudd. Unfortunately, Dr. Mudd would not be granted the privilege of explaining his deeds to the court. Under the existing rules of military court-martial he, as defendant, was considered to be an incompetent witness. He could not testify.

However, the defense hoped to introduce Dr. Mudd's testimony indirectly, and for that purpose Ewing called to the stand Dr. George D. Mudd. The witness explained that he practiced medicine in Bryantown. Dr. Samuel A. Mudd had studied under him for several years. Sam's father and George's father were first cousins. "State whether or not you saw Dr. Mudd on the Sunday after the assassination of the President," asked Ewing.

"Yes, sir," replied George Mudd. "I saw him at church. He overtook me after that on my way home to Bryantown and I rode with him as far as his house."

"State whether he said anything to you about any persons having been at his house."

Judge Holt stopped the witness with a sharp command: "You need not answer that question! The government has not introduced the declarations of the prisoner Dr. Mudd at that time."

The witness temporarily faded into the background while Ewing addressed himself to the court: "I propose to offer that statement for the purpose of showing that Dr. George Mudd, a resident of Bryantown, and who I will prove is a man of *unquestionable* loyalty, was informed by the prisoner at the bar that there were two suspicious persons at his house on Saturday morning; he told him of the circumstances of their coming there; expressed to him a desire that he should inform the military authorities, if he thought it advisable, of the fact of their having been there; stated to him that he wished him to take it direct to the military authorities, and *not* tell it at large about the streets, lest the parties or their friends might assassinate him for the disclosure."

On a table before Ewing lay a stack of law books with markers in place. He reached for one and began to quote from it to the court. He cited, from book after book, the precedents which would allow him to include the sought-after statement in the record. Ewing wanted to nullify Detective Lloyd's claim that Mudd had concealed the fact of Booth's visit. "This statement," Ewing continued, "was made before he could have known that any suspicions were directed against him. It was an act done during the time of that silence and alleged concealment by reason of which they seek to implicate him as an accessory before and after the fact in the assassination. That conversation with Dr. George Mudd accounts for the silence; that conversation broke the silence. If the fact of his having been silent is to be urged against him, may not the fact that he broke the silence and communicated all the facts to the military authorities be introduced in his behalf?"

Ewing argued forcibly against Holt's objection and subtly managed to interweave into his argument most of the information he had hoped to draw from the witness in the first place. But Judge Holt was no novice at influencing juries, whether civilian or military. He had his own interpretation of the law. "The *res gestæ* in which he was involved," Holt said, speaking of Dr. Mudd, "and which is the subject of arraignment on the part of the government, had closed the day before. That consisted in his having received and entertained these men, and sent them on their way rejoicing, having fed them, having set the leg of the one whose leg was broken, having comforted and strengthened and encouraged them, as far as his hospitality and professional skill could do, to proceed on their journey. That is the *res gestæ*, the transaction on which the government arraigns him, and that was complete at four o'clock on Saturday evening. Now on a subsequent day, on Sunday, after carefully reviewing his own conduct, he proposed to introduce a line of declaration on his part, nearly twenty-four hours afterward, by which he seeks to relieve himself of the imputation which the law attaches to his previous conduct, which has been the subject of the testimony before this court. I say it is not competent for him to do so."

The choice, according to Holt, was either Mudd the lamb, caught in a web not of his own weaving; or Mudd the devil, who, after aiding the killer, now sought to cover his cloven-hoofprints. But the defense would not yield. "The Judge Advocate says that the transaction was wholly closed," argued Ewing. "Not so! The charge here is a charge of concealment among others, and the concealment, as they have sought to prove it, was a concealment not only of their presence when they were in the house, but a concealment extending until Tuesday or Friday, of the fact of their having been there."

The stern Judge Advocate seemed to bend: "If the gentleman will frame his question so as to bring out simply the conduct of the party in the act he did, I shall not object, but I must object to his declarations."

"I cannot prove how he informed the government without proving the words he used," said Ewing.

Assistant Judge Advocate Burnett offered a compromise: "The question could certainly be asked, 'Did Dr. Samuel A. Mudd direct you to go to the authorities and inform them that these parties had been there?'"

"I claim more than that," said Ewing. "I claim the whole statement."

But Ewing would not gain his point. The commission sustained Holt's objection, and Ewing's appeal to legal precedent came to no avail. The attorney for Atzerodt—William E. Doster—would later note somewhat bitterly: "To appeal to soldiers with a legal document had been about as sensible as asking the Supreme Court to decide on a question of strategy."

Ewing finally continued: "State whether you had communicated to the military authorities in Bryantown the fact of any suspicious persons having been in the house of Dr. Samuel A. Mudd on Saturday."

"I did," replied George Mudd. He had sat silently while the tempest over competency raged around his head.

"State to whom you communicated."

"I communicated, I think, to Lieutenant Dana who was the principal in command of the military there at that time."

"When did you communicate it to him?"

"I think it was on Monday morning."

"What statement did you make to him?"

"I stated to him that Dr. Mudd had informed me that two suspicious persons were at his house, that they came there a little before daybreak on Saturday morning, and that one of them had a broken leg which he bandaged."

George Mudd stated that on the day after informing Lieutenant Dana, he had gone to Sam Mudd's house. "Name the officers that went with you," Ewing directed the witness.

"One was named Lloyd, the other Gavacan, and the others were Lieutenant Lovett and Mr. Williams."

Ewing had another important question: "State whether or not anything was said by either of these gentlemen about Dr. Mudd having denied that the two men were at his house."

Bingham objected. Ewing withdrew his question, apparently having learned his lesson. But a week and a half later the court changed its mind and permitted Dr. George Mudd to return and tell what his cousin had said. Judge Holt considered the admission of such a statement "irregular," but nevertheless finally agreed to let George Mudd speak. "I had very little conversation with Dr. Mudd at church," the witness said. "He remarked that he regarded the assassination of the President, to use his own expression, as a most damnable act."

If George Mudd could be believed, Sam Mudd apparently had no sympathy with the assassination. Still, he could hardly be classified as a Union man. One of the military members of the court had already probed in this area: "What is the record of Dr. Sam Mudd for loyalty or disloyalty?"

"From my association with him," George Mudd had replied, "I have had to consider him as sympathizing with the South."

Holt had probably smiled at this admission by a relative of the defendant. Unfortunately for the prosecution, the court had asked one question too many: "Did you ever know him to harbor Rebels or disloyal persons?"

"Never," George Mudd had said. "I have never known him to commit any treasonable act. I have generally considered Dr. Samuel Mudd as very temperate in his discussions and expressions relative to the war. His ordinary manner of discussion was the right of legality of secession, which he maintained. He has generally, however, spoken very temperately and never used any disapprobative epitaphs against the heads of government. He was much more temperate on that subject, I may state, than many other citizens." Perhaps unwittingly, George Mudd had painted the most accurate portrait of Dr. Mudd yet presented at the trial of the conspirators. The doctor's political views hardly paralleled those of, say, an Edwin Stanton. However, he was a temperate and soft-spoken man, not one given to violence. If Samuel Mudd were living in the South in the mid-twentieth century, one could most accurately classify him as a moderate. He might have sympathized with an abduction plot; he would never have advocated assassination.

Benjamin Gardiner, who also had seen Dr. Mudd at church on Sunday the sixteenth, appeared to testify. After another legalistic fight no less pronounced than the first, the court permitted him to repeat Sam's statements. Gardiner had asked Sam Mudd if it was true that the President had been assassinated? "Yes, such seems to be the fact," said Mudd, according to Gardiner. "We ought to immediately raise a home guard and hunt up all suspicious persons passing through our section of the country and arrest them and deliver them up to the proper authorities, for there were two suspicious persons at my house yesterday."

Assistant Judge Advocate Bingham derided this statement when he made the summation for the prosecution: "It would have looked more like aiding justice and arresting felons if he had put in execution his project of a home guard on Saturday, and made it effective by the arrest of the man then in his house who had lodged with him last fall."

One of Mudd's household servants, John F. Davis, had seen Lovett and the other officers arrive on Tuesday. They had sent Davis out to one of the fields to summon his master. Ewing asked the servant what George Mudd had told Sam Mudd just before Sam entered the house. "Objection," cried Bingham. Ewing said he wanted to show that Mudd knew *why* the detectives were at his house. "He could not, after that, as a rational man," protested Ewing, "have gone into the room and *denied* that there were two persons in his house on Saturday morning." Again the court sustained the prosecution's objection. Ewing introduced several witnesses who had been in Bryantown on Saturday and who had not realized that Booth was being hunted. That could mean that Mudd had not heard Booth's name. Some confusion did exist over the identity of Lincoln's killer, but as the prosecution later tried to show, not in the case of Dr. Mudd. After the defense had closed its case, Holt introduced two rebutting witnesses who said that Mudd, on Saturday afternoon, had quoted Booth's name as the killer. Ewing objected that this did not qualify as rebutting evidence. His objection was overruled.

On the nineteenth of June, the many defense attorneys began to summarize their cases. After they had finished, Bingham presented one argument to answer them all. On that first day of the defense's summation, Reverdy Johnson's argument against the legality of the court was read; Johnson did not appear himself. A court reporter read a similar argument by Frederick Stone. Walter S. Cox made his arguments in defense of Arnold and O'Laughlin. Ewing argued for Spangler on the twentieth of June, and, the following day, William E. Doster presented arguments for Paine and Atzerodt. On the twenty-third, Ewing argued for Arnold, disputing the jurisdiction of the court, and finally he argued for Mudd.

Ewing developed his defense of Mudd logically. After questioning the right of the court to try his client, he attacked the omnibus charges laid against Dr. Mudd. Step by step, he dismissed the evidence presented by nine of the prosecution's witnesses, including that of Mary Simms, Daniel J. Thomas, Marcus P. Norton, William A. Evans, and Louis Wiechmann. "I venture to say," Ewing declared, "that rarely in the annals of criminal trials has the life of an accused been assailed by such an array of false testimony as is exhibited in the evidence of these nine witnesses—and rarely has it been the good fortune of an innocent man, arraigned and on trial for his life, to so confute and overwhelm his accusers."

Ewing summarized well his contention that Dr. Mudd had not recognized the disguised Booth. "Now, I ask the court," he explained, "what is there up to this point to indicate that Mudd knew or had any suspicion that the broken-legged man was implicated in the crime? If there is anything in proof showing that fact, I fail to find it. True, he had met Booth twice in November—five months before; had seen him that dark, cloudy morning at daybreak, faint with fatigue and suffering, muffled in his shawl and disguised in a heavy beard; had ministered to him in the dim light of a candle, whose rays struggled with the dull beams of the opening day; had seen him perhaps sleeping in the darkened chamber, his mustache then shaved off, his beard still on, his effort at concealment still maintained. And here let me remind the court, that there is nothing in the evidence showing that Booth *spoke a word*—but where either of the men are referred to as saying anything, 'the smaller man' was the spokesman. Let it be remembered too that Booth was an actor, accustomed by years of professional practice to disguise his person, his features, and his tones—so that if Mudd had been an intimate associate, instead of a mere casual acquaintance, it would have been easy for Booth to maintain a disguise even when subjected to close scrutiny under circumstances favorable to recognition."

Ewing accurately gauged the spirit that moved the court when he said: "The very frenzy of madness ruled the hour. Reason was swallowed up in patriotic passion, and a feverish and intense excitement prevailed most unfavorable to a calm, correct hearing and faithful repetition of what was said, especially by the accused."

"Let it be also remembered," the lawyer later argued, "that anonymous letters have been picked up in railroad cars, found in pigeonholes at hotels, rescued from the waves, and that the continent has been traversed and the ocean vexed in search of proofs of the conspiracy, its instigators, leaders, and abettors, and that in all this written and oral testimony there is not a word making the remotest allusion to Dr. Mudd."

Ewing then added: "Can, then, Dr. Mudd be convicted as a conspirator, or an accessory before or after the fact in the assassination? If this tribunal is to be governed in its finding by the just and time-honored rules of law, he cannot; if by some edict higher than constitutions and laws, I know not what to anticipate or how to defend him."

When Ewing asked if the tribunal was governed "by the just and time-honored rules of law," he unwittingly may have touched on the one flaw that jeopardized the defense of Dr. Mudd. Whether Mudd was guilty or not, the prosecution had failed to present enough evidence to convict him. The military court not only lacked sufficient evidence to convict Mudd of conspiracy, it had not presented enough unrepudiated evidence to convict him of being an accessory after the fact. Yet Mudd was not facing a judge, he was facing a juggernaut. He was a victim of hysteria. He had not even been able to testify in his own behalf, but had been forced to attend the trial as a passive observer, unable to utter a word in his own defense. All his skills as a doctor could not help him in this court of mock justice. Nor did Ewing's skill as a lawyer prove to be of much use.

Ewing was not appealing to jurists; he was appealing to soldiers. They would settle the case not on points of law, but on passion. In their defense it can be said that in 1865 a legitimate jury might have treated Mudd no better. "These nine soldiers constituting the judges in this case," wrote the observer, Judge Watts, "had but little sympathy or patience with the sentimental saying that 'it is better that ninety-nine guilty escape than one innocent should suffer.' The suffering of the innocent during the last four years had filled the measure. There was no place for sympathy here."

A trickle of witnesses remained and then Bingham delivered the final case for the prosecution against all the alleged conspirators: Paine, Herold, Atzerodt, Mrs. Surratt, Arnold, O'Laughlin, Spangler, and Dr. Mudd.

"The conspiracy here charged and specified," he began, "and the acts alleged to have been committed in pursuance thereof, and with the intent laid, constitute a crime the atrocity of which has sent a shudder through the civilized world." Bingham dwelled on the arguments of the defense, and of Ewing in particular, that the court had no jurisdiction over civilians: "Martial law and military tribunals are as essential to the successful prosecution of war as are men, and arms, and munitions." The Judge summarized the evidence linking Jefferson Davis and other Confederate officers to the conspiracy, then began his case against Dr. Mudd.

He told of Booth's visit to Mudd in November and their later meeting with Surratt and Wiechmann in the hotel in Washington. He thought it of little importance whether the meeting had occurred in December or in January. Then Bingham shifted his fire to O'Laughlin and Arnold, describing their early acquaintance with Booth. He discussed the most damning piece of evidence against Sam Arnold: the letter Arnold had written to Booth in an attempt to back out of the plot only a few days before the assassination. Bingham snorted at the notion that Arnold had thus exonerated himself: "If he abandoned the conspiracy, why did he not make known the fact to Abraham Lincoln and his constitutional advisers that these men, armed with the weapons of assassination, were daily lying in wait for their lives?"

Bingham traced Atzerodt, Herold, Paine, and Booth to Mary Surratt's boarding house: "If not one word had been said, the mere act of Paine, in flying to her house for shelter, would have borne witness against her strong as proofs from Holy Writ." Ned Spangler, said Bingham, aided Booth's escape from the theater. Mudd set Booth's leg and later hid this fact from the authorities.

"I leave the decision of this dread issue with the court," ended Bingham, "to which alone it belongs. It is for you to say, upon your oaths, whether the accused are guilty."

On the twenty-ninth of June, Major General David Hunter stretched himself and for the last time arose from the chair he had occupied during these sessions for the better part of two months. Major General Lew Wallace laid down his pencil. Brigadier General T. M. Harris sighed and moved on to scrutinize other bumps on other heads in other places. The six other officers in somewhat ruffled blue uniforms followed the lead of their superiors and left the courtroom. Judge Holt, without a glance at the attorneys who had opposed him, left with his assistants. His task was not yet completed. In line with the rules of military trials, he would sit with the nine judges to assist them in their decisions. The guards nudged the prisoners and they shuffled for the last time through the prison door at the rear of the dock. The clanking of their chains echoed in the courtroom long after they had disappeared from sight.

Thomas Ewing, Jr., stuffed his papers into a briefcase and moved toward a door on the opposite side of the courtroom. He nodded politely to General Hartranft as he left. The representatives of the press closed their notebooks, and with a sigh of relief—"Thank God, that's over"—left the arsenal grounds to concentrate on less earth-shaking axe-murders, rapes, wife-beatings, and kidnapings. But before their duties ceased, they would have an execution to attend. Benn Pitman gathered his notes from the court recorder's table and headed toward the carriage which would take him to his office. Late that night he added the five-thousandth page to the trial record. The spectators who had witnessed that last session rushed home to place their entrance passes in a drawer, so that some day years later they might exhibit them as souvenirs. After the last person had moved from the small, whitewashed room with its cocoa matting floor and new furniture, a detail of soldiers entered and with brooms and mops started the job of cleaning up the scene of the trial of the Lincoln conspirators.

Chapter 10

WRITING MANY YEARS AFTER the Civil War had ended, R. A. Watts, referred to earlier, did some speculating. "As to the actual guilt of Atzerodt, Herold, and Paine," he wrote, "there was no room for doubt. In the cases of Arnold, O'Laughlin, Spangler, Dr. Mudd and Mrs. Surratt, there was much contradictory testimony. If the government witnesses were entitled to credit, the verdict was justified. If the witnesses for the defendants told the truth, there was room for doubt, and for reasonable doubt, particularly in the cases of Arnold and Spangler.

"But here entered the serious difficulty for these defendants. All or nearly all the witnesses for the defense were either active sympathizers with the rebellion, or at best of most doubtful loyalty to the government. More than all else, however, every one of the defendants were most bitter in their hatred of Mr. Lincoln and the United States government. These facts were the terrible makeweights that condemned them, where otherwise there might have been hope. What a boon to Arnold, Spangler, and Mudd would a fair reputation for loyalty have been!"

At ten in the morning on the twenty-ninth of June, 1865, the nine members of the military commission (with Judge Advocate General Holt advising them) met behind closed doors. They deliberated for six hours, then adjourned until the following day. At about this time General Wallace wrote to his wife: "I have passed a few words with my associate members, and think we can agree in a couple of hours at farthest. Three, if not four, of the eight will be acquitted." But early the next morning, when the commission had finished its deliberations, it decided that *none* would be acquitted. All eight conspirators were found *guilty*—but in varying degrees.

Paine, Atzerodt, and Herold were sentenced to death by hanging. To obtain the death penalty, a two-thirds majority—six of nine voters—had been necessary. Mrs. Surratt had been found equally guilty, but a petition for mercy (reportedly signed by Hunter, Kautz, Foster, Ekin, and Tompkins) was attached to the findings sent to the President for approval. It was not heeded. In later years a storm of protest arose against the severeness of her punishment. President Johnson, who signed her death sentence, claimed that Judge Holt had never shown him the petition for mercy. Judge Holt claimed otherwise. It has never been established which of the two men told the truth.

The four other prisoners, for whom Wallace had predicted acquittal, would not hang. Perhaps this fitted the general's definition of "acquittal." The court sentenced Arnold, O'Laughlin, and Dr. Mudd to life imprisonment at New York's Albany Penitentiary. Spangler was sentenced to six years at the same penitentiary. Mudd's attorney, Fredrick Stone, later agreed with the judgment against his client. In 1883, Stone informed a reporter from the New York *Times*: "The proclamation of the government was straightforward, that death should be the penalty for any man who could give information about the convicts and would not do it. Yet Dr. Mudd was saved, and it is understood that the vote stood five to four. One more vote would have hanged him." Stone's opinion to the contrary, Dr. Mudd somehow would not, in the years following, feel "saved."

It could not be denied, however, that Dr. Samuel A. Mudd had passed within the shadow of the gallows. Shortly after the trial had ended, a revealing item appeared in the letters column of the New York *Times*. It came from a "friend" of General Hunter who reported on a conversation with the general. "The court never believed that Dr. Mudd knew anything of Booth's designs," General Hunter was said to have told his friend. "Booth made him a tool, as he had done with others. Dr. Mudd was the victim of his own timidity. Had he acknowledged to the soldiers whom he saw in search of Booth the day after the assassination that Booth had got his leg set at his house and went off, and had he like a man come out and said he knew Booth instead of flatly denying it to the courts, he would have had little trouble." Hunter never denied the statements of the letter-writer.

On the fifth of July, President Johnson signed the order which sentenced Paine, Atzerodt, Herold, and Mrs. Surratt to death. At noon the next day, Major General W. S. Hancock, Hartranft, and a turnkey, visited four cells to inform the three men and the woman that they would be executed the next day. "I am entirely innocent," insisted Mrs. Surratt. Lewis Paine later agreed with this statement.

Sam Arnold described the day before execution: "That same afternoon the noise of hammers was distinctly heard as if some repairing about the building was being done. I tried to concentrate my thoughts in an attempt to unravel its meaning, never for an instant dreaming they were erecting the scaffold to launch human souls into endless eternity in such quick and sudden haste. The hammering continued throughout the afternoon until late, when the noise from the hammers ceased. The next morning there was an unusual movement of feet hurrying to and fro, the rattling of chains and dragging of ponderous balls over the brick pavement in front of my cell."

About two o'clock that day, General Dodd visited Arnold's cell and sat down on a small box. "Have you noticed anything of an unusual nature today?" he asked the prisoner.

"I judge from all the noise other prisoners have arrived," answered Arnold.

"No," replied the General. "Four of the conspirators have been executed."

Arnold remembered being "completely thunderstruck." He, O'Laughlin, Spangler, and Dr. Mudd would not discover their own fate, or even that they would not be executed, until the government chose to inform them ten days later.

At his last Cabinet meeting on the morning of April fourteenth, Lincoln had expressed his ideas on punishment for the vanquished South. "I hope that there will be no persecution," he had said, "no bloody work after the war is over. No one need expect me to take any part in hanging or killing these men, even the worst of them." Lincoln might not have been so forgiving to a criminal offense as serious as murder, but he would certainly have frowned at sentencing a young doctor to life imprisonment for "timidity," and at the execution of a mother because she "feathered the nest where the eggs were hatched." Mrs. Surratt's attorney, William Doster, attended the execution, saw the traps fall, and hurriedly left the arsenal grounds. He reported that a large crowd around the exit shouted: "Judicial murder!" The New York *Times* apparently did not concur with the crowd's judgment. On the day of the executions it editorialized: "The justice of the verdict in the case of the conspirators of the fourteenth of April is such as to command the approval of the whole country, and what is of high importance in this instance—of history."

Today this statement seems ironic indeed, especially when one considers the questionable aspects of this "justice." The defendants had had no opportunity to obtain lawyers until after the trial had begun. The prosecution had summoned witnesses to court without giving the defense any notice. The reliability of the prosecution witnesses, as Ewing indicated in his summation, struck a new low mark in the history of American law. One witness, Sanford Conover, had sought to involve Jefferson Davis and the entire Confederate administration in the assassination. Later the federal government tried him for perjury and sentenced him to ten years in jail. Daniel Thomas, who had accused Dr. Mudd of predicting Lincoln's assassination in advance, was later arrested, tried and convicted on a charge of fraud involving pension funds. (He died in the penitentiary.) The defense requested that witnesses be retained one extra day should there be need of recalling them. Hunter agreed, but Holt protested so vigorously that the presiding officer decided in Holt's favor. Witnesses were obliged to face the court at all times, even when being questioned by defense attorneys who were seated at tables in the rear. If a witness attempted to turn in a natural desire to face the person addressing him, he was halted by a sharp command: "Face the court!" Of fifty-four objections made by the prosecution, the court overruled only three; of twelve objections made by the defense, the court overruled every one. The prisoners' appearance in court in irons could hardly be said to have demonstrated that the government believed in innocence until proven guilty.

Dr. Mudd himself bitterly resented the treatment he had received from the military commission. "Not a man of them sat on my trial with an unbiased and unprejudiced mind," he years later told a New York *Herald* reporter. "Before a word of evidence was heard, my case was prejudiced and I was already condemned on the strength of wild rumor and misrepresentation. The witnesses perjured themselves and while I was sitting there in that dock and listening to their monstrous falsehoods I felt ashamed of my species and lost faith forever in all mankind. That men would stand up in that court and take an oath before heaven to tell the truth and the next moment set themselves to work to swear away by unright perjury the life of a fellow man was something that I, in my innocence of the world, never thought possible." Dr. Mudd was only thirty-one years old—but he was learning rapidly.

Despite Dr. Mudd's life sentence, a flicker of hope remained. When Ewing learned that his client, by court order, would spend the remainder of his life in Albany Penitentiary, he quickly charted his next move. He would go to New York as soon as Mudd reached the penitentiary and ask for a writ of habeas corpus. Brought before a judge in a civil court, the legality of Mudd's trial before a military tribunal could be challenged. The case, on appeal, might even go up to the Supreme Court; and the highest judicial body in the country could be expected to rule justly on the usurpation of a constitutional right by the military. A civil retrial at a later date, in a calmer time, might win Mudd acquittal. Certainly the prosecution would no longer dare to utilize either Daniel Thomas or Mary Simms as witnesses. At the worst, the sentence of life imprisonment might be reduced.

But Mudd's attorney did not have an opportunity to ask for a writ of habeas corpus. On the seventeenth of July, guards dragged the remaining four conspirators—Arnold, O'Laughlin, Spangler, and Mudd—to the offices of General Hartranft. He informed them that they had been found guilty. That night, once more at midnight, the conspirators were taken from the arsenal grounds as they had been brought there: wearing irons and marching between two columns of armed guards. At the wharf they were ushered aboard a steamboat, which immediately moved downriver. The next afternoon, near the mouth of the Potomac, the guards temporarily removed the irons from the prisoners' wrists. The four men were then transferred to a small tugboat. Soon after that, in a third move, Mudd and the others found themselves scrambling up a ladder onto the deck of the gunboat *Florida*. And the following morning the Washington newspapers announced that, instead of being taken to the Albany Penitentiary, the conspirators had been dispatched to Fort Jefferson in the Dry Tortugas, a lonely outpost on a small cluster of islands in the Gulf of Mexico. The prisoners would remain completely under military control.

The change had been ordered by Secretary of War Stanton. Stanton was a shrewd man and trained in the law. Perhaps he had anticipated Ewing's next move and, like a skillful chessplayer, had moved his pieces to a safer area on the board. Ewing was temporarily outwitted. "If their destination is as supposed," he wrote a friend, "they are beyond the reach of law. We will have to await the course of events to bring their relief."

In the meantime, Samuel Cox and Thomas A. Jones, the two Marylanders who had hidden Booth and Herold in the swamp for a week, were quietly released from jail. They had spent an uncomfortable six or seven weeks in prison, but they would never be tried by either civilian or military court. The Confederate soldier, Willie Jett, who had taken Booth to Garrett's farm, also was set free. So were the Garretts. Dr. Stewart, the Virginia physician who had refused to treat Booth, probably shuddered when he read of Dr. Mudd's fate. John Lloyd returned to his inn at Surrattsville and presumably got drunk again. His testimony, along with that of Wiechmann, had condemned Mary Surratt to death.

Ewing displayed no anxiety when, a week and a half after Stanton's decision, he wrote to Dr. Mudd's wife: "If he is sent to the Tortugas, the place is better for his health than almost any other. The island is dry and the climate good. Rely on it, wherever he has gone, his sanguine temperament will buoy him up."

Dr. Mudd was badly shaken by the prospect of living out the remainder of his life on a narrow sand island. According to Captain George W. Dutton, who helped guard the prisoners on board the *Florida*, Mudd reacted more despairingly than any of the other three men. "There is no hope for me," he was reported to have said. "I cannot live in such a place." Within three months after his arrival on the Dry Tortugas, Mudd was plotting escape as the only way to prolong his life.

Captain Dutton had other interesting reminiscences of his cruise toward the Gulf with Mudd, Arnold, Spangler, and O'Laughlin. Upon his return to Washington on the twenty-second of August, he went to the offices of Judge Holt. "During a conversation with Dr. Mudd, on the twenty-second of July," Dutton swore in an affidavit, "he confessed that he knew Booth when he came to his house with Herold on the morning after the assassination of the President; that he had known Booth for some time, but was afraid to tell of his having been at his house on the fifteenth of April, fearing that his own and the lives of his family would be endangered thereby. He also confessed that he was with Booth at the National Hotel on the evening referred to by Wiechmann in his testimony; that he came to Washington on that occasion to meet Booth by appointment, who wished to be introduced to John Surratt; that when he and Booth were going to Mrs. Surratt's house to see John Surratt, they met, on Seventh Street, John Surratt, who was introduced to Booth, and they had a conversation of a private nature."

General Dodd, in charge of the conspirators on the trip south, leaked a similar report of a Mudd confession to the newspapers. Dodd attempted to clarify whether or not Mudd had talked only to Surratt in the passageway outside Booth's room. The general added about Mudd: "He said that the military commission, in his case, had done their duty, and as far as they were concerned the sentence in his case was just, but some of the witnesses had sworn falsely and maliciously." Mudd later denied having volunteered any such statements to either Dutton or Dodd aboard the *Florida*. He claimed that Dutton and Dodd's testimonies were "notoriously false." Mudd's "confession" was one of several equally strange confessions which allegedly were made after the trial, and which conveniently supported the judgments of the military tribunal.

About the same time, the papers printed a confession by George Atzerodt. Atzerodt, by then, was no longer alive to make denials. Shortly after the execution the Baltimore *American* had received a "special report prepared by one who knew him [Atzerodt] since his arrest." The *American* did not reprint the confession in its entirety, probably because the paper did not actually have it. In this death-row confession, reported third person, Atzerodt seriously implicated Dr. Mudd in the abduction plot: "Booth was well acquainted with Mudd and had letters of introduction to him. Booth told Atzerodt, about two weeks before the murder, that he had sent provisions and liquor to Dr. Mudd for the supply of the party on their way to Richmond with the President." However, the Baltimore *American*, three and a half years later, inadvertently exposed the falseness of its own earlier report. After John H. Surratt had finally been arrested (and then acquitted by a civilian court), the paper decided to publish in full Atzerodt's last words to the world. The confession, a rambling discourse which gave a good discription of his movements following his failure to kill Vice President Johnson at Kirkwood House, did little to implicate others. Atzerodt said he believed Spangler innocent. No mention in the confession was made of Mudd!

Within a few days after she received Ewing's letter on her husband's destination, Mrs. Mudd traveled to Washington to see the Secretary of War. She walked briskly into the office of Edwin McMasters Stanton, the most fearsome man in the country. "I would like to send my husband money and clothes to make him comfortable," she said.

Stanton looked at the woman for a few moments with the same stare that had so often dismayed his generals. "Mrs. Mudd," he said. "As long as Dr. Mudd is in prison, the government will furnish him with what it thinks necessary for him to have, and he can have *no* communication whatsoever with the outside world." Mrs. Mudd left without another word.

Sarah Mudd visited Washington frequently during the years of her husband's imprisonment, in an attempt to secure his pardon. While at Ewing's office during one such trip, she met the wife of Secretary of the Interior Orville H. Browning. Mrs. Browning told Mrs. Mudd a rather interesting story. She and her husband often breakfasted in a restaurant where General Lew Wallace frequently appeared. One morning, while the trial was still in progress, Wallace had remarked: "If Booth had not broken his leg, we would never have heard the name of Dr. Mudd."

"Why don't you then send Dr. Mudd home to his wife and children?" asked Mrs. Browning.

Wallace replied: "The deed is done. Somebody must suffer for it, and he may as well suffer as anybody else."

The question later arose whether the author of *Ben Hur* (*The Tale of the Christ*), would ever have uttered such un-Christian sentiments. Forty years later when questioned by Dr. Mudd's daughter Nettie, the late general's wife could not remember that her husband had ever made such a statement. Samuel Mudd himself mentioned in a letter that a Judge Turner had made a similar remark to him. The idea that "somebody had to suffer" had perhaps become a generally accepted cliché to be employed when anyone felt it necessary to explain why so harsh a punishment had been meted out to Dr. Mudd.

The doctor-prisoner had his own opinions on the subject. "My conscience rests easy under all the grossly false and frivolous charges, notwithstanding their approval by an unjust, bigoted, and partisan court," he wrote from the Dry Tortugas. "I scorn the idea, the doctrine, that the innocent should suffer to satisfy a bloodthirsty and vindictive people. Was Pilate justified in sanctioning the death of our Savior to appease the wrath of the multitude, who cried out for his blood? They who contend that the multitude, the mob, must rule, though innocence and justice be trodden under foot, are walking exactly in the footsteps of poor, weak old Pilate."

As for Dr. Mudd, his real suffering had hardly begun.

III. *Somebody Had to Suffer*

Chapter 11

FORT JEFFERSON HAS BEEN CALLED, with some justification, America's Devil's Island. The very name was said to cause hardened criminals to shudder. We can imagine then its effect on the phlegmatic and timid Dr. Mudd. However, some have claimed that Fort Jefferson fell short of the reputation it had earned as a kind of island Siberia. One of its defenders was the New York *Herald*, which solicitously provided its readers with reports on the Lincoln conspirators during their early days in the Dry Tortugas.

"When these state prisoners were put upon the *Florida*," wrote a *Herald* correspondent on August 2, 1865, "they were totally ignorant of their destination, and they were sadly disappointed when informed that their prison house would be on the arid wastes of the Dry Tortugas of which they had undoubtly heard enough to inspire them with a desire to be sent almost anywhere else upon the footstool.

"But on the twenty-fifth of July when they reached the island, they were rather agreeably surprised to find that all the horrors they had imagined of the spot had been figments of the brain and had no existence in reality. The Tortugas, an island of some thirteen acres in extent, has no particular claims to present as a delightful place of protracted residence, being dry, barren, and sand-covered with but few trees and less green grass and vegetation. But it is not Hades exactly, nor is it Pandemonium and the conspirators may congratulate themselves that they have the freedom of its barren heaths and arid sandbanks rather than the close dreary cells of the Albany penitentiary where their fettered limbs would chafe and their hearts beat against only four hard, naked, and cheerless stone walls."

No doubt the *Herald* correspondent had paid no more than a brief visit to Fort Jefferson. Had he been imprisoned there, he might have painted quite a different picture for his readers. The Florida Keys admittedly offered a mode of life not available elsewhere on the American continent. The islands of the Keys started at the foot of Florida's east coast and stretched westward into the Gulf of Mexico. The Keys were not a chain of islands, but one long coral reef with sand and grass clinging where the coral had massed above the ocean surface.

During Dr. Mudd's lifetime, the second oldest city in Florida—Key West—could be reached from Washington only by a boat trip which took several weeks. The name Key West derived not from the island's western position in the Florida Keys, but rather from a mistranslation of the name originally given the island by Spanish explorers. Discovering that the island had been used as a burial ground by natives and was thus covered with bones, the Spaniards called it *Cayo Hueso*, or "Bone Key." The Englishmen who appeared centuries later anglicized the name to Key West. The overseas highway now linking most of the Keys with the mainland ends at Key West, but the Keys do not. They trickle off into the Gulf of Mexico for another sixty-eight miles westward and end —just beyond a stretch of open water—at the Dry Tortugas. The latter are not a single island (as the *Herald* correspondent seemed to think), but a cluster of seven tiny islands.

Ponce de Leon, while in search of the Fountain of Youth, discovered the Dry Tortugas in 1513. He found no youth, and no fountain; he did not find even water on these seven specks of sand and shell that rise only a few feet about the surface of the sea. He did, however, find turtles by the thousands, and named the island *Tortugas*, or "turtles." Cartographers later added the adjective "dry" to warn mariners not to expect water.

Yet, dry or not, the Tortugas appeared to the *Herald* reporter to lie at the end of the rainbow. The Gulf Stream sparkled with colors: yellow ochre over the sand bars, royal blue in the deep Gulf Stream ditch, pea green elsewhere. Tarpon splashed off in the distance, and beneath the water shuttled the ominous shadow of the manta ray. The latitude and the water tempered the climate: seldom did the temperature rise over ninety; rarely did it go below fifty. Each evening the sun dropped into the ocean like a huge orange ball. At night the stars twinkled like diamonds. But idyllic though the scene might have appeared to the journalist, Fort Jefferson was no paradise.

In the fall, fierce tropical storms boiled out of the southwest, stirring the waves to frenzy and, sometimes, washing whole islands away. The sun beat unyieldingly on the laborers during the summer. The moisture hung in the air like wet down, and coated the casemate walls with slime. So enervating was this atmosphere that twenty men were needed in Fort Jefferson to do what three might accomplish on the mainland. In addition, mosquitoes attacked with fury and brought with them disease, especially the dreaded yellow fever. A bucket of sea water left standing a few hours seemed to sour and give off a rank, stagnant smell. Any article left outside would rot. Here men's souls, too, corroded.

To this add inadequate rations, cruel and vengeful guards, and the despair of men condemned for life, and one obtains an accurate picture of Fort Jefferson at the time of the Civil War. Garden Key, on which Fort Jefferson stood, was about sixteen acres in area (not thirteen, as the *Herald* reported), but three-fourths of it was covered by the fort. In addition to guards and laborers, 550 prisoners were crowded into the fort in the summer of 1865— although this number would soon decrease.

The Dry Tortugas was a strategic base for buccaneers in the Gulf long before the United States decided to build a fort there. The Gulf Stream served as a natural sea-highway for travel to the Caribbean countries. Ships moving east sailed mid-channel, depending on the strong currents for extra speed. Ships moving in the other direction sailed thirty miles to the north, much as a barge going up a wide river might hug the less turbulent river bank. The galleons of Spain unfurled their canvas on this sea lane, a point not lost on the pirates of that era. Privateers would anchor in the shallow and weather-protected waters around the Tortugas and, on sighting a sail on the horizon, pull up anchor and clear their decks for action.

Shortly after Spain sold Florida to the United States in 1821, the pirates were driven from the Keys. Thereupon, the Tortugas were considered a logical site for a fortress to defend the Gulf. Newspaper writers often sneered at the idea, claiming Fort Jefferson was so isolated that enemy vessels could sail past without ever coming within range of its guns. Such reasoning, with its implication that forts on land could similarly be by-passed, betrayed a lack of understanding of military matters of the time. Generals who moved their troops past any fort did so at the risk of having their supply lines cut, and so it was with Fort Jefferson: American cruisers could moor beneath its protecting guns, and no enemy would venture in from the Gulf with such a threat on its flank.

Thomas Jefferson was the first to conceive of a chain of forts stretching along the nation's coastline. He was convinced that the chain would provide protection against the territorial ambitions of Great Britian. Jefferson hired Simon Bernard of France to build and design the forts. Bernard, who had been Napoleon's aide-de-camp and was considered the world's foremost expert on defense, did not completely design Fort Jefferson—that was done by Montgomery Meigs—but the basic plan followed Bernard's outline. Work on the fort began in 1846 and dragged behind schedule from the beginning. The workmen's quarters should have been erected in two months; the task required a year. At the end of ten years the walls had been raised only a few feet above the surrounding waters. The vile climate hampered much of the work, but the slow progress on the fort was due also to the massiveness of the plan. Fort Jefferson eventually became America's largest fort. The distance around the hexagonal outer walls was almost a half-mile. The walls rose fifty feet above the foundation. An estimated forty-two million bricks, shipped from Mobile, Alabama, and Pensacola, Florida, went into these walls. Stone both for the embrasure lintels and for the flagging were brought all the way from New England. Four hundred and twenty gun emplacements were built on three separate levels within the walls, but only 141 would ever be mounted. None were ever fired in combat. One hundred and nine cisterns in the foundations stored the rain water caught on the roofs. Slaves, hired from their masters at twenty dollars a month, did most of the labor. Brick masons recruited from New York and Boston, most of them Irish, were paid $1.12 a day plus subsistence. All laborers worked a six-day, sixty-hour week.

Horatio G. Wright, a lieutenant and military engineer from West Point, was in charge of construction initially. Captain Daniel Phineas Woodbury of New Hampshire soon relieved him. To Woodbury the fort lacked the normal graces of army social life, so he tried to extend the borders of his command to include Charleston and Havana. He spent so much time merrymaking in these two cities that General Joe Totten, supervisor of the entire project, censured him for dereliction of duty. Woodbury, unbowed, immediately sailed off for Havana, but this time he returned with the Spanish defense plans for Havana harbor in his possession. Washington quickly forgave him for his previous indiscretions.

On the eve of the Civil War, the fort, with $1,250,000 spent, was still uncompleted, but the walls had begun to sink. The engineers had assumed that the Tortugas, like the rest of the Keys, were coral islands and capable of bearing any weight. Instead, the islands were mainly heaps of sand and shell which had been tossed up into mounds by whirling ocean currents. The weight of the walls squeezed the sand out from under the foundation, as one writer in the *Saturday Evening Post* put it, "like jelly oozing from between two slices of bread." In 1860 the designer of the fort, Captain Montgomery Meigs, relieved Captain Woodbury. There was now fear that the fort would fall into Southern hands. There had been rumors that in the event of secession, Florida would attack the island. Reinforcements were sent to strengthen the defenses. Meigs quickly closed the holes that had been left in the walls by the workmen to permit the movement of construction materials. He built a drawbridge before the sallyport (or entrance). The mounds of brick that were to be a fort had at last become a stronghold. However, one serious weakness remained. There was not a heavy gun on the island.

Help, of a sort, was on the way. On January 4, 1861, Major General Lewis G. Arnold, then in command of Fort Independence in Boston Harbor, received a telegraphed order from General Winfield Scott to engage steam transportation and to head southward with his men. The next day, General Arnold was instructed to depart immediately. The strictest secrecy prevailed. The North was eager to conceal its plans from the South. General Arnold sailed for Fort Jefferson under sealed orders. His troops went aboard ship in ignorance of their destination. But when the steamer had raised anchor, the Boston papers published full details of the significance of the departure.

On his arrival in the Tortugas, General Arnold assembled heavy guns and ammunition from the naval station at Key West. He had no carriages for his unwieldy fifteen-inch cannons and had to improvise mounts from lumber. Within a few weeks he had amassed ten thousand pounds of gunpowder and a four-month supply of food. Although by no means invulnerable, the unfinished fort was at least prepared to defend itself.

Shortly after this, an armed schooner arrived from Florida. It anchored in the channel, and sent a landing party ashore with a simple message for General Arnold: "We demand the surrender of your fort."

The Little General, as Arnold's men called him, was not to be intimidated. His reply was clear enough: "If you aren't gone from the vicinity of this fort within ten minutes, I'll blow you out of the water!"

Arnold had four guns in place, but they could not be trained on the schooner, since the traverses were not ready. He could have ordered his men to fire their muskets at the schooner, but the ten thousand pounds of gunpowder were entirely useless without heavy guns. However, Arnold won his bluff. In the long history of Fort Jefferson this was the only time it was ever threatened. The many massive guns, once in place, would never be fired—except in practice. It is therefore difficult to evaluate the role played by Fort Jefferson in the Civil War. It simply sat in the Gulf, more threat than threatening. On the other hand, had Confederate forces been able to take Fort Jefferson, they could have opened a trade route from New Orleans to Cuba and from there to Europe.

The era of the fortress in defense was coming to an end. Fort Jefferson became obsolete even before it was completed. The cannon balls of pre-Civil War days would only have ricocheted from the eight-foot-thick walls. The deeply planted cannon in the fort could have discouraged the most resolute foe. But in the nineteenth century, gunsmiths discovered that an internally grooved cannon barrel caused a shell to spin as it was fired. The sharp, spinning shell would crash and dig into mortar rather than ricochet from it. Such rifled cannon made it possible to reduce a once impregnable fort to rubble in a matter of days. Fort Pulaski, one of Fort Jefferson's sister fortifications, was the first fort to suffer the fire of rifled cannon. After the fall of Fort Pulaski there no longer seemed to be any reason for the construction of huge fortresses—or to complete the work on those still unfinished. Firepower had made such aged bastions of defense obsolete.

Though Fort Jefferson had practically no military value after the Civil War, it was important as a prison. In this role Fort Jefferson became a law unto itself. Here was a military post surrounded only by water, an island lying outside the land boundaries of any state, an extremely effective reserve for the isolation of prisoners—especially political prisoners. Thus, in July of 1865, the four prisoners—Mudd, Arnold, Spangler, and O'Laughlin—were sent to the fort. Later these four would be joined by a member of another conspiracy: Colonel George St. Leger Grenfell, a wiry English soldier of fortune. Many other prisoners were quartered within Fort Jefferson's brick bastions, but none of them achieved the notoriety of these five.

Chapter 12

DURING THE ENTIRE LENGTH of Dr. Mudd's incarceration in the Dry Tortugas, his loyal wife labored for his release. Not long after the *Florida* sailed south with its cargo of political prisoners, Ewing, who still considered himself Mudd's lawyer, thought he detected a more relaxed attitude in the flint-hard Judge Holt. The latter talked to Ewing several times about Sarah Mudd and even asked about the children. "I think you have made some impression on the old gentleman," Ewing wrote to Mrs. Mudd toward the end of August. "In all these matters, his opinion will guide the action of the President."

The astute Ewing proved to have assessed the matter correctly. When Mrs. Mudd visited Washington some days later to ask Andrew Johnson to sign papers authorizing the release of her husband, the President said to her: "If Judge Holt will sign the papers, I will."

Mrs. Mudd left immediately for Holt's office. But she met again with disappointment. "Mrs. Mudd, I am sorry," the Judge Advocate said. "I can do nothing for you."

Arnold, O'Laughlin, Spangler, and Dr. Mudd had already arrived at Fort Jefferson. They had their first sight of the prison on July 24, 1865. As the *Florida* approached the deep channel south of the island, a small gunboat fired a signal gun and moved toward them from the wharf. The *Florida* waited. An officer from the small boat boarded the *Florida*. "What's the purpose of your visit?" he inquired.

"To deliver state prisoners to the fort," was the reply.

"Right! We've been expecting you."

The change in destination of the prisoners—from Albany Penitentiary to Fort Jefferson—was due neither to accident nor to indecisiveness. The order could have come only from Stanton. In the far-off Dry Tortugas, the conspirators could not rouse public sympathy by getting word of their conditions to reporters. More important, Fort Jefferson was a military reserve where military rules prevailed. The prisoners would be marooned far from the arm of the civil courts, which might grant them a further hearing on a writ of habeas corpus.

Colonel Charles Hamilton, commanding officer of the fort, greeted the four state prisoners after they had been transferred by small boat to the island. He stated plainly the regulations in force. "We have a dungeon for those who do not obey," he said. Arnold, O'Laughlin, Spangler, and Mudd would soon get to know that dungeon quite well, but not because they disobeyed regulations.

"Do you have any special instructions relative to us?" asked Arnold.

"No. You have the same privileges of the island as any person confined here."

That night the fort's officers acted the part of good hosts to the visiting officers of the *Florida*. Perhaps they wanted to exhibit the advantages of army duty. None could deny that the liquor supply at the Fort Jefferson officer's mess was ample for warding off malarial chills. The officers drank deeply and swapped tropical yarns. Sam Arnold reported that the next morning one naval officer had to be carried to the wharf in a wheelbarrow.

Mudd and his fellow conspirators, as Colonel Hamilton had said, at first suffered no special restrictions. The War Department had not ordered restrictions. But even ordinary life in the Dry Tortugas was far from attractive. The prisoners lived and worked in flannel shirts, which were excellent in the damp evenings but sweltering under the sun during the daytime. However, thick clothing offered the only protection against the swarms of mosquitoes that seemed to be more firmly possessed of the islands than was the United States government. The humidity seldom fell below the saturation point because fresh winds could not circulate through walls designed, not for ventilation, but for resistance to cannon balls. For beds the prisoners had only wooden planks. Ned Spangler later employed his skill as a stage carpenter to nail together crude bedsteads, which he covered with canvas.

For breakfast the prisoners had coffee, butter, and bread. For lunch they had coffee, butter, and bread. For dinner they had coffee, butter, and bread. Now and then they had a treat: either potatoes or onions and perhaps a small portion of meat. Vegetables were perishable in the hot and moist climate. Fruit was plentiful on the mainland of Florida, but the prisoners seldom got any. Dr. Mudd sampled the prison's pork and beef, then wisely decided to forego eating it. Those who did not follow his example often wished they had, for the meat apparently spoiled in the heat and caused cramps and diarrhea. Occasionally, when he could buy it, Mudd supplemented his diet with molasses. Fresh fish was a much desired, yet all too rare delicacy, although the Tortugas were in an excellent fishing area. In the hours between the unpleasant meals, the dreary life at the prison offered nothing but boredom.

Colonel Hamilton had assigned jobs to the prisoners. Ned Spangler labored as a carpenter. An easy-going workman, quick to jest, he perhaps suffered less from despair than the others. But with a sentence of only six years, Spangler could look forward to a day of freedom. The others, imprisoned for life, could only hope for a reduction of their sentences. Michael O'Laughlin apparently abandoned all hope of ever seeing Maryland again. Only brief mention of him or his work appears in the tales told of life on the island. From the instant that he stepped ashore he vanished almost completely from the annals of history. Sam Arnold had the handsome features of a riverboat gambler and the dainty penmanship of a scribe. Had he remained undetected in Baltimore, he could have found employment as a clerk; he was given such an assignment at the fort. Because he worked at post headquarters, Arnold had special privileges. His cellmates (except for Dr. Mudd) continued to wear chains, even while at work, but Arnold's chains were soon struck off. The officers were disturbed by the clanking of his chains as he moved around in the offices. At another time, an officer ordered Arnold to move from the dank cell he occupied to the more habitable guardhouse. Arnold asked, however, to return to his friends: The changing of the guards at all hours disturbed his sleep.

Dr. Mudd went to work at the post hospital as ward master. Although he recognized his hospital job as an improvement over hard labor in the sun, he was distressed by what he witnessed. "Four prisoners have died here during the short time I have been here," he wrote several months after his arrival. "Not a single soldier- or citizen-laborer has died or suffered with any serious sickness, thereby showing something wrong, and a distinction made between the two classes of individuals. Every case of acute dysentery or diarrhea among the prisoners either dies in the onset or lingers on and terminates in the chronic which eventually kills."

Even in these early days of his imprisonment, Dr. Mudd observed another disease. He had encountered it once or twice while at medical school, and thus could recognize the symptoms; but he had not seen it as a rural doctor practicing in Lower Maryland. He wrote: "We have a disease here which is termed bone fever, or mild yellow fever, which has attacked at least three-fourths of the inmates of the fort. It lasts generally but two or three days; during the time, the patient imagines every bone will break from the enormous pain he suffers in his limbs." Mudd added: "None has died with it." He could not make such a statement two years later.

If life at Fort Jefferson began quietly for the four conspirators, it did not long remain quiet. Lafayette Baker, head of the United States Secret Service, saw to that. He reported on August 17, 1865, from Louisville: "I have important papers. I think the commanding officer at the Dry Tortugas should be put on his guard against an attempt to rescue the state prisoners in his charge. A company is organizing in New Orleans for that purpose. I have all the facts from a reliable source."

Stanton immediately dispatched a fast steamer from Fort Monroe to deliver Baker's warning. A second note, from Baker to General Sheridan, prompted another steamer to churn the waters of the Gulf. Finally, from Tallahassee on the third of September, came an order for the Fort Jefferson commander to prepare the garrison against possible uprising among the prisoners. "Take measures to ferret out the leaders," wrote General Newton, "and place them in irons."

The officers at Fort Jefferson acted promptly. They threw the four conspiracy prisoners into irons. Colonel Hamilton posted additional sentinels. "Muskets," he decreed, "will be kept loaded day and night." He ordered gun crews strengthened. At the same time, the ranks of those imprisoned at the fort began to thin. Prisoners would be freed from the island by the hundreds within the next few months—perhaps in a conscious effort to remove possible dissenters, perhaps in an attempt further to isolate the conspirators, but more likely because the end of the Civil War had diminished the need for military prisons. However, for Fort Jefferson the war was not yet over. The guards stood by their posts with loaded muskets, anticipating attack any moment.

Not long after the first warning from Lafayette Baker, a tense drama began to unfold. "Sail on the horizon!" a lookout shouted one afternoon. No boat was due from Key West that day. The soldiers in the fort quickly took up their positions, expecting an attack to begin. Slowly, a large, brig-rigged schooner appeared in the lookout's spyglass.

"Any flags flying at the masthead?" asked the officer of the day.

"None, sir," replied the lookout. "Neither pilot nor distress."

The officer frowned. Though there was hardly a trace of wind, the schooner was attempting to tack with only one small topsail. The lookout, his glass trained on the ship, reported only two men on deck. The schooner drifted closer until sundown, then tacked north and disappeared into the dusk. Because of the warnings from Lafayette Baker, the vessel's movements seemed sinister. In 1902, W. R. Prentiss related this incident for *McClure's* magazine: "It was easy to imagine that she carried a heavy cargo of treason between decks."

That night no one at the fort could sleep. A double guard watched the prisoners. The sentinels guarding the boats outside the fort were on the alert. Crews stood by their guns ready to fire at a signal.

In the morning, the schooner reappeared and tacked past the fort three times. Unable to suffer the suspense any longer, the commander sent a pilot out in a small boat to hail the ship and learn her intentions, if possible. Within two hours the pilot returned. "Our mysterious brig is from Portland, Maine," he declared. "She's been to Aspenwald with ice and is now homeward bound in ballast. Every man on board is either sick or dead with Panama fever."

The pilot stated that the captain of the schooner could move around on deck and change the course, but that he lacked the strength to run up a signal. The ship had sprung a leak and had more than nine feet of water in her hold. The commander of the fort dispatched a group of men, including prisoners with nautical experience, to bring the ship into the harbor. The men pumped out the hold and buried the dead. And thus ended Lafayette Baker's plot.

Security measures, with or without the vivid imagination of the Secret Service chief, were stringent enough at the fort. After retreat (the lowering of the flag at sundown), the guards marched the regular prisoners to their casemate quarters. All soldiers at the fort who were being punished for infractions of the military laws went to the guardhouse. A single sentinel stood at the prisoners' bastion, permitting no movement in or out without proper authorization. Another sentinel guarded the sallyport, and permitted no exit after tattoo (the call to quarters). A third sentinel watched the small fishing and pleasure boats which were moored at one of the wharfs. After retreat, he would lock the boats within a wooden enclosure. Still another sentinel guarded a second wharf. Neither sentinel would permit any boat to leave the fort without strict scrutiny by either the corporal or sergeant of the guard.

Yet prisoners constantly sought to escape, and some did succeed in getting away. According to Sam Arnold, nine out of ten who attempted to escape were caught. This would imply that the tenth man succeeded. Dr. Mudd indicated in letters to his wife that escape was a simple matter. "I have had several opportunities to make my escape," he wrote, "but knowing, or believing, it would show guilt, I have resolved to remain peaceable and quiet, and allow the government the full exercise of its power, justice, and clemency. Should I take French leave, it would amount to expatriation, which I don't feel disposed to do at present." So was Sam Mudd's resolve on September 5, 1865, a month and a half after his arrival at the Dry Tortugas.

Thus far, Dr. Mudd's life in prison had not been unbearably harsh. He had a reasonable amount of freedom—for a political prisoner. He was usually free of chains, and he had no hard labor to perform (as had actually been prescribed in his sentence). He slept in the hospital instead of in the casemates with the other prisoners. His lawyers and relatives buoyed his hopes with talk of writs of habeas corpus and appeals. As basically an honest man, he still had faith that only the guilty remained in jail. The conspiracy trial had been a miscarriage of justice because of the hysteria after the death of the President. His case would soon be reappraised, perhaps retried.

But within another three weeks Mudd was confronted with what he considered an intolerable situation. The 161st New York Volunteers, a group of men who, he admitted, had treated him with decency and humanity, left for home. In their place arrived the 82nd United States Colored Infantry. The doctor felt that he knew what the Negroes would think: Abe Lincoln had freed the Negroes, Sam Mudd had shielded the man who had murdered their emancipator. The New Yorkers, as they left, had warned Mudd of their replacements: "As soon as we leave you'll lose your former privileges. Your life will be in their hands."

Mudd did not greatly fear the loss of privilege, but as a former slaveholder, he shuddered at the thought of being abused by Negro troops. "It is bad enough to be a prisoner in the hands of white men, your equals under the Constitution," railed the

Marylander in him, "but to be lorded over by a set of ignorant, prejudiced and irresponsible beings of the unbleached humanity was more than I could submit to."

On September 25, 1865, the *Scott* lay moored at the wharf, preparing to take the New York volunteers aboard and to sail for home. Mudd decided to join them. He had been allowed to bring several suits of clothing with him, but until this time had worn the prisoner's regular garb. Now he took out one of his suits and put it on. His plan seemed deceptively simple. It required only nerve—or foolishness. He would stroll up the gangplank of the *Scott* and nod cordially, as if he had every right to be there, to any officer on deck. Once aboard, Mudd would conceal himself somewhere. He had no wish to become a fugitive from justice; so he later said. He would instead, at some point where a writ of habeas corpus could be obtained in his behalf, surrender himself to the authorities. He had not lost faith in the courts of the land, only in military tribunals.

Mudd did not engage in this scheme alone. "I had the advice of many and was promised aid by one of the quartermasters on the boat," he later wrote Ewing. "I was persuaded, believing my chances sure with only the proper effort on my part."

After boarding the *Scott*, Mudd quickly sought out the seaman Henry Kelly. The doctor had talked to Kelly earlier and probably had offered him money to aid in the escape. Kelly took Mudd down into the lower hold and pried up several planks. "Get under here," he said.

Mudd, it would seem, was aware of every security regulation but one: no ship would sail until the fort's commander had accounted for every prisoner in his charge. The guards conceivably might ignore, or fail to note, the absence of a burglar, or a murderer, or a rapist—but not of a conspirator. Even as he lay in the lower hold, barely daring to breathe, Mudd was missed. "Mudd's gone!" a sentinel reported to the sergeant of the guard.

"Go search the *Scott*," the sergeant ordered.

Soon the *Scott's* deck clattered under the heavy feet of the soldiers of the guard. "Now that you mention it," one of the mates on the *Scott* may have said casually, "I did notice a strange man in civilian clothes come aboard. He had a thick beard and a balding head. I think he went below."

The soldiers moved up and down ladders, ran through the passageways and peered into the closets. In the lower hold, they began to thrust their sabers through the narrow slits between the planks. Suddenly one of the sabers struck something soft. "I think we've caught our fish," said a soldier. Dr. Mudd had received a slight wound, the location of which was never recorded, not even by him.

The guards dragged him up and hustled him before Major George E. Wentworth, the new commander of the fort. "You did not get down into that hold alone," said Wentworth. "Who helped you?"

Mudd would not answer.

"Out with it. Or I'll string you up by your thumbs."

That mode of persuasion would become increasingly popular with the authorities in the Dry Tortugas. Mudd had already gone to prison for sheltering one man. He did not want to suffer torture by shielding another. "A seaman named Kelly," Mudd said.

Later, when the guards threw Kelly into the same room with Mudd, the doctor apologized to him. "The commander is a fool to think he can hold me," Kelly retorted. Even as he was tied down with chains and flung into the dungeon, the seaman began to plot his escape. A cellmate named Smith joined Kelly in the plan. One night, they broke their chains and ripped the iron grating from their window. Using their irons as a rope, they slid from the window into the moat below. They stole a boat from the otherwise well-guarded wharf. Less than a week had passed since Mudd's unsuccessful attempt, and these two were out. As Kelly and Smith watched the squat silhouette of Fort Jefferson slipping away on the horizon, they must have laughed at the doctor who was so inept as to be caught. But Mudd could never accomplish what they had done with such apparent ease.

Mudd wrote his wife that four other prisoners had escaped undetected on the *Scott*; he later amended that figure to six. He indicated that thirty to forty men had either made their escape, or had attempted to do so, during his first two months on the island. Nothing, he said, was done to them: no additional punishments, no loss of privileges. But the absence of a Kelly or a Smith would cause few heads to turn in the North. The escape of Dr. Samuel A. Mudd would have brought banner headlines across the country. The officers at Fort Jefferson had to keep Mudd, right or wrong, for better or for worse. Sitting in judgment on their actions was the stern, cold Secretary of War, the most powerful man in the country.

"Why should I be expected to act more honorably than my persecutors who sent me here?" rationalized Mudd. He spent two days in the guardhouse with chains on his hands and feet. For Mudd's indiscretion, Arnold, O'Laughlin, and Spangler also suffered. The commander removed them from their former jobs. He threw them into the dungeon beside Mudd and let them out only to serve at hard labor during the day.

If life had now become more difficult at Fort Jefferson, it would soon, as the soldiers of the 161st New York Volunteers had promised, become intolerable. Whether in retribution for Mudd's escape attempt, or because of War Department orders, the heavy hand of discipline fell on the fort and, especially, on the conspirators.

Mudd went to work wheeling sand and cleaning old bricks. "I worked hard all day," he wrote bitterly, "and came very near finishing one brick."

Chapter 13

"I AM VERY WELL," wrote Dr. Mudd to his wife on October 23, 1865, "although at present confined to a small, damp room with Arnold, O'Laughlin, Spangler, and a Colonel Grenfell, formerly an English officer, but recently of the Confederate Army. What has led to this treatment, we are at a loss to account."

Three weeks after Mudd's attempt to escape, Major Wentworth moved the conspirators to one small cell and kept them chained during the daytime. Retribution on the part of the prison officials could not have accounted altogether for this change in treatment. Colonel George St. Leger Grenfell had only recently arrived. He had not even been inside the fort when Mudd had tried to flee. Yet Grenfell shared in the treatment reserved for the Lincoln conspirators. Perhaps Lafayette Baker's warning was responsible for the restrictive measures. Perhaps the new officers thought that the dungeon-like cell was an effective means of demonstrating their power over the conspirators. Perhaps it took three weeks for the news of Mudd's offense to travel to and from Washington. It isn't hard to picture Stanton pounding his fist on his desk and thundering: "Throw them in irons!"

Whatever caused the stringent orders, Major Wentworth followed them diligently. Each day the conspirators stumbled off to work trailing their leg irons and shadowed by an armed Negro guard. They were not permitted to talk to other prisoners on the island. Only Arnold, because he worked at post headquarters, retained any vestige of privilege. He still did not have to wear leg irons, yet he continued to grumble. "Coffee was brought to our quarters in a dirty, greasy bucket," wrote Arnold, "always with grease swimming upon its surface: bread, rotten fish, and meal all mixed together, the one spoiling the other by contact." The enlisted men, who were on the island voluntarily, fared little better at their mess table.

The 82nd Colored Infantry, so feared at first by Dr. Mudd, remained only a few months at Fort Jefferson. Soon the 5th Artillery replaced them. The prisoners cheered when they heard that white troops would again be in charge of them, but as Arnold later said: "We had traded off the witch for the devil." However, the enlisted men—either white or black—rarely abused the prisoners. Officers caused most of the suffering.

The guards had originally told the state prisoners that they must wear chains only when a boat was at the wharf, but chains soon became a permanent part of their attire. The cells were not merely damp; often there was a foot of water on the floor of Dr. Mudd's cell. And not only mosquitoes, but bedbugs, roaches, and scorpions became his cellmates. Shortly after the 5th Artillery arrived, a pompous lieutenant named William Van Reed, acting as officer of the day, visited the conspirators in their dungeon. O'Laughlin rose to make for him a rare complaint. "Why are we in irons?" he asked. "It is not in conformity with the findings of the court. Our sentence did not call for inhuman treatment."

Van Reed glared. "Sir, your sentence is nothing. We can do with you, and to you, just as we please."

The officers could thus punish the conspirators (as well as the other prisoners) as their whims dictated. A cruel regime was the result. Yet only rumors about the true wretchedness of conditions at Fort Jefferson drifted out in Sam Mudd's correspondence with his wife. Perhaps he feared censorship. Perhaps also he did not wish to alarm her. One rare letter of complete candor was mailed on January 22, 1866. Mudd wrote: "Imagine one loaded down with heavy chains, locked up in a wet, damp room, twelve hours out of every twenty-four during working days, and all day on Sundays and holidays. No exercise allowed except in the limited space of a small room, and with irons on. The atmosphere we breathe is highly impregnated with sulphuric hydrogen gas, which you are aware is highly injurious to health as well as disagreeable.

The gas is generated by the numerous sinks that empty into that portion of the sea enclosed by the breakwater, and which is immediately under a small porthole—the only admission for air and light we have from the external port. My legs and ankles are swollen and sore, pains in my shoulder and back are frequent. My hair began falling out some time ago, and to save which I shaved it all over clean, and have continued to do so once every week since. It is now beginning to have a little life. My eyesight is beginning to grow very bad, so much so that I can't read or write by candlelight. During the day, owing to the overpowering light and [to bad] health, my eyes are painful and irritated, and can't view any object many seconds without having to close or shade them from the light. With all this, imagine my gait with a bucket and broom, and a guard, walking around from one corner of the fort to another, sweeping and sanding down the bastions. This has been our treatment for the last three months, coupled with bad diet, bad water, and every inconvenience. The greatest wonder is, that we have borne up so well."

Soon, however, the prisoners obtained some relief. Mrs. Mudd wrote President Andrew Johnson complaining of the treatment her husband suffered. She pleaded once more for his early release. The President had his own problems, the least of which was Dr. Mudd. Congress had returned to Washington threatening to undo the plans for a gentle reconstruction, as originally proposed by Abraham Lincoln and endorsed by Johnson. Led by Representative Thaddeus Stevens of Pennsylvania and Senator Charles Sumner of Massachusetts, the Radicals in Congress had concocted a broth of hatred. President Johnson had such men to contend with; it is amazing that he gave any thought at all to Samuel A. Mudd.

Mudd's wife was not alone in her pleas for mercy. Mrs. Jefferson Davis wanted her husband released from Fort Monroe. The president of the late Confederate States of America had never even been brought to trial, nor would Davis ever be tried, although eventually he was freed. President Johnson did not entirely ignore Mrs. Mudd. He did ask General Hill, the commander at Fort Jefferson at that time, to remove the chains and to provide more humane treatment. Hill followed the President's request more faithfully than Congress would later follow the President's request for mercy for the South. Mudd's chains were taken off. The prisoners were moved from the lower level to "more salubrious quarters" above the sallyport. They had moved from Hell to Purgatory.

The state prisoners were not the only ones who suffered at Fort Jefferson. For disobedience of regulations, the guards often strung up the ordinary prisoners by the thumbs until the joints were nearly pulled from their sockets. They roped prisoners and dunked them into the Gulf. They whipped their naked flesh. They tied them to branches of trees and left them to swing throughout the night. A cruel sergeant named Murphy beat a French Canadian prisoner so severely with his musket butt that the prisoner died. (Murphy in time was promoted to a lieutenancy.) One day, before the eyes of a large number of prisoners and guards, a Negro prisoner accidentally fell into the moat. Unable to swim, the Negro splashed desperately with his arms and legs, gulping and coughing for help. No one moved. The guards did not care. His fellow prisoners may have thought him better off dead. The man drowned.

The enlisted men on the island led a life better only by a degree than that led by Dr. Mudd and the other prisoners. A soldier named Wheeler, to save money to send to his family at home, mended his own uniform rather than pay the company tailor for the work. The tailor apparently had influence, for soon Wheeler's company commander sent for him. "But I'm too poor to pay to have it done," the soldier pleaded. He was ordered to carry an iron ball for one month, day and night, two hours on, two hours off—for daring to do what? Simply for mending his own garments.

Carrying heavy iron cannon balls was a common punishment. These balls each weighed twenty-four pounds or more. Every day ten or fifteen men could be seen trudging in tight circles around the parade grounds, carrying such weights and thus paying for wrongs real or imagined. Failure to salute an officer brought punishment, although the officers often failed to wear their uniforms. Any one of a hundred other infractions could send men to the ring on the parade grounds to carry the heavy iron balls.

One soldier, Christian Conrad, a German, began to suffer from fits after he arrived in the Tortugas. He was soon unable to perform his company duties and had to go to the hospital. There he encountered a frowning assistant surgeon named John Bell. Bell did not have the compassion of a Samuel A. Mudd. During Bell's career as an army doctor he had probably encountered many malingerers. Now the surgeon displayed no sympathy at all when Conrad claimed that he had lost his sense of feeling in his lower limbs. "This is mere pretense!" snorted Bell. "We'll give you some work that will bring you around to duty."

Bell's prescription was to order Conrad to the guardhouse. The sergeant of the guard told Conrad to carry a twenty-four-pound log. Arnold described the scene: "The man trembled like an aspen all over from the exertion required to execute the imposed task, his limbs being dragged along, devoid of life or action." Conrad began to suffer a new fit. The sergeant would not permit anyone to go near him.

In civilian life an ambulance might have taken the convulsing man to a hospital. At Fort Jefferson they threw Conrad into the guardhouse. Whenever he had another spasm, the guards doused him with buckets of water. After another week of fits, they did remove him to the post hospital, and even the suspicious Bell could no longer refuse to accept him. "Dr. Bell is trying to kill me," Conrad groaned to anyone who would listen. Whenever the doctor entered the ward, the sick man trembled with terror. At last, they discharged from service what was left of Christian Conrad. They hauled him to the wharf on a stretcher. Later a steamer took him home, maimed and crippled, unable to stand up or to move his lower limbs.

Mail came slowly to the Dry Tortugas. Boats visited but once every few weeks. Letters were censored both coming and going. If the prison officials came upon any word that reflected on the government, the mail would not be dispatched. Money mailed to the prisoners often found its way into someone else's pocket. But then, regulations clearly stated: prisoners would be allowed only three dollars a month. At one point Dr. Mudd waited for the arrival of a trunk which he had been informed would contain, among other items, two bottles of Burdu Whiskey. His companions, too, waited for that trunk. But when it arrived, there was no whiskey. That night several officers toasted the Maryland doctor for the generosity of his wife.

New officers arriving at Fort Jefferson quickly discovered that there were two main forms of amusement: punishing the men and getting drunk. Often the two amusements could be combined. Each boat carried, in addition to the food necessary for the men, the liquor necessary for the officers. When supplies ran low between sailings, the officers frequently made a midnight requisition of the alcohol reserved for the hospital. Furthermore, they eagerly sought entertainment for their parties, and Dr. Mudd, who had played the violin at wedding receptions for his friends, now fiddled at the drunken orgies of his captors.

The enlisted men began to dread the hangover-inspired orders of their superiors. They dreaded even more the demands made by officers who were drunk on duty. More and more soldiers began to desert rather than submit to this tyranny of alcohol. As a result, passes to Key West were no longer issued. The soldiers, like the prisoners, were inmates on the island.

The paymaster arrived one day at Fort Jefferson by supply boat. As usual, the prisoners were marched to the wharf to unload the supplies for the commissary and the quartermaster. It was the unhappy fate of one James Dunn to be among these prisoners. Dunn worked with two guards unloading liquor and, before long, was thoroughly drunk. When the officer of the day, Brevet Major C. C. McConnell, learned of it, he flew into a rage. He ordered Dunn placed in the ring on the parade grounds.

The sergeant of the guard, Edward Donnelly, dragged Dunn to the punishment area and told him to start carrying the heavy cannon ball. Dunn turned sightless eyes on him and snickered.

"If you're too drunk to carry the ball, we'll get you sober," said

Major McConnell. "Sergeant, string this man up." The major seemed in little better shape than Dunn. That day, Sam Arnold encountered him in a hall near headquarters and offered him some official papers. Major McConnell stumbled past toward his room and tripped three times going up the stairs.

Meanwhile, Sergeant Donnelly dragged Dunn to the guardhouse and tied the drunken prisoner by his wrists to a bell post. It was now eleven o'clock in the morning. Dunn was left to hang in this position for four hours. Then, still unconscious, he was moved to an iron railing near the sallyport, just beneath Mudd's window. There he was suspended by his thumbs. Sam Arnold saw him hanging and described the man's plight: "He was in drunken insensibility, swinging to and fro, by his thumbs, bound around by a small rope, his legs stretched outwardly, and the whole weight of his body resting on his thumbs. The ends of the thumbs were fearfully swollen and puffed out, having the appearance of a mortified piece of flesh, his head was drooping backwards, the burning rays of the sun striking him full in the face; and the face— red, blue and in some parts nearly black; the veins in the neck swollen and extended like cords, there being no circulation of the blood."

Dunn hung by his thumbs until five in the afternoon. The commander of the post, General Hill, chanced to walk by the sallyport and saw the figure swaying like a carcass from a hook in a butcher's shop. "What is this man doing here?" roared the general.

"He's drunk, sir," volunteered a guard.

"No man in this condition will be punished in this manner again," said the general. "Cut him down!"

The general disappeared into the fort, and left the guards to execute his command. As they cut the ropes holding Dunn, the man fell heavily to the ground. So deep was his stupor that he did not awake. They dragged him to the guardhouse and threw him into a cell. At retreat, Major McConnell strolled by the fort entrance to inspect the guard.

"Where's Dunn?" he asked.

"In the guardhouse," said Sergeant Donnelly.

"Take him out and make him carry a ball."

They gave Dunn a forty-five-pound cannon ball, but he could not grasp it. The guards lifted the ball onto his shoulders only to see him totter and fall to the ground, scraping his face on the coral sand. Blood dripping from his chin, Dunn arose. As he stumbled once more the heavy weight crashed down on his chest. Sergeant Donnelly finally strapped the ball in a knapsack to Dunn's back. Dunn reeled around the ring, each drunken lurch accentuated by the heavy weight. Then, with a rip, the straps of the knapsack broke. The ball dropped from his shoulders and crashed to the ground again. Dunn fell.

"Back into the guardhouse with him," ordered Major McConnell. "Take him out again in two hours."

At eight that evening, they once more dragged Dunn from his cell. Nine hours had passed since James Dunn had begun his temperance lesson, and he was now sober. He stood bent before the cannon ball and reached down. He could not grasp it with his hands. The guard pointed a bayonet at his throat. Dunn turned to Sergeant Donnelly. "I am willing to carry the ball," he cried, pressing his palms together as if in prayer. "God knows the truth of what I say. But I can't do it. Look, *look!*"

The sergeant gazed coldly at the bleeding and swollen hands: "You must carry the ball."

Dunn looked up at him silently.

"Sentinel," said the sergeant. "If he refuses to carry it, obey your orders. Run him through with your bayonet."

Dunn grasped the ball and raised it to his knees. He staggered a step, then two, and crumpled to the ground. "Sentinel, perform your duty," he groaned. "Bayonet and kill me."

The sentinel pricked him again and again with the bayonet, but Dunn was apparently insensitive to the pain. "String him up again," said Sergeant Donnelly. The guards rolled Dunn over and began to twist cords around the bleeding wrists. "*Mercy! Mercy!*" the victim screamed. His cries merely echoed from the hard brick walls of the fort.

At least one person could stand the agony of James Dunn no

longer. The lighthouse keeper, a man who lived on the island with his family, called on Major McConnell. He complained that the guards were butchering this man outside his window. "Can't you do something?" the lighthouse keeper asked. "He's spoiling my supper."

At McConnell's direction, the soldiers pulled Dunn from the vicinity of the lighthouse and tied him beneath some stairs. They gagged him with a bayonet, thus effectively muffling his cries. Dunn dangled there throughout that night. In the morning, the guards cut him down. Now they had to turn him over to the hospital. He lay there for four months. The doctors talked of amputating one gangrenous hand, but that was unnecessary. When he left the hospital at the end of his prison sentence, Dunn had lost nearly all use of his left hand, but at least he was alive when he was sent home.

James Dunn's ordeal did not go unnoticed. Above the sallyport where Dunn's tortures had begun was the cell of Colonel George St. Leger Grenfell as well as that of Mudd. Grenfell had soldiered for four decades with armies in many lands. "Bloody American savages," he must have thought. He had seen barbarism in his day, but this matched the worst of it. What happened to James Dunn would, in time, have repercussions on Grenfell himself.

Sam Mudd meanwhile wrote his wife: "I am very well and the island continues quite healthy. Yellow fever and cholera are reported prevailing at Key West about sixty miles distant; precautions have been taken to prevent its introduction here."

Chapter 14

OF THE FIVE POLITICAL PRISONERS who were kept at Fort Jefferson in those years after the Civil War, only one was not even remotely associated with the conspiracy against Abraham Lincoln. Yet Secretary of War Stanton seemed to harbor resentment, if not hatred, for Dr. Mudd's most flamboyant roommate—Colonel George St. Leger Grenfell. This British soldier of fortune had been involved in another conspiracy, perhaps second in importance only to the plot against Lincoln.

A group of Confederate soldiers, Northern spies, and Copperheads had conspired to free the prisoners at Camp Douglas in Chicago and then to sack that city. After Union detectives uncovered the plot and corralled the ringleaders, a military tribunal sat in judgment in Cincinnati. "His sword has gleamed in every sun," said the order condemning George St. Leger Grenfell to the Dry Tortugas for life, "a fit instrument to be used in this enterprise."

Grenfell's sword had indeed gleamed in every sun. The personality of this swashbuckling Englishman contrasted vividly with that of the taciturn Dr. Mudd, who became his cellmate. Grenfell used to gallop into battle swinging a saber, dressed in a blue English staffcoat, and wearing a scarlet skullcap perched on his silver-haired head. In this garb, he should have been a ready bull's-eye for Union sharpshooters, but Old St. Lege (as his troops called him) flitted in battle like a butterfly. Few marksmen apparently could draw a bead on him. Once when he was leading a group of Morgan's Raiders in a Kentucky brawl, he was exposed to a line of fire. Bullets creased his scarlet cap and knocked it from his head. They shot the horse out from under him. They perforated his English staffcoat. Altogether, eleven bullets peppered him and his mount. Yet Grenfell continued to attack and was unharmed. He was a fiery man even when not on the battlefield and was given to bursts of temper. Grenfell's men recalled that he once became so provoked with a finger infected with a boil that he chopped the finger off with his knife.

The Confederate troops thought their English gentleman a dashing figure, but they saw him only in the twilight of his career. George St. Leger Grenfell had been born more than a half-century before, of a distinguished family in Great Britain. At an early age he decided that a respectable business life would be frightfully dull. "I've decided to join the British army," he informed his father, who promptly vetoed the notion. Thereupon, young Grenfell left home and joined not the British but the French army. For three years he served in Algiers with a French lancer regiment. He rose from private to lieutenant, then retired to become a counselor agent at Tangier in Morocco. When the French later bombarded the town, Grenfell, in true soldier-of-fortune spirit, joined the Moors. He immensely admired the Moorish commander, Abd-el-Kader. "He has everything needed to succeed in life except membership in the Church of England," Grenfell declared.

At another time Grenfell fought the Riff pirates. He also served in Argentina beside Garibaldi. In the Crimean War he commanded Turkish cavalry of the bashi-bazouk, but found the garrison life too dull for him. Late in life, while raising sheep in South America, he heard of the American Civil War. It was quite in keeping with his nature to choose the side of rebels. Grenfell ran the blockade to Richmond and presented himself to General Robert E. Lee. The latter sent him to General Beauregard. The Englishman remained with Beauregard for only a while. He had heard of Morgan's Raiders.

Sooner or later a man with the dash of Colonel George St. Leger Grenfell would have had to encounter a Colonel John Hunt Morgan. Many Southern officers looked askance at Morgan because he was not a West Pointer. But the lack of formal military education did not prevent Morgan from making his own rules for successful guerrilla warfare. More precisely, he helped write them. Three generations ahead of his time with his blitzkrieg tactics, Morgan employed a highly mobile force that could strike suddenly and with concentrated power in a particular locale, then vanish before his enemies could muster enough troops to defeat him—or even to find him! Morgan's Raiders, a free-living band—rowdies, some called them—spent the Civil War ranging through the hills of Tennessee and Kentucky. On occasion they ventured into Ohio and Indiana. But Morgan's triumphs came not from his skirmishes alone, but also from his success in keeping Union troops, who might have been better employed elsewhere, bottled up in defensive positions. The Federals could never guess where he might strike next.

One day early in 1862, Morgan's men looked in wonder at a new arrival in their camp. No stranger sight had ever before crossed Rebel picket lines. As Colonel Grenfell rode into Morgan's camp, mounted on one horse and leading another, three hunting dogs trotted behind him. He was clad in his blue English staffcoat and his scarlet skullcap. The Rebel troops might have joked about this foppish-looking man. But when they saw him in action, all joking stopped. Grenfell was the soldier par excellence.

Morgan wisely appointed Grenfell his adjutant general, although Grenfell had held only the rank of private in the Confederate forces. Grenfell easily earned his promotion. Tutored in the British school of firm military discipline, he began to use the blunt end of his sword to pound respect into the loyal but unruly soldiers under Morgan's command. With Grenfell leading charges, Morgan's men rode to victory after victory. However, the English gentleman apparently could not abide their manners after battle. He liked the sight of a quick cavalry thrust, the smell of gunpowder, the sound of bullets whistling past his graying head, but he did not care for the miserable aftermath of battle. "They're a band of horse thieves and plunderers, carrying on a system of warfare which is revolting to my nature," he later said of Morgan's men. Then Morgan and he fell out over the appointment of a junior officer to brigade command, and Grenfell resigned. Morgan regretted the loss, for the Raider's greatest victories had come while Colonel George St. Leger Grenfell wielded a steel fist of discipline over his men.

Grenfell gathered his swords, his saddles, his horses, and his hunting dogs, and shifted his allegiance to General Bragg. For Bragg he was inspector of cavalry. He later served in Virginia on General Jeb Stuart's staff. Grenfell encountered Morgan again in Richmond, late in the war. The raider chief had been captured once, but had successfully escaped from the Ohio penitentiary. Grenfell agreed to rejoin Morgan as his representative in the Confederate capital, but the playing of politics soon disillusioned him. President Jefferson Davis seemed to be interested in helping only his friends—and neither Grenfell nor Morgan qualified as such.

On June 12, 1864, Colonel Grenfell, having traveled to Washington via Nassau and New York, presented himself to Secretary Stanton. "I want to obtain a parole so I can return to England and live my last few years in peace," said Grenfell. Stanton's eyes sparkled as Grenfell rattled off numbers, positions, and movements of Confederate troops throughout the Southern states. The Secretary promptly dispatched this valuable information to his generals. The generals soon relayed to Stanton that not a single fact Grenfell had told him was correct. If Stanton then could have laid hands on the Englishman, Grenfell would have languished in the Dry Tortugas a year earlier than he did.

Grenfell had no intentions of returning to England—at least, not at present. While in Richmond, he had encountered, besides Morgan, Thomas H. Hines, a former captain on Morgan's staff. Hines, a slender young soldier who delighted in reading the classics, earlier that year had planned Morgan's escape from the Ohio penitentiary. Now Hines had a more important escape to engineer. Camp Douglas in Chicago held ten thousand Rebel prisoners of war. Hines proposed to free them and to lead them on a raid of the city. Copperhead sympathizers in Chicago and Canada, he was confident, would co-operate readily. Jefferson Davis hoped that a general uprising in the Northwest would compel the Federal government to seek terms to end the war. All that the secessionists desired was stalemate, since that would force the Union to compromise on the question of slavery; and such a compromise would be a victory for the South.

Hines apparently met Grenfell in Richmond and there told him of the plans. "How would you like to go along with us to Chicago?"

Grenfell must have accepted the invitation. He appeared next in Toronto, Canada, where he pretended he was about to embark on a sightseeing tour of Georgian Bay. Captain Hines meanwhile had difficulty securing the men and money he needed. Months passed before he could obtain the co-operation he had thought he would get quickly. Late in August of 1864, as the Democrats met in Chicago for their national convention, Captain Hines, with seventy-four carefully picked men, left Toronto by train. The conspirators traveled to Chicago in pairs. Several of the Confederate undercovermen were understandably shocked when Grenfell arrived at the train depot in a gray uniform, with a hunting dog on a leash. "They'll mob you in Chicago when they see that gray uniform."

"This is an English battalion uniform," Grenfell blandly informed them. "I have my English papers, my gun, and my dog. If they ask what I am doing, I will say I'm going prairie-chicken hunting." The rumor started among the conspirators that Grenfell had volunteered for the Chicago enterprise only because Hines had promised to let him wear his uniform and lead a mounted charge on Camp Douglas.

In Chicago Hines's men registered at the Richmond House. They immediately hung placards over their doors: "Missouri Delegation." But the jail-break plans, originally to mature while the convention was in progress, failed to materialize. The Northern Copperheads at first had promised to provide thousands of armed men to aid in the assault on Camp Douglas. Now they confessed that they could perhaps provide several hundred. When the roll was called only twenty-five appeared. Infuriated, Hines left for southern Illinois. Whatever Grenfell thought, he went off with his hunting dog to visit an English friend named Baxter in Carlyle, Illinois—and to hunt prairie chickens.

By the seventh of November, Hines had returned to Chicago. He was determined to put his plan into action with or without support from the Copperheads. His attacking force would divide into four groups. Each band would meet after dark at one of Camp Douglas's four sides. Carts and wagons brimming with arms and ammunition for the escaped prisoners would be wheeled into the nearby bushes and thickets. A skyrocket lighting the night sky would announce the attack. The prisoners, apparently informed that the attack would come, would mob their guards. The wires linking the city to the rest of the country would be cut. Other conspirators would burn the railroad depots and seize the federal ordnance warehouses. The plan, if executed properly, would have devastated the city of Chicago and torn a gaping hole in the Union's home defenses.

Unfortunately for Hines, too many people had known of the plot for too long. Word had leaked to the authorities. Even the newspapers that morning reported rumors that Camp Douglas would be attacked. The plot was exposed when the prison commandant located a deserter from Morgan's Raiders and bribed him to enter the prison as a counterspy. Since prisoners from Morgan's Raiders were at the heart of the plot, the spy had little difficulty in obtaining all the details.

On the day of the attack, instead of the plotters converging on Camp Douglas, the Union authorities converged on Richmond House. In Colonel Grenfell's room they found the soldier sitting before the fireplace, a brandy in one hand, his hunting dog at his side. He was trying to cure a cold, he said. He cured it later—in prison. Of the plotters, only Captain Hines escaped. Detectives raided the home of Dr. E. W. Edwards, but failed to find Hines, as they had expected. The captain had stuffed himself inside a box mattress on the bed where the doctor's wife lay ill. Two days later, Dr. Edwards sorrowfully announced that his wife was dying. Friends and neighbors visited to offer their sympathies. The guards posted at Edward's house failed to notice that one more neighbor left than had entered. Hines escaped on the next train to Cincinnati.

The trial of the Camp Douglas conspirators lasted from January to April, 1865. Grenfell was the only one of the plotters sentenced by the military court to be hanged. While making his closing argument in the case, on the seventeenth of April, the Judge Advocate, H. L. Burnett, received a dispatch from the Secretary of War. Report to Washington to take part in the trial against the Lincoln conspirators, the order read.

Dr. Samuel A. Mudd, shortly after his unsuccessful escape, wrote home about his new cellmate: "He is quite an intelligent man, tall, straight, and about sixty-one or sixty-two years of age. He speaks fluently several languages, and often adds mirth by his witty sarcasm and jest. He has been badly wounded and is now suffering with dropsy, and is allowed no medical treatment whatever, but loaded down with chains, and fed upon the most loathsome food, which treatment in a short time must bring him to an untimely grave."

How had Colonel Grenfell escaped the noose? President Johnson, perhaps prodded by the British government, had commuted the old soldier's death sentence to life imprisonment. At the cruel tortures performed on the drunken and helpless James Dunn, Grenfell fell into a rage. He could do nothing to help Dunn, but he could complain vociferously. Mudd, whatever his feelings, said and did nothing. Grenfell wrote a blazing letter to his friend Bradly Johnson in Richmond, Virginia, and for some reason the normal surveillance of outgoing mail failed and the letter went out. Johnson forwarded the letter to the New York *World*. The paper published it anonymously. An officer at the fort who escorted four prisoners to South Carolina bought a copy of that issue of the *World*. As he read the article his eyes blazed. When he returned to the island, he and the other officers ransacked Grenfell's cell. They uncovered a diary in which the Englishman had written down the name of every officer on the island alongside the atrocities each had committed. They also found a copy of the letter that had appeared in the New York *World*.

The officers had their foe, but they could not punish him immediately. General Hill had ordered all tortures to stop; no punishments were to be inflicted except by his order. This proved to be but temporary relief. Rather than discontinue the punishments, the officers simply changed the scene. Instead of punishment in the ring there was punishment behind the guardhouse, out of Hill's sight. Grenfell was thrown into solitary confinement. To make his life doubly uncomfortable, the entrance to his cell was boarded up. He could survive only if he carefully mended his ways, for one step out of line, and his enemies would surely destroy him.

Once, Arnold saw him in the prison yard: "One morning every feature in his face plainly showed his condition, proving in most unmistakable terms that he was quite ill. He had never made it a habit to visit sick call since incarcerated upon the island, stating the cause for not doing so, his fear that poison might be administered to him, as every officer was deeply prejudiced against him on account of the article he had published. Sickness in this instance forced him against his convictions to attend sick call."

At sick call Grenfell told Dr. J. Holden that he had been unable to eat for six days. "I cannot work," he said. The doctor merely stared at him. Grenfell next appealed to the provost marshal, Lieutenant Frederick Robinson. "Have you been to see the doctor?" asked the lieutenant.

"Yes."

"What did he say?"

"The doctor refused to exempt me from labor."

"Then I am powerless to act."

In the yard, Grenfell's work was to move heavy lumber from one pile to another. The hot sun beat down on his back. He was soon unable to perform any work. The provost marshal found Grenfell sitting exhausted on a pile of boards. "Why aren't you working?"

"I cannot bend my back."

Robinson ordered that Grenfell should be bound with cords and tied to the same bars where James Dunn had once hung. "They could not forget," wrote Arnold, "that his was the voice that broke their slumbering security and forced thus their cruel routine of punishment to be suspended for a while."

Grenfell remained bound to the bars the entire morning. At two o'clock, Robinson, accompanied by two other lieutenants—George W. Crabbe and Albert Pike—returned to the guardhouse. "Cut him down and march him to the wharf," they ordered.

They sent all other prisoners inside the fort. No one would be allowed to witness how they punished this man. The Englishman, forced out on the deck of a scow tied to the wharf, turned to the officers. "Do you intend to submerge me in the sea?" he asked.

"Yes," was their reply.

Grenfell did not wait to be thrown. He jumped. The sergeant who was holding the rope tied to the prisoner's back tried repeatedly to force him under the water by yanking on the rope. But Grenfell managed each time, to keep his head above water.

At last, they hauled him out. "Send to the blacksmith-shop for some weights," ordered Robinson. The sergeant busily scurried around the wharf picking up bricks. Grenfell, still in possession of himself, gazed at them scornfully. "Gentlemen, if it is your intention to murder me, do it in a respectable manner, and I will thank you for the act."

"Damn you!" shouted one of the officers. "You deserve to die for the crimes you have been guilty of."

"I have God to judge between us, which is the worse, you gentlemen, or I."

Bricks and iron weights, nearly forty pounds in all, were hung about Grenfell's feet, and he was cast, like a huge bait with enormous sinkers, into the sea. A small boat, on which were visiting ladies, touched the wharf at the moment that Grenfell's head popped above the surface. The sergeant had yanked him up for a breath of air. "*Murder!*" screamed the colonel. "*Murder!*" The ladies covered their ears with their hands and fled toward the fort, as Grenfell disappeared beneath the waves again. When they finally dragged Grenfell from the water again, he was unconscious.

He lay on the dock like a creature of the sea. Lieutenant Robinson kicked the old soldier in the ribs. "Either I'll make you work, or I'll kill you!" he shouted.

The guards returned Grenfell to his cell. Soon after, most of the officers at Fort Jefferson were transferred to other posts. In May, 1867, Major Valentine H. Stone arrived to take command. Stone proved to be a stern disciplinarian, but he disciplined his officers as well as the enlisted men and prisoners. Under him, the severe punishment and harassment of Grenfell ceased. Dr. Mudd and the others breathed their relief. But within a few months the men at Fort Jefferson would face a threat deadlier even than the cruelty of men in authority.

Chapter 15

AMONG THE MANY RESIDENTS at Fort Jefferson, one, A. *aegypti*, was by far the most anti-social. A. *aegypti* was neither a coldhearted officer nor a sadistic guard. He, or rather it, was a mosquito of the species that transmits the deadly yellow fever.

This fearsome disease had spread throughout the Americas for two and a half centuries after the colonization of the New World. Medical authorities believe that slave traders brought the mosquito *Aëdes aegypti* from West Africa in the middle of the seventeenth century. In those days sailing vessels carried open casks of drinking water on their decks for the convenience of the crews and passengers; these casks were refuges for breeding mosquitoes. Between 1793 and 1900 an estimated half-million cases of yellow fever occurred in the United States. As late as 1905 a yellow fever epidemic broke out in New Orleans. In such outbreaks fatalities could be as low as 5 per cent of those stricken or as high as 50 per cent. No one could say how one might guard against the ravages of yellow fever. For no one knew what caused it, and no one knew how to treat it. Even today there is no effective treatment for yellow fever aside from keeping the patient quiet, regulating his diet, and meeting the symptoms as they arise.

In Dr. Mudd's day, medical men believed that yellow fever was a contagious disease: one that could be passed from person to person through simple contact. As Major Walter Reed later discovered in his experiments with volunteers in Havana in 1900, yellow fever is infectious and not contagious. The virus travels from person to person via the proboscis of a mosquito. Nineteenth-century doctors did not recognize this human-mosquito-human cycle, although Dr. Carlos Finlay of Cuba suspected it in 1881. After an individual is bitten by an infected mosquito, the yellow fever virus multiplies in the area of the bite. Then, within two to four days, the virus begins to circulate through the blood stream. Within a week, the body will manufacture antibodies, which combat the disease by neutralizing the virus. If such antibodies are not produced in sufficient numbers the victim dies. If, during this early stage of virus circulation, another mosquito should bite the victim, this second mosquito will become infected and carry away the virus of the disease. The mosquito itself suffers no harm; it acts only as a carrier. Ten days after the mosquito has acquired the infection, the deadly virus multiplies within its body and contaminates him. Fortunately, the life cycle of the mosquito is only three months. Mosquitoes do not pass the infection to offspring. But a single infected mosquito may bite other humans who may be bitten by other mosquitoes who may bite other humans and the cycle may reach epidemic proportions. The critical elements in the spread of yellow fever are the first victim and the next mosquito. The disease cannot spread except under conditions where mosquitoes abound.

However, those charged with the health of Fort Jefferson knew nothing about the manner in which yellow fever spread. On July 31, 1867, the Spanish frigate *Francisco de Assisi* arrived in the Dry Tortugas. Within a few hours a second ship arrived—the *Narva*, a steamer which was laying underwater cable between Key West and Cuba. Both the *Francisco de Assisi* and the *Narva* had come from Havana, a port which was then ravaged by yellow fever. Somewhere on board the *Narva*—or perhaps on the *Francisco de Assisi*—was that "first" yellow fever victim.

On the island was that "first" mosquito that would bite a yellow fever sufferer and start the terrible cycle.

The Tortugas had experienced an exceptionally wet summer. That year, 37.20 inches of rain fell in the months of June, July, and August—within two inches of the average fall for the entire year. Much stagnant water stood in the unfinished moat along the southeast side of the fort. From the middle of May to the end of August an unseasonable wind blew from the southeast, bringing larger swarms of mosquitoes through the fort than normally appeared. In addition, about one hundred new and unacclimated recruits had arrived during the months of May and June.

On the tenth of August, the eve of the yellow fever outbreak, Mudd sat calmly writing to his wife. "My health is not good, but much better than formerly," he assured her in a rare mood of introspection. "Our fare consists principally of salt pork, bread, and coffee—fresh beef two or three times in every ten days. We had issued yesterday to us, eight in number, about a peck of Irish potatoes, the first vegetables of any kind since last January, with the exception of corn and beans occasionally.

"As regards my looks, being an interested party, I might be inclined to flatter; but to answer your inquiry, I must pass a judgment or opinion no matter how incompetent. Therefore, agreeable to the best estimate I am capable of forming, my appearance is about the same as when I left home, with the exception that my hair is considerably thinner, consequently the bald head more perceptible, and no doubt larger in circumference. I have no wrinkles, and wear constantly a mustache and goatee. Owing to the peculiarity of my skin, and not much exposed to the sun, I am paler or fairer than when I left home. I may be a few pounds lighter, perhaps about a hundred and forty-four or five. My manners about the same, impulsive, etc. Generally, have but little to say, but think a great deal. I am very weak, though in appearance strong. This I think is attributable to the climate and the want of free exercise. The rules governing the fort are very rigid and severe, more barbarous than ages bygone—refusing to work or obey an order is punishable with instant death by shooting."

While Mudd sat in his cell composing this letter, the yellow fever virus may already have been incubating within at least one *A. aegypti* mosquito. Infected mosquitoes could have come along on the *Narva* or *Francisco de Assisi* from Cuba. The time element, however, causes one to believe that there was an infected man on one of these ships. The two vessels had arrived at the island on the thirty-first of July. As noted before, it takes about ten days for the virus to develop within the mosquito's body. Mosquitoes usually feed every three days. Once a man has been bitten, two to four days pass before yellow fever symptoms appear. On the eighteenth of August, prison officials hospitalized the first soldier with what seemed to be yellow fever. And a week later, Dr. Mudd again wrote his wife, this time with somber news which he nevertheless tried to report calmly: "We have had one case of yellow fever here since I last wrote, which proved fatal. It originated here and was not imported. A general renovation has ensued, which for the future will prevent its recurrence. I have no fears regarding it, which is its greatest preventative."

Even if Mudd truly harbored no fears, the victims would be pitifully fearful. An attack of the disease usually begins with a severe headache, followed by pains in the back and neck and a rise in temperature. The virus attacks the liver and kidneys, and colors the skin as in yellow jaundice. In the acute stage, the mucous membranes rupture. Streaks of blood appear in the victim's vomit; later, the vomit turns the color of coffee and, finally, black. Few patients survive the black vomit. Most fatalities occur around the sixth or seventh day after the infection. Of course, the infection usually escapes immediate detection. "Sometimes the poor creatures are struck with delirium from the beginning," wrote Dr. Mudd, "and are perfectly wild and unmanageable; some die the same day they are taken, but most live to the third day. More die for the want of proper nursing and care than for lack of medical attention."

Within three days after the first soldier had been stricken, the disease claimed three more victims. The first four men had shared a room along the southern side of the fort just above the moat. Dr. Mudd visited the infected casemate with hammer in hand rather than with his stethoscope. He now worked in the carpenter's shop alongside Ned Spangler and had orders to barricade the room where the soldiers had slept. This apparently was the "general renovation" he had mentioned to his wife. But wooden walls would not halt the spread of yellow fever. Other soldiers who bunked nearby soon became ill. The disease spread as though it were blown by the wind, and Dr. Mudd suspected that it might be spread by some poison in the air and not by contact, as was commonly believed. His observations were not without merit; they did contribute in a small way to the discoveries later made by Carlos Finlay and Walter Reed.

One company's quarters lay behind a bastion that effectively blocked the steadily blowing southeast wind. This company remained free of disease. However, one evening, a small rain cloud drifted over, and a heavy wind blew at the men's quarters from the opposite direction for about twenty minutes. Within two days, nearly half of that company of thirty men had contracted the disease.

In the early stages the prisoners joked about the spread of the fever, for it struck down only their guards. "It is just a little Southern opposition to reconstruction," said one man. "The matter should be reported to Congress in order that a law might be passed lowering the temperature below zero. That would put an end to the disloyalty."

Those historians who are inclined to magnify minute bits of evidence into great theories might see a link between yellow fever and a Confederate plot. For when the disease had finally run its course, only two prisoners had died from it. The officers at the fort suffered the most. "Doctor," remarked another prisoner to Mudd, "the yellow fever is the fairest and squarest thing that I have seen in the past four or five years. It makes no distinction in regards to rank, color, or previous condition—every man has his chance, and I would advise you as a friend not to interfere."

But Dr. Mudd could no more ignore the advance of the epidemic than he could have ignored the pleas of the man who had come to his door with a broken leg. There was only one surgeon, Dr. J. Sim Smith, at the fort. On the fourth of September, Mudd learned that yellow fever had claimed Dr. Smith as its victim and left the fort without a physician. The only individual qualified to treat the sufferers was in the carpenter's shop.

The next morning after breakfast, Mudd asked Sam Arnold to talk to Major Stone, the commander, in his behalf. He had decided to approach the major, but did not want to speak up himself. He was a prisoner here, not a doctor, but his knowledge and skill were needed. Perhaps it was pride that kept him from going to the major directly; perhaps he wished that tiny bit of satisfaction that his jailer, by summoning him, could give him. "Tell him," said Mudd, "if he wants my help in curing the sick, I have no fear of, no objection to, performing whatever aid there is in my power toward their relief."

Arnold started across the parade grounds, only to meet Major Stone coming toward their cell. The prisoner spoke of Mudd's offer. "That is good," said the major. "I was just coming to ask for the doctor's help."

Dr. Mudd was immediately placed in command of the post hospital. There could be no question of his value to the entire fort now, for within three days Dr. Smith was dead.

Mudd advised the commander to move his troops to another island nearby where they might be safe from contamination. Such advice might have been accepted from a regular physician. It could not be considered coming from a prisoner-doctor, especially not from Samuel A. Mudd. So Major Stone ignored the advice. Later, Dr. D. W. Whitehurst, a sixty-year-old civilian physician, arrived from Key West. At the outbreak of the Civil War he had been expelled from the fort because of Confederate sympathies. Whitehurst repeated Mudd's advice, and the majority of the soldiers were moved to another island. Not one who left was stricken with yellow fever.

In dealing with the sick, Mudd employed a different strategy. The commander had erected a temporary shack on Sand Key to serve as a hospital. He hoped thereby to keep the infection from spreading inside the garrison. His intentions were good, but to obtain treatment at the hosptial, the sick men had to be transported across several miles of open sea. Often they had to lie at the wharf for hours while waiting for the boat to arrive. Many times, the sick patients had to lie beside a coffin being shipped to Sand Key for burial. From both a psychological and a physical standpoint, it was better to bring the hospital back to the fort.

Mudd took action to accomplish this; apparently, no one vetoed his counsel here. He later boasted that all who were admitted to the hospital during the periods in which he was in command—a total of three weeks—survived. His procedure was simple: prompt treatment and constant care.

Dr. Mudd toiled like a truly dedicated physician. Yet the yellow fever epidemic raged at Fort Jefferson, and the living showed little respect for the dead. "No more respect is shown the dead, be he officer or soldier," said Dr. Mudd, "than the putrid remains of a dead dog. The burial party are allowed a drink of whiskey both before and after the burying, which infuses a little more life in them. They move quickly, and in half an hour after a man dies, he is put in a coffin, nailed down, carried to a boat, rowed a mile to an adjacent island, the grave dug, covered up, and the party returned, in the best of humor for their drinks. Such are life and scenes in Tortugas."

Arnold painted a similar picture. "In many instances," he said, "coffins were brought into the hospital, and placed alongside of the bed to receive the body of someone expected to die." Sometimes the hospital attendants were overzealous and had to remove the coffin when a patient recovered. The desperately ill patients could not have been cheered by the sight of the coffins.

With three-quarters of the troops quartered elsewhere, and most of those who remained soon in serious condition, the strict security regulations could not be enforced. One night the corporal in charge of the burial detail arrived at the wharf. The lone sentinel guarding the boats nodded recognition. He had been instructed to allow burial parties to pass at any time, day or night. The corporal rowed out in the direction of the burial island—and rowed on and on—far from the Tortugas to a more healthful climate. With him fled three other soldiers and a former murderer whose death sentence had been commuted to life imprisonment in the Tortugas. With fewer guards to balk escape, several of the prisoners, too, got away to freedom. Mudd himself realized that now was the time to accomplish what he had failed to do two years earlier. "Little or no guard duty is performed," he wrote, "and but little difficulty presented to those who might be disposed to escape. I have resigned myself to the fates and shall no more act on impulse."

The victims of *A. aegypti* fell daily. "Fear was depicted upon the countenance of everyone on the island, each looking for his turn next," reported Sam Arnold. Dr. Smith's son, a three-year-old named Harry who used to turn somersaults to amuse Dr. Mudd, died. Mrs. Smith left the island with her only remaining child, a girl. Four out of six officers died. A fifth survived only because of careful nursing by Colonel Grenfell, who apparently bore no ill will against the class of men that tormented him most. Mrs. Stone, the wife of the company commander, died. Soldiers died singly, in pairs, four at a time. Arnold observed further: "The officers who died of the disease were coffined and borne to their lasting resting place by the prisoners of the post, no respect being shown by the other officers. Even wives were carried in like manner to the grave, the husband remaining in his quarters, callous to everything around, void of attention or respect to the loved dead."

Finally, death narrowed the ranks of the conspirators. Michael O'Laughlin died of the yellow fever. Of the state prisoners, he is the least mentioned in the voluminous records. While staying together in prison, O'Laughlin and Mudd apparently became close. The doctor found that he could talk more easily with O'Laughlin than with any of the other prisoners, yet in his letters home he alluded only occasionally to the despair of Michael O'Laughlin. Reporters had usually ignored O'Laughlin, and when he died, even Arnold did not note the passing. O'Laughlin, like nearly every other mortality at Fort Jefferson, was a victim of yellow fever, but his case at first had not seemed severe. He persevered through the early stages of the disease. "Stay in bed," Dr. Mudd warned him sternly, but had so many others to attend that he was unaware that his patient disobeyed orders. When the doctor left him one morning, O'Laughlin bounced out of bed and paced the room seeking books and newspapers. Perhaps it was the additional exertion that felled him. That evening at five o'clock he collapsed.

For thirty-six hours, O'Laughlin hovered on the thin edge separating life from death. "O'Laughlin had a convulsion a few minutes ago," Mudd wrote to his wife. "My heart almost fails me, but I must say he is dying. God only knows who will be the next. There will be likely two or three more deaths during the day."

O'Laughlin, who had escaped the gallows only to die hundreds of miles from home, in a prison hospital, expired from the bite of an insect. Shortly before his death he had gazed into the eyes of his friend, Samuel Mudd. "Doctor, Doctor," he pleaded. "You must tell my mother all." Then he called Spangler to his side and offered his hand. "Good-bye, Ned." On the morning of September 23, 1867, Michael O'Laughlin was dead.

The next day Mudd wrote to his wife: "I am not feeling so well today. My head aches. It may be from sitting up so much, but I fear it is the premonitory symptoms of the prevailing epidemic. Five were buried this morning, including O'Laughlin. The hospital is full, and scarcely nurses enough to attend the sick. I have been acting physician and nurse for a considerable time, until I am nearly exhausted. My heart sickens at the prospect which is before me. Were an enemy throwing shot and shell in here a more horrible picture could not be presented—a useless expenditure of life and money."

After Stone's wife had died of yellow fever, the major hoped to leave the island to protect his only son from the reach of the terrible disease. Mudd felt that not only the commander should leave the island but that everyone should be taken off. He went to see the major. "There is no abatement in the disease," he declared. "Instead of becoming milder, it is becoming more malignant. In a short time this garrison will be without officers. And it will be death to send any unacclimated officer here."

"Perhaps the disease will eventually wear itself out," the major replied.

"In this climate," insisted Mudd, "the disease is likely to continue an indefinite period, because there is little temperature change with the season."

Dr. Mudd was not altogether correct. Cold weather might indeed kill the infected mosquitoes, but so would time. Eventually the island became yellow-fever-proof. The disease seemed to burn itself out for want of new victims to feed on. "I will talk to General Grant," Major Stone promised, "and tell him what you have said."

Unfortunately, Major Stone never obtained that interview with the commander of the army. He left the island on the twenty-first of September. Five days later the schooner *Matchless* returned to Fort Jefferson with some sad news for Mudd and the rest of the garrison. The day before Major Stone had died of yellow fever in Key West. "He was very kind toward us," Mudd wrote his wife, "and had promised to make known to the authorities at Washington the service I had rendered the garrison during the recent epidemic, which he thought would have considerable weight in restoring me to liberty, and to my family. Now that he is dead there is no one here whom I can expect to take any interest in my behalf, and the future may not be so propitious with me."

Mudd labored on. "No deaths have occurred today," he wrote on September thirtieth, "although there is one not likely to live until morning. I was interrupted a few minutes ago, and told that he was breathing his last by his nurse. I went to him, and with the application of a pitcher or two of cold water to the head he was relieved of the convulsion, and is now doing as well as can be expected. With good and proper attention he would get over it, but that is impossible here. The nurses are ignorant and careless, and I can't act both the physician and nurse. Colonel Grenfell is quite sick; his case is doubtful. More were admitted in the hospital today. There are not more than a dozen on the island yet to have it. We will call them up tomorrow and learn the reason why they did not have the disease."

The disease thus continued through August, September, and into October. "During the prevalence of the fever, the island had assumed a different shade," explained Arnold later. "The island which before was more like a place populated by fiends, than anything else it could be compared with, suddenly became calm, quiet, and peaceful. Fear stood out in bold relief upon the face of every human soul. Some attempted to assume the tone of gayety and indifference, but upon their face could be readily traced other feelings." One night a prisoner, terrified at the threat of the fever, jumped through a porthole into the moat. He sank to the bottom, where his feet became entangled in seaweed. The next morning the guards, looking down into the moat, saw what they thought was a man standing upright in ten feet of water. Ironically, the man's pardon arrived the very next day.

A new doctor, Edward Thomas, a contract physician from New York, had come to the island toward the end of September. Old Dr. Whitehurst returned home to Key West. Mudd hoped to turn the responsibilities of the post hospital over to Thomas, but the New Yorker soon revealed himself to be a poor replacement. With a bottle of liquor in his hand Thomas retired to his room and shut the door. He had no interest in ministering to the victims of yellow fever; he wanted only to keep himself out of the path of the disease.

Meanwhile, Dr. Mudd, too, fell ill. Spangler and Arnold put him to bed in their prison room. These men knew nothing of medicine, but they had seen Mudd prescribe for others. They had stood beside the doctor during his futile attempt to save O'Laughlin's life. First Arnold and then Spangler watched over their fever-stricken friend. Mudd recovered, but not once during his illness did Dr. Thomas come near him. (Arnold reported that Thomas remained in his quarters in a state of drunkenness until the government revoked his contract.) Mudd was grateful for the care provided by his fellow prisoners. He said to Spangler and to Arnold, "Without your watchfulness, I would have died."

The disease, at last, began to subside. In three months, 270 persons had suffered from it. Of these, only thirty-eight died: a comparatively small percentage if one compares it to others recorded in the annals of yellow fever. Only two prisoners had died:

O'Laughlin and a newcomer who perhaps had not had sufficient time to build up the natural resistance that must accrue to those who live in the tropics for some time. Much of the credit for containing the disease and for helping its victims went to Dr. Mudd. He reported: "The news had spread around through the garrison of the neat and comfortable appearance of the hospital and the improved condition of the sick, which had the effect to gain for me a reputation, and the confidence of the soldiers—all I could desire to insure success. It was not long before I discovered I could do more with nine cases out of ten by a few consoling and inspiring words, than with all the medicine known to me in the *materia medica*."

Yellow fever left Fort Jefferson after the middle of October, for reasons which now are easy to understand. Those who had suffered and survived became immune to further attacks. The infected mosquitoes themselves died within two or three months, and the virus died with them.

Mudd mentions one last name on the roll of the sick; none other than Dr. Edward Thomas who had taken refuge in the bottle and had discovered that alcohol was not an effective remedy against yellow fever.

Having luckily escaped death himself, Mudd now pondered whether he would have any new luck with his pardon. "When the apples are ripe," he wrote, "they will fall without human intervention—so with my release. When I am released from here, I shall thank no mortal man for it, but shall look upon it only in the light of every other thing in nature, that it was ordained, could not be otherwise."

The officers and men of the fort knew whom to thank for their lives. Dr. Mudd, whether guilty of a part in the Lincoln conspiracy or innocent of anything except helping an injured man, had bent over them tenderly during their sufferings. All the soldiers on the post signed a petition requesting that he be pardoned because of his role in fighting the epidemic. President Johnson, however, never saw that petition.

Chapter 16

"TODAY, BEING NEW YEAR," Dr. Mudd wrote to his wife on January 1, 1868,* "I will begin it by dropping you a few lines to let you know that I am spending the day soberly & thoughtful of you & little ones. I sometimes fancy I can see the dear little creatures coming in with chattering teeth & little snotty noses shivering with cold. I have felt great concern to know how you are provided with fuel & fire. Since the darkies have been turned away. Jere in his last told me he had been down though did not state wheather he had obtained anyone to see to affairs during the winter. Your last letter led me to a different conclusion which the one preceding was calculated [to hide], had I not seen through the myth. Anyone would judge from the former that my release was immediate—all that had to be done was to present the petition and etc. with the long list of Hon. Names to obtain the desired boom. Your last postpone the happy day four months longer—planting time. I can't see there is so much virtue in Honorable Names & letters—or even for meritorious services rendered. These are hard things to overlook. I have no doubt saved dozens of lives & thousands worth of property to the nation & can say from my inmost heart that I have never so much desired the death of an individual—yet you with me and the children are suffering for a crime which I am sure never entered our brains. This is justice I would like to see visited upon those who have so cruelly wronged me, that they may be brought to a sense of their guilt & may atone for their crime. I have seen mention of the action of the Medical Confraternity in my behalf, but of what use, if it will not secure my release. My

---
* This letter is printed in its entirety. The spelling and punctuation are Dr. Mudd's own.

pride is not elevated by seeing my name paraded in the Newspapers as deserving the clemency of the Government for the services I have rendered. Why don't they take up the case & prove my innocence and confound my infamous calumniators. This would be doing the world a service, besides relieving the injured—I don't say satisfy.

"My darling Frank [Mrs. Mudd] you ask me to write something cheering? Nothing would afford me more pleasure than to be able to comfort & console you in your present unhappy & helpless condition. So long as the Government is controled by men without souls & less honesty I can[not] promise you nor myself anything. The spirit of infidelity pervades the whole Country. This is not only in regard to God, but to the laws and the Constitution of the Country. They are materialists & think only of self gratification—exulting in the ruin & misery they cause others. I have had no means except by reading to arrive at the truth of our political woes. The soldiers are a very ignorant class generally and there is no one here in civil life who is capable of advising. The Officers I rarely have anything to say to. You can now judge of the facilities I have of acquiring knowledge, even upon the most unimportant matters. The Gentleman whom I have been expecting down—has not made his appearance. I will be prepared to undergo his bread and water administration upon his arrival. I think I have acted wisely. I shall certainly not make any statement—until I am placed right before the law. The only comfort or consolation I can give you is that I am well with a very good prospect of living until planting time. You arc in a situation to know more than myself, consequently you should look to those better informed & receive cheer. If you believe all that is told you I am sure you ought not to despond on my account. Two Companies of soldiers have been ordered from here to New Orleans & will leave upon the first steamer that arrives. The two remaining Companies have orders to be in readiness to move, but their destination is not known. From what I have heard & can judge, this Post will soon be guarded by negro troops—perhaps early in the Spring. Owing to the damp and unhealthy condition of the Fort, the

Commandant has recommended that the Garrison & Prisoners be removed to one of the Islands near & erect temporary sheds to shield us from the heat of the sun & rain. The truth is beginning to be manifest.

"Tell Lilly Pop has nearly completed her little work box. It is made of mahogany & inlaid with crab wood. Three little leaves representing a branch is inlaid in the corners of the top—a fancy piece in the center with the enetials of her name in German letters engraved & inlaid, which looks quite nice. I have the sides yet to finish. I have several little crosses made of crab wood which I will send to be distributed among you all. We received the box & barrel of Potatoes in good order. There is no objection to our receiving anything. The jug of whiskey was a great treat to us—it lasted us over a week—so you can judge our moderation. Maj. Andrews has given us permission to receive anything our friends chose to send us not excepting whiskey. Remember me to dear Pa & Ma & family to all of our household—kiss our darling little children & tell them Pop loves them with all his heart & they must be good & learn their little lessons well & learn to write to Pop."

Life thus dragged on in the Dry Tortugas. Dr. Mudd's friends employed every means they could to secure his freedom. After an attempt failed to obtain a writ of habeas corpus in Key West Mudd despaired of ever obtaining justice. Soon after his arrival at Fort Jefferson he had inscribed on the door of his prison cell: "Abandon hope all ye who enter here." Mudd had indeed abandoned hope. Meanwhile, the government regularly rotated the officers and men assigned to this unpopular island post. Some of the men who were sent here were brigands, and may have deserved imprisonment more than those over whom they stood guard. A few demonstrated human qualities. New prisoners arrived on the island, then, at the expiration of their terms, were sent home. But certain factors remained unchanged: the sun, the heat, the bugs, the dampness, the poor food, the sagging brick walls of the fort itself, and the state prisoners. Five had come here in the fall of 1865. The yellow fever epidemic had reduced the number to four. Now in the early months of 1868, one of these four left.

On the fifteenth of January, the prison gardener, Colonel George St. Leger Grenfell, wrote to a friend: "I was set up in a closed dungeon for ten months, every orifice carefully stopped up except one for air, denied speech with anyone, lights, books, or papers. I could neither write nor receive letters. I was gagged twice, tied up by the thumbs twice, three times drowned. I am not exaggerating, and all this for having written an account to a friend of severe punishment inflicted to soldiers and prisoners here: the bare truth only, the statement which General Johnson published in the New York *World*. I fear therefore giving publicity to anything. Not that I am afraid of Major Andrews. I have really not a fault to find with him. But tigers have claws and sometimes use them. While you are blowing your finger ends from cold, I sleep close to an open window with one blanket only and that oftener off than on. I have tomatoes, peppers, and melons in full bloom, salad radishes, and peas and greens in maturity in the open air of the fort. In fact, I am obliged to use sunshades from ten to three all through the garden, for be it known to you that they have turned my sword into a shovel and a rake and I am at the head of my profession here. What I say on horticultary is law."

Grenfell added: "Wonders never cease, but my paper does."

Claws or not, Dr. Mudd and Colonel Grenfell had little time to appreciate the presence of a benevolent commander. In March of 1868, Major George P. Andrews left the fort. To replace him appeared Brevet Major C. C. McConnell, the officer who had presided over the cruel treatment of prisoner James Dunn. Nearly dismissed from the service because of Grenfell's letter exposing his conduct, the major may have dreamt of revenge. Grenfell certainly anticipated new punishment. McConnell appointed Lieutenant Frank Thorpe as provost marshal. "What Major McConnell could not conceive," said Sam Arnold, "Lieutenant Thorpe could, as deceit, treachery, and hatred were stamped upon every lineament of his face. Each studied out the most cruel measures to adopt, in persecuting prisoners and what the one could not devise, the other would." The new provost marshal, undoubtedly remembering Grenfell's incriminating letter, opened all letters that came in and all that went out. This so enraged Dr. Mudd that he vowed never again to use the mails. The next year of his ordeal at Fort Jefferson is obscure because Mudd apparently corresponded only when he could have his letters carried from the fort and mailed in Key West.

Thorpe picked for his provost guards, according to Arnold, "the most contemptible men of the garrison, who abused, cursed, struck and maltreated the prisoners under their charge in every conceivable manner." Almost at once, McConnell relieved Grenfell of his garden duties and sent the old soldier to hard labor. Forgotten was his service in nursing several officers during the yellow fever epidemic. "If they have started to kill me inch by inch," Grenfell told Arnold and Mudd, "I might as well have a go at escape. A watery grave is better than these indignities."

Grenfell did not have to search far for someone willing to go with him. William Noriel, a soldier who hated Major McConnell as much as any of the prisoners did, agreed to accompany Grenfell. Joseph Holroyd (some sources say he was a prisoner, others that he was a guard) also wanted to desert. A prisoner named J. W. Adair, who had already attempted to escape twice before, brought experience to the group.

Three years earlier, Adair and a Negro prisoner had crawled out a window and paddled to Loggerhead Key on a wooden plank. Stealing one of the lighthouse boats on that island, the two sailed to Cuba, where Adair tried to sell his friend into slavery. The Negro brought the account of the treachery to the Spanish authorities in Havana, who promptly returned the escapees to Fort Jefferson. A year and a half later, Adair tried to duplicate his initial escape, this time alone. Though weighed down by a thirty-pound ball and chain, he crossed to Loggerhead Key, again on a plank. This time, however, there was no waiting boat to give him passage to Havana. Guards routed Adair from the underbrush, and he was brought back once more.

Grenfell accepted one more equally desperate prisoner in the group. James Orr's reputation matched Adair's. A year before, the assistant military storekeeper, a mulatto named George T. Jackson, had caught Orr sitting down when he should have been working. Jackson ordered him to work, and threatened to report him to the provost marshal. If reported, Orr would spend the night carrying an iron ball around the prison ring. The furious Orr waited for a chance to take revenge. Later that day he told Jackson that an officer wanted to see him behind the stable—then he followed Jackson. Orr yanked a pen knife out of his shirt and lunged at Jackson. One result of Orr's assault was that Secretary Stanton in Washington ordered sentinels to shoot or bayonet anyone refusing to work. Not long after the issuance of this order, a guard used it as an excuse to gun down a drunken prisoner.

On the sixth of March, Grenfell decided to make his break. That night his soldier-accomplice, William Noriel, was scheduled to guard Post No. 2, which commanded the fort's locked boats. For a week a storm had been lashing the waters of the Gulf, but Grenfell probably reasoned that they could not afford to wait for better weather. Besides, no one could say when Noriel would get the post again. The waves might reduce their chances for success, but the storm might also discourage pursuit. Noriel went on duty at ten o'clock. The night was dark. Scudding clouds masked the stars. Grenfell and his accomplices eluded the sentinel within the fort and quietly slipped through a porthole into the moat. At eleven o'clock the first sentinel called the hour. Noriel answered the call, stepped into the boat which he had pulled next to the wharf, and paddled to where Grenfell and his men were waiting at the breakwater. Raising sail, the five escapees headed out into the Gulf and vanished into the night. The phlegmatic Mudd, observing this escape at a safe distance, probably wondered how a man like Grenfell could be so daring.

At midnight, Sentinel No. 1 once more called the hour. Only his echo returned. He called again. Still no answer. "Probably asleep at his post," the sentinel muttered. Advancing toward the dock with the corporal of the guard he found a boat missing—and Noriel gone. Soon the sentinels were tramping down the long corridors of the fort. The guards jostled prisoners out of their beds and searched their cells. They soon reported the bad news to Major McConnell: "Grenfell has escaped, sir."

This information must have struck Major McConnell hard. His career had already been jeopardized by Grenfell, because of his letter about the treatment of James Dunn. Now that same complainer, one of the four most important prisoners in the fort—if not in the entire country—had escaped. Secretary Stanton would hardly be pleased.

The survey steamer *Bib* stood by the wharf. McConnell sent her in pursuit of Grenfell, but the ocean was vast and Grenfell's boat but a speck on it. After a day battling the stormy waters of the Gulf, the *Bib* returned—no Grenfell. McConnell reported to Washington that Grenfell had possessed a large sum of money and had bribed a sentinel. Sam Arnold denied the charge: "He could have gone without a dollar, as the rule of the place was as disgusting to the soldiers as it was to those confined." McConnell, with little apparent evidence to back his claim, also reported Grenfell dead by drowning. No open boat, he reasoned, could have long survived such rough seas.

Perhaps McConnell was right, for here the story of Colonel George St. Leger Grenfell, soldier of fortune, conspirator, prisoner, ended. But not quite. Seventy years later, A. W. McMullen, who once lived on the Gulf coast in Florida, told a story of a mysterious visitor. The visit occurred during his youth; he thought the year had been 1866 or 1867. The stranger (McMullen informed the readers of *The Confederate Veteran* in January, 1929) had just escaped from the Dry Tortugas. He had left Fort Jefferson one night expecting to reach Key West the next morning. But strong winds blew him out into the Gulf. For five days he steered by the sun during the day and by the North Star at night, and sustained himself on small rations of food and water. "The name he gave I can't recall," wrote McMullen, "but I think he was English. I very well remember he and my father discussing the Crimean War and the bombarding of Sevastopol." This mysterious stranger rested a few days at the McMullen house, then left, in the direction of

Pensacola. McMullen's remembrance added a final touch of scarlet to the already impressive Grenfell legend. If one accepts the story, it is the last account in Grenfell's saga. Shortly after the escape, Southern papers reported that Grenfell reached Havana and waited passage back to England. These accounts have been discredited, chiefly because his family claimed that he never came home. One can choose from two pictures: that of the red skullcap bobbing on the turbulent waters of the Gulf, its owner dead by drowning, as his foe McConnell reported; or, if one credits McMullen's account, that of the Old Soldier who, having escaped from the major's clutches, returned to raising sheep in Argentina and quietly faded from the pages of history.

Chapter 17

AFTER GRENFELL ESCAPED, the regulations at Fort Jefferson became increasingly suppressive. Arnold stated: "No one after retreat was permitted to place his head out of the aperture of his casemate under the penalty of having a musket ball come crashing through his brain." Soldiers might no longer talk to the prisoners. Work in the hot sun continued from morning till night with no rest periods. One day carpenters appeared and boarded the three state prisoners—Arnold, Spangler, and Mudd—into their cells.

"What are we accused of?" they demanded.

"You are accused of nothing," the officer in command replied. "There is a rumor of the escape of some of the prisoners." The boards were to serve as a barricade to prevent the prisoners from crossing the guardhouse shed to the corridor beyond and so out into the fort enclosure. It mattered little that anyone entering this area would have to do so in full view of the guardhouse. A poor excuse is better than none, snorted Arnold.

During these prison years Dr. Mudd's hopes that justice would prevail had risen and fallen like a fisherman's cork float. In January of 1866, Dr. Mudd had been able to speculate with some logic: "An early release on my part would be a virtual acknowledgment of the injustice of the court-martial; therefore, my conclusions are—I will have to remain here some time yet to keep up appearances." He had been sentenced to life imprisonment, but in his heart he was unable to accept the sentence. His friends wrote encouraging letters, perhaps merely to buoy his spirits, maintaining that his release was not only inevitable but not far off. Mudd, understandably, when their claims of a pardon within a short time continued, became provoked. For at last they seemed idle words to him. "I want you to state in your next what you consider a short time," he wrote testily to his wife. "I am becoming tired of these expressions, because they don't comport with my reckoning. Perhaps you call one, two, or three years short—it seems very short after it is passed, but distressingly long to view in my present position and condition."

In the spring of 1866 he had reason for optimism when the Supreme Court announced its decision *ex parte Milligan*. Lambdin P. Milligan, an Indiana lawyer, had worked undercover for the Southern cause during the Civil War. Loyal Unionists probably detested Copperhead sympathizers nearly as much as they despised assassins. Brought before a military tribunal in Indianapolis in 1864, Milligan was accused of treason. Henry L. Burnett, who subsequently labored for the prosecution against Grenfell and then went off to sift evidence in the Lincoln conspiracy trial, sought Milligan's conviction. He succeeded; the military commission sentenced Milligan to death. But Milligan did not hang. The stakes were too small in Indiana. There was neither public nor government sentiment to hasten the Copperhead to the gallows without permitting an appeal.

In a federal court Milligan's attorneys argued that their client had been deprived of his constitutional right to trial by jury. They maintained that the military trial was illegal. The government argued in defense of military tribunals, citing Lincoln's suspension (with the authorization of Congress) of the right of habeas corpus in cases where military authorities arrested civilians for war crimes. The machinery of justice, however, functioned admirably in Milligan's case. The case finally reached the Supreme Court. Although the United States was at war, a military commission, so ruled the court, should not have taken jurisdiction in this matter, for the civil courts in Indiana were still functioning properly at that time. Civilians were not to be tried by military courts except where the civil courts had ceased to function because of invasion or disorder. After spending eighteen months in custody, Milligan was set free.

The similarity of Mudd's case to Milligan's seemed to be clear. Mudd was a civilian who had been tried by the military. At the time he was tried, the courts of the District of Columbia and

Maryland were still functioning. Moreover, Mudd was tried in Washington for a crime (aiding Booth) that had presumably been committed in Maryland. The Milligan decision, however, had caused the Radicals to raise a storm of protest, and the Supreme Court consequently hedged on several other controversial points of law. With Chief Justice Chase eyeing the 1868 Presidential nomination, the Court had small reputation for courage. Had Mudd's case instead of Milligan's been brought before the Court, the machinery of justice might have ground to a halt. With Mudd exiled to the Dry Tortugas, the question of the legality of the tribunal that had tried him seemed moot and academic. *Ex parte Milligan* would not benefit Mudd.

But it would benefit another conspirator. In January, 1867, the authorities finally captured John Surratt. Like Arnold and O'Laughlin, Mrs. Surratt's son had lost faith in Booth's plots when the repeated attempts at the abduction of Lincoln had failed. After the last failure, Surratt had fled from the capital. Testimony at his trial and his own assertions later seemed to prove that he spent the night of the assassination not in Washington (as the 1865 military commission insisted), but in Elmira, New York. Hearing of Booth's death and realizing that he would be implicated, Surratt fled to Canada. He remained undercover for several months in the home of a Catholic priest, which fact later caused more than one rabble-rousing writer to speculate that Lincoln's death had been the result of a papal conspiracy.

Northern newspapers villified Surratt as a coward because he did not come forward to help his mother. But he could have done little to alter the course of military justice. In all likelihood, his would have been one more body swinging from the gallows. It was said that Mrs. Surratt's lawyers, who were in touch with him, warned him to stay away. Few actually expected the woman to be executed. John Surratt had little reason to give himself up.

Surratt's life reads as though it had been lifted from the pages of some adventure magazine. Between the assassination and the trial, Louis Wiechmann, accompanied by federal detectives, traced him to Montreal. Surratt saw them; they missed him. In

November he sailed for England, but he was recognized in Liverpool, and the news of his appearance was relayed to the United States. Instead of taking action to apprehend him, whether through official channels or by special agents, the American government responded strangely by canceling the twenty-five-thousand-dollar reward on the fugitive's head. He was therefore able to proceed unhindered on his journey to the Continent. Eventually, one of Wiechmann's friends found Surratt in Italy, where the latter was in the uniform of a papal Zouave. On discovering Surratt's identity, the papal authorities, waiting for no requests from America, ordered him arrested. Surratt was placed under guard. The next day, as he was being transferred to another prison, he leaped off a balustrade and into a deep gully. The fall knocked him unconscious. He regained his senses to hear bullets whistling around his head. He managed to stumble into a nearby woods and, though still clad in the resplendent uniform of a Zouave, managed to elude fifty pursuers. He reached Naples, and went on. He was not arrested again until he reached Alexandria, across the Mediterranean in Egypt. From there he was returned to the United States.

Fortunately for Surratt, *ex parte Milligan* had removed the props that supported military trials for civilian offenders. In Surratt's trial, in which he was charged with assassination, the coals of the original conspiracy trial were raked over again. But the jury disagreed and declared itself deadlocked. The case was dismissed. The situation of a hung jury was a strange victory for authorities who had maintained two years earlier that an unbiased jury could not be found to try the conspirators; with one exception the jury men in the Surratt trial voted along partisan lines. One Pennsylvanian, one New Englander, and two foreign-born voted guilty. Three Virginians, two Marylanders, two from the District of Columbia, and one New Yorker found him not guilty. The government announced that it would try Surratt again, this time on charges of conspiracy and treason—charges less difficult to prove than assassination—but no second trial was held. The statute of limitation (two years in such cases) had run out, and Surratt went free. Dr. Mudd saw hope in Surratt's release, but he was again to be disappointed.

If Mudd could not look to the Supreme Court for help, if he could not expect the freeing of John Surratt to enlist public sympathy for his cause, he could at least look hopefully toward Andrew Johnson. As President, Johnson had the right to pardon any and all criminals. A simple stroke of his pen would have granted Mudd freedom. The President apparently felt some sympathy for the convicted doctor. Each came from a Border State—Mudd from Maryland, Johnson from Tennessee—and perhaps Johnson had some understanding of the pressures to which Mudd had been subjected after his arrest, or perhaps he felt the doctor had been altogether a victim of Stanton's power and lust for revenge. While Mudd's friends sought his release, John Ford, owner of the theater in which Lincoln had been shot, worked diligently to obtain the release of his former stagehand, Ned Spangler. Jere Dyer, Mudd's brother-in-law, learned of Ford's effort and sent news of it to his sister: "Ford told me he had a long interview with the President the day before, and had every assurance he would release Sam at the earliest moment he could consistently do so; the President also remarked to him, he [Sam] was a mere creature of accident, and ought not to have been put there, but in the present state of political excitement he did not think it prudent in him to take any action, as it would be another pretext for the Radicals to build capital on. He also stated that the issue between the President and the Radicals would be made within a few days, and if they still persisted in their extreme measures, he would then take a decided stand against them; so my dear, you will still have to exercise the virtue of patience yet awhile longer."

This letter was written February 18, 1866. Congress had reconvened a few months earlier for the first time since the assassination. Johnson soon learned that, "decided stand" or not, he would have no success with the Radicals. They controlled the necessary two-thirds majority to override his veto on any legislation they enacted. Johnson had inherited the policies of his predecessor:

sympathy for the vanquished foe, the "malice toward none" credo of the Second Inaugural Address. But he had not inherited his predecessor's reputation as the savior of his country. Lincoln had fallen martyr to the derringer of John Wilkes Booth, but the assassin's bullet may have spared him an even grimmer fate. Johnson fell martyr to the Radicals in Congress who, determined to throttle the South politically and economically, peppered Lincoln's reconstruction plans like a paper target. Perhaps Lincoln could have forced his program upon Radicals; Johnson could not.

After Mudd's heroic battle against yellow fever in the fall of 1867, the doctor probably expected some expression of gratitude from the federal government. The officers and men at Fort Jefferson had signed a petition that recommended freedom for their prisoner-physician. That petition was sent to Washington. Mudd himself had done nothing to encourage the petition; apparently he did not believe it would make any impression in the capital. He wrote, "Knowing the great prejudice pervading all classes of society toward all the so-called conspirators, I have but little hope of a favorable result." In this respect he was not disappointed. The petition reached the War Department, and seemed to die there. President Johnson probably never saw it. However, a petition signed in Mudd's behalf by the entire United States Army probably would not have been forwarded to the President. At this time Congress, eager for an excuse to remove the only obstacle in the way of its carpetbagger legislation, was hearing for the third time the evidence of the Lincoln assassination. The President's foes hoped to prove that Johnson himself had been guilty of supporting Booth. In such an atmosphere, the President could not have been expected to pardon Dr. Mudd even had the petition been placed on his desk.

"Judging from papers," wrote Mudd, "the old ship of state is adrift, floating without a rudder, without a captain, and they threaten to throw overboard the chief engineer, the President." When Congress sent an investigator to Fort Jefferson, Dr. Mudd became elated, thinking that his case would be reconsidered. But the investigator was only seeking evidence to incriminate the President. He had no interest in exonerating Mudd. Arnold at first refused to see the man; then, characteristically, he argued the accuracy of the statement he was asked to sign. Mudd and Spangler talked freely, but said nothing new. The congressional investagator uncovered no evidence to aid the men who were planning the President's impeachment.

A year later, Congress attempted to remove Johnson on another charge: he had dismissed Secretary of War Stanton from his Cabinet post. This action, claimed Johnson's foes, violated the newly passed Tenure of Office Act (an act that later was held to be unconstitutional). Congress failed, by only one vote, to convict Johnson.

But Johnson's troubles finally came to an end with the close of his term. A few weeks before leaving office, he took care of some unfinished business. On February 15, 1869, by order of the President, at six o'clock in the evening, four soldiers uncovered the body of a man who had been dead almost four years. The body was removed from its secret resting place beneath the flagstone floors of a warehouse on the grounds of Washington Arsenal. The dampness had rotted the wooden coffin. The body inside was black and decomposed. The soldiers wrapped the remains in two blankets, placed it in a white-pine box, and lifted it into a red expresswagon. The Negro driver of the wagon could not read, so the name on the box may have meant nothing to him. The body was delivered for identification to a funeral home in Baltimore, where souvenir hunters cut up the two blankets that had covered it. News of the arrival of the body caused crowds to gather around the funeral home; perhaps the people wanted to follow the hearse to the burial. However, to avoid demonstrations, the dead man's family had to wait several months before they would place the body in a grave in the family plot at Greenmount Cemetery in Baltimore. A simple marker was placed over the grave to identfy it as the last resting place of the once able actor, the perpetrator of the worst crime of the century, John Wilkes Booth.

Two days before the disinterment of Booth's remains, a special messenger left the White House and headed on horseback into

Lower Maryland. Again there was a knock on the door of the Mudd farmhouse; this time it brought no tragedy. The messenger handed Sarah Mudd a note from President Johnson. The President, so it read, asked Mrs. Mudd to come to Washington to receive her husband's pardon. She left for Washington immediately, and arrived there the next morning. Dr. Mudd's brother-in-law, Dr. J. H. Blandford, accompanied her to the White House. "I'm Mrs. Sarah Mudd," she told the doorkeeper. "I would like to see the President."

When she walked into his office President Johnson had her husband's pardon on his desk. She asked if the papers could go safely through the mails.

"Mrs. Mudd, I will put the President's seal on them," Johnson replied. "I have complied with my promise to release your husband before I left the White House. I no longer hold myself responsible. Should these papers go amiss you may never hear from them again, as they may be put away in some pigeon hole or corner. I guess, Mrs. Mudd, you think this is tardy justice in carrying out my promise made to you two years ago. The situation was such, however, that I could not act as I wanted to do."

He signed the papers, sealed them, and handed them to Mrs. Mudd. "Thank you, Mr. President," she said.

That stroke of the pen was one of Johnson's last acts in office. Two and a half weeks later, Ulysses S. Grant became President. Grant had played the part of gallant conqueror at Appomattox, but with his Radical backers now dictating his moves as President, he might not have been able to display much sympathy for Mudd. Fortunate, indeed, that Andrew Johnson, despite the burden of his own problems, did not forget the promise he had made to the pleading wife of an unhappy man.

Pardon in hand, Mrs. Mudd rushed to Baltimore. She missed by two hours passage on a steamer for the Dry Tortugas. Two or three weeks would pass before another steamer would be available. She could not wait. Perhaps she feared that the pardon might be revoked. She sent the pardon express to her brother, Thomas O. Dyer, in New Orleans. Dyer is said to have paid a man named

Loutrel five hundred dollars to have the papers delivered in person to Fort Jefferson. On March 8, 1869, more than three weeks after the pardon had been signed, the commanding officer ordered the release of Samuel A. Mudd.

Time and new turbulent events had done much to subdue the public rage at the conspirators. The newspapers, which had suffered through "that interminable trial," were occupied with items currently more newsworthy than the assassination of Lincoln. Four years earlier, Mudd's name had been the subject of bitter headlines. Now only a few lines of type, buried in the central sections of most newspapers, noted that he had been pardoned. A few days before he left Fort Jefferson, a company of the 3rd Artillery aboard a transport saw him walking on the parapet of the fort and cheered him. Mudd was no longer the conspiratorial physician who had set Booth's leg; he was the compassionate healer of the yellow fever epidemic.

Mudd reached his home on March 20, 1869. Nine days after the doctor returned, Arnold and Spangler were freed. The authorities at Fort Jefferson delivered the last two conspirators to Key West and left them to make their way home on their own resources. "Like justice," Arnold wryly reported, "followed my footsteps from beginning to end."

The New York *Herald*, which had covered Dr. Mudd's internment at Fort Jefferson, now, with his release, displayed new interest. The paper returned as if, in publishing tradition, to write "thirty" to the story. A *Herald* reporter soon appeared at the Mudd farmhouse and asked for an interview. But Dr. Mudd declared that newspaper publicity was the thing in the world he least desired. "Nothing was ever printed in connection with my name that did not misrepresent me," he said. "A burned child dreads the fire, and I have reason to be suspicious of everyone. It was in this way that Booth came to my house representing himself as being on a journey to Washington and that his horse fell on him fracturing his leg and otherwise injuring him. Six months or so from now when my mind is more settled and when I understand what changes have taken place in public opinion regarding me I shall be prepared to speak freely and fully on these matters you are so anxious to know about. At present for the reasons stated, I would rather not say anything."

It was a fine speech, but he could no more turn away the reporter than he could have turned away the injured Booth. He invited the correspondent to stay overnight and the visitor got his story. "The world went well and smoothly with him previous to that unhappy event," *Herald* readers soon learned. "His house was furnished with all the comforts of a country gentleman's residence. He had his horses in town and in the sporting season was foremost in every foxhunt and at every manly outdoor sport. He had robust health and a vigorous athletic frame in those days. But it is very different now. Above the middle height with a reddish mustache and attenuated nose, his appearance indicates a man of calm and slow reflection, gentle in manner in a very domestic turn. He says he was born within a few miles of this house. He has lived all his life in the country. His whole desire now is to be allowed to spend the balance of his days quietly in the bosom of his family. In his sunken, lusterless eyes, pallid lips, and cold, ashy complexion, one can read the word Dry Tortugas with a terrible significance. In the prime of his years looking prematurely old and careworn, there are few indeed who could gaze on the wreck and ravage in the face of this man before them without feeling a sentiment of sympathy and commiseration."

In three and a half years the New York *Herald* had somewhat changed its attitude toward life in the Dry Tortugas. "It is not Hades exactly, nor is it Pandemonium," the paper informed its readers when Mudd's exile began. Now it seemed willing to admit that Fort Jefferson was both Hades and Pandemonium. The *Herald* offered one last view of Dr. Samuel Alexander Mudd.

"You must have felt seriously agitated after being arrested in connection with this matter," prodded the reporter.

"No, sir," replied Mudd. "I was just as self-possessed as I am now. They might have hanged me at the time and I should have faced death just as composedly as I smoke this pipe."

Chapter 18

AFTER THREE MONTHS of confinement in and around Washington, D.C., and three years seven months and twelve days of imprisonment on the Dry Tortugas, Dr. Mudd was once again with his family. Years later, his daughter Nettie described her father's homecoming: "On the twentieth day of March, 1869, sixteen days after President Johnson's term of office had expired, my father arrived home, frail, weak, and sick, never again to be strong during the thirteen years he survived. It is needless for me to try to picture the feelings and incidents of his homecoming. Pleasure and pain were intermingled—pleasure to him to be once more in his old home surrounded by his loved ones, and pleasure to them to have him back once more; pain to them to see him so broken in health and strength, and pain to find his savings all gone and his family almost destitute."

Photographs and descriptions of Dr. Mudd often make people think of him as an old man. Yet when he returned from Fort Jefferson, his vigor already gone, he was only thirty-five years old.

Concerning Dr. Mudd's return to life on the farm, Nettie wrote: "Again we find him, after a brief period of rest, engaged in the struggle to regain in a measure his lost means and position. This he never accomplished. He found himself surrounded by exacting duties, yet handicapped by innumerable disadvantages. There were no laborers to cultivate the farm; the fences had fallen down or had been destroyed by the Federal soldiery, and the fields were unprotected against intrusive cattle; buildings were out of repair, and money almost unobtainable. His hardships in prison, however, had in a measure taught him to be patient. Gradually things became brighter. When the warm glow of summer passed into harvest time, he was encouraged by the fact that a generous yield of earth's products rewarded him for his labor."

Ned Spangler came to call shortly after he was released. The doctor introduced his prison friend to his wife. "Mrs. Mudd," said Spangler, "I came down last night, and asked someone to tell me the way here. I followed the road, but when I arrived I was afraid of your dogs. So I roosted in a tree." Spangler was accustomed to nap in unusual places. Before Lincoln's death he had slept backstage at Ford's Theater. On the night of the assassination, when he heard cries of "Burn the theater," he had moved his bed to a carpenter's shop nearby.

Dr. Mudd, with the generosity that became a mark of the man, gave his erstwhile cellmate five acres behind the house, and Spangler lived there and did carpentry for the neighbors. Eighteen months after he had left Fort Jefferson, he was caught in a sudden cloudburst on his new land and, before he could take cover, was thoroughly drenched. Yellow fever had not destroyed him, but now the exposure brought him to the sickbed. After a short illness, he expired. He was then only in his mid-forties.

The Mudds buried Ned Spangler in the simple cemetery at St. Peter's Church. No trace of that grave can be found today. (Sam Arnold died in Johns Hopkins hospital in Baltimore in 1906. John H. Surratt outlived all the other conspirators; he died in 1916.)

According to members of the Mudd family, Dr. Mudd, not long after his return from the Tortugas, accepted a position with the United States Public Health Service and traveled through the South doing research in yellow fever. It has been claimed by the Mudd family that he may have been the first to suggest that the mosquito was the carrier of the disease, though no proof of this claim exists. Because the pay was so poor, Dr. Mudd had to leave his government appointment and return to his farm and to his local practice, meager as it was. In the spring of 1876, neighbors elected him to the Maryland legislature as a Republican. Apparently he was nominated and elected without his approval, for he had no love for the party of the Radicals.

Dr. Mudd's return home from Fort Jefferson was not an unalloyed triumph. As his daughter wrote: "He only partially regained his practice. While he was confined in prison many of the families he had attended employed other physicians. Many of these families sought my father's services on his return, but some did not. Apart from this, the people of the neighborhood had become comparatively poor by reason of their losses occasioned by the war. A great deal of his attention and skill was therefore given gratuitously."

A tragedy reversed should end with proof that some retribution was made to the man who had suffered so much. But there was little to give Samuel A. Mudd any deep and abiding satisfaction except that, at last, he was again a free man. He lived in relative obscurity and struggled to earn a living for his family.

While visiting patients during the winter of 1882, he contracted pneumonia. At least that is generally accepted as the circumstance of his final illness. On January 10, 1883, Dr. Mudd died at the age of forty-nine. He was buried near Bryantown at St. Mary's Church, the same church where, eighteen years earlier, he first met a man named John Wilkes Booth. The Mudd family in recent years has replaced the orginal wooden marker with a marble monument.

In the story of the doctor there were always more versions than one of any incident in which he was involved. No wonder then that there is even a second version of how he took cold and succumbed. Reverend Southgate, the pastor of St. Mary's Church, told historian Osborn H. Oldroyd, two decades later, that one Sunday in January, 1883, Dr. Mudd arrived at church a half-hour before the service, that he remained outdoors talking to friends although he had no overcoat, and that he thus caught cold. He took to his bed and, ten days later, was dead. Reverend Southgate also reported that the doctor, upon resumming his medical practice, had been very successful, which is sharply at variance with other accounts.

In the year the doctor died, a reporter from the New York *Tribune* interviewed Frederick Stone, who had been one of Mudd's attorneys. Stone, reminiscing, said of his famous client: "The court very nearly hanged Dr. Mudd. His prevarications were painful. He had given his whole case away by not trusting even his counsel or neighbors or kinfolks. It was a terrible thing to extricate him from the toils he had woven about himself. He had denied knowing Booth when he knew him well. He was undoubtedly accessory to the abduction plot, though he may have supposed it would never come to anything. He denied knowing Booth when he came to his house when that was preposterous. He had been even intimate with Booth." It is difficult to assess how Stone arrived at these conclusions. He probably was speaking not from what Dr. Mudd may have confided, but from what he may have thought Dr. Mudd should have confided. Thomas Ewing, Jr., who had done so much for Mudd as his chief counsel, never offered any comment.

In 1901, historian Oldroyd traveled in Booth's footsteps through Maryland. Besides the priest at St. Mary's Church, he met the adopted son of Colonel Cox, Samuel Cox, Jr., who, as a twelve-year-old, had been sent by his father to the house of Thomas A. Jones with the news that John Wilkes Booth was hiding in the swamp. By a strange coincidence, years later, young Cox and Samuel A. Mudd ran for state office at the same time. "On frequent occasions during the campaign when we were alone together," Cox told Oldroyd, "Mudd would talk about the assassination and the part for which he was tried and convicted and sent to the Dry Tortugas. He had been pardoned by President Andrew Johnson, and had been home several years when these conversations took place. He told me that he had never admired Booth, who had forced himself upon him twice before he came to his house the morning after the assassination; that several years before he had refused to be introduced to Booth in Washington, and that some months afterward Booth came to the Roman Catholic church at Bryantown, of which Dr. Mudd was a member; that seeing Booth there he had spoken to him, and studiously avoided inviting him to his house, but that when going home from church Booth had followed him uninvited; that he never saw him again until the morning of the fifteenth of April, 1865, when Booth came to him with a broken leg, and told him he and Herold had just come from across the Potomac, and that soon after leaving the river his horse had fallen and broken his rider's leg; that he believed the statement, and knew nothing different while he was ministering to Booth's sufferings; that after he had made Booth as comfortable as he could, he left him and rode to Bryantown to mail some letters, and when he arrived within a half-mile of the village he found the place surrounded by soldiers, and was stopped by a sentry, by whom he was told of the assassination of the President the night before, and that Booth was the assassin.

"He then said his first impulse was to say, 'Come with me and I will deliver him to you.' But instead he rode back home with the full determination to warn Booth and to upbraid him for his treachery and the danger he had placed him in; that he felt outraged at the treatment he had received at the hands of Booth, and that he did threaten to deliver him up. He then said Booth, in a tragic manner, had appealed to him in the name of his mother not to do so, and he yielded to the appeal, but made them leave his premises forthwith. This statement was made to me by Dr. Samuel A. Mudd several years after he had been released from the Dry Tortugas, when he could have no motive in telling me what was untrue as to his part in assisting Booth. From statements made to me I believe Mudd was aware of the intention to abduct President Lincoln, but am confident he knew nothing of the plan of the assassination."

Several inconsistencies with known facts raise doubt of the complete accuracy of Cox's statements. But he was talking a quarter of a century after this conversation with Mudd and thirty-six years after the actual events had taken place. Although these revelations come to us twice removed from their alleged source, the basic fact—that Mudd recognized Booth—can probably be accepted. After his release from prison Dr. Mudd made no more "official" statements, although his wife made several after his death. She continued to insist that Booth had indeed come in disguise and had left still unrecognized.

Shortly after being arrested, David E. Herold, who might have provided the most accurate information on Mudd's relationship with Booth, gave the authorities a statement that was a compound of distortions and falsehoods. Even though he had been captured in the company of Booth, Herold was apparently under the impression that the government could prove nothing against him. His statement was an alibi, and no mention was made of Dr. Mudd. Herold, like the other prisoners, could not testify during the trial; and since he was kept in isolation until his hanging shortly after the trial, he never had an opportunity to revise his version of the assassination and the escape.

The person who, to this date, has made the most exhaustive study of the life of Dr. Mudd is his grandson, Dr. Richard D. Mudd, a physician for the Chevrolet-Saginaw Gray Iron Foundry in Saginaw, Michigan. There is scarcely a detail in the life of his grandfather into which Richard Mudd has not inquired. In his home he has the sofa upon which Dr. Mudd first examined Booth's leg. In his office are files of information concerning the conspiracy and his grandfather's alleged part in it. "I have never officially taken any position as to my grandfather's guilt or innocence," says Richard Mudd. "I feel privately he was innocent. My grandmother would never feel any different. He had a right to treat Booth. He did report it. He didn't destroy the boot. He guided the soldiers in the direction of Booth. He couldn't have known of the assassination unless Booth told him."

Certainly Dr. Samuel A. Mudd was no simple martyr. Today, almost a century after the trial that nearly took his life, it seems likely that he was guilty only of being an accessory after the fact. When arrested, Mudd told how two strangers had pounded on his door in the morning after Lincoln's assassination. He claimed that he did not recognize the actor whom he had met twice before, and that Booth had worn a beard and concealed his features with a shawl. It was dark and raining—but Mudd saw his guest later that morning in the light of day. According to Mudd and his wife, the two men used assumed names—but Cox's son claimed years later that Booth had made no attempt to shield his identity. Indeed, at no other stop did Booth wear a beard, and at no other stop did Booth and Herold use the aliases Tyler and Tyson. Elsewhere they either admitted their identity or said they were the brothers Boyd. There seems to be no other possible interpretation of these facts than that Dr. Mudd recognized Booth before the actor left the Mudd household.

Mudd treated Booth's broken ankle and put his patient to bed. He tried unsuccessfully to borrow from his father a carriage for his guests. Then Mudd rode off with Herold toward Bryantown. Although Mudd never admitted it, and Ewing tried to prove otherwise at the conspiracy trial, Mudd probably learned of the assassination (and more important, the name of the assassin) on this trip. Cox's son claimed that a sentry at the edge of town gave that information.

Herold had turned back earlier, perhaps frightened when he spied the soldiers. By the time Mudd returned home, following his own account, the two strangers were leaving. He continued to insist, even during his imprisonment at Fort Jefferson, that he had not at that point realized it was Booth. The junior Cox contradicted this. He said that Mudd, on learning of the crime committed by his unwanted guests, returned home to *demand* that they leave. Mudd, who had no love for Northern authority, was undoubtedly apprehensive, aware that he would have difficulties explaining his two previous encounters with Booth.

He may have known of Booth's earlier plans for the abduction of the President, but he may not have been in sympathy with such plans. Certainly, he was not a man who would have sympathized with, or participated in, an assassination. If he had heard nothing about the assassination from Booth and Herold, the doctor must have been badly shaken when the news was related to him in town. However, he did not go to the authorities, but rode slowly home, thinking of his terrible plight. By not going to the detectives in town, he became a *de facto* accessory to the assassins.

Sarah Mudd later insisted that after Booth left that night, she persuaded her husband not to go to the authorities at once. So he waited until morning. Even then, Mudd, either from fear or from indecision, did not go straight to the law. Again his decision was to withhold the information about the assassins. Perhaps he still needed time in which to formulate a story that would not implicate him in the conspiracy, perhaps he could not act because he could not determine a just course of action. He wanted family counsel; he needed the comfort of talking to someone in whom he could confide completely. After church he talked to George Mudd, his cousin, whom he encountered. Although neither admitted it in so many words, Sam probably asked George the question: What shall I do now?

George Mudd was a Union man; he undoubtedly advised his cousin to tell all. Perhaps Sam agreed to do so; perhaps he procrastinated. It is possible that George Mudd went to the authorities on Monday of his own accord when Sam could not bring himself to do so. Only when Lieutenant Lovett arrived in Bryantown on Tuesday did the military rivet its attention on the home of Dr. Samuel A. Mudd. That was three days after Booth and Herold had disappeared into the thicket. Had Mudd delayed to give them more time, or were the delays circumstantial, as both George and Samuel Mudd claimed them to be?

Understandably chary of Northern justice, Mudd volunteered only the information which the detectives sought. Had he actually forgotten about his guest's boot, so that he did not produce it until the second visit of the detectives on Friday? If he had wanted to foil the authorities, or if he had wanted to erase all trace of his guests, why did he not destroy the boot? When faced with the indisputable evidence—the assassin's initials in the boot—he grudgingly admitted that the two men who had stayed at his house must have been Booth and Herold. Had he really associated the boot in his possession with the assassin, either he or his wife could have burned it or buried it.

Mudd's counsel, Frederick Stone, stated that the doctor's prevarications were painful. In answering his interrogators, Mudd did tell at least one lie when he denied to Colonel Wells that he had seen Booth between November and April. After his conviction, Mudd admitted that he had encountered Booth in Washington. But to this day no one can say with absolute certainty whether the meeting was accidental or whether Mudd had actually, at the time of their first meeting, promised Booth to introduce him to John Surratt.

Justice ceased to function for Samuel Mudd beginning the day Colonel Wells and Lieutenant Lovett called to take him to Washington. Mudd thought he was going there to testify at the trial of David Herold, never imagining that he would be tried in chains as one of the conspirators. Of course, as later underlined by the Supreme Court decision in the Milligan case, such accused should not have been tried by the military, but by the civil courts, which were still functioning. However, the War Department, under Secretary Stanton, was determined to employ a military tribunal to take revenge for the murder of the Commander-in-Chief.

Mudd was a rational, well-educated man who had been trained to deal scientifically with any problems that confronted him. But nothing in his studies or in his previous experience could have prepared him for the series of events that began at four o'clock, the morning of April 15, 1865. From that moment, he became a pawn in a deadly game in which nothing he might have said or done would have spared him.

He was moved by the invisible forces in control. Mudd could only sit in the prisoner's dock as a helpless observer while his fate was being decided.

At Fort Jefferson, his single attempt at escape was a failure. His friends were unsuccessful in their attempts to obtain either a retrial or a pardon.

His great day came when a challenge for which his previous training had amply prepared him arose: the yellow fever epidemic. Now he thrust aside the painful memories and the anguished present—he was at last able to act. He worked heroically to save the lives of officers, guards, and prisoners alike. His battle with yellow fever did not alone secure his pardon, but at least his conduct caused those who hitherto had regarded him scornfully to see him not as an arch-criminal but as a plain country doctor who, through strange circumstances indeed, had been entrapped in a web that others had spun.

He was pardoned in 1869, four years after his conviction. But another ninety years passed before he was officially vindicated. In October of 1959, Congress passed, and President Dwight D. Eisenhower signed into law, a bill providing for a bronze memorial at Fort Jefferson commemorating Dr. Samuel A. Mudd's service during the yellow fever epidemic. The bill carefully avoided any consideration of the doctor's innocence or guilt in the episode that was responsible for his incarceration in the fort.

Epilogue

FORD'S THEATER had a short, glorious, but unhappy career. The building (or buildings) on Tenth Street, N.W., between E and F streets, was originally the First Baptist Church. The members of this congregation built the church in 1834. Twenty-five years later they united with another congregation and sold the building to John T. Ford, a theatrical producer from Baltimore and Philadelphia. In 1861 Ford converted the structure into a theater, Ford's Atheneum, only to see it destroyed by fire the following year.

Ford completely rebuilt his theater. He laid the cornerstone on February 28, 1863, and completed the construction six months later. Architects acclaimed it as the finest theater in the United States. The new Ford's Theater was built entirely of brick and could seat seventeen hundred people. In addition, eight private boxes, four on each side of the stage, accommodated special guests in celebrity-conscious Washington. On the night of April 14, the Lincoln party occupied two of the upper-level boxes to the right of the stage.

The unconscious Lincoln was carried to a narrow three-story house (now operated as a museum) across the street from the theater. There he died. Immediately after the assassination, the War Department placed guards before Ford's Theater; there had been rumors that it might be burned to the ground. Secretary Stanton canceled all scheduled performances. Ford himself, a victim of the dragnet that took hundreds of other innocent people into custody, temporarily went to prison. He regained possession of his theater in June and announced that his first play would be *Octoroon*. A grumbling public, however, caused the government to prohibit permanently the reopening of the theater. Congress passed a bill authorizing its purchase for $100,000. On August 17, 1865, the government began ripping out the woodwork in order to remodel the interior. The surgeon general's office claimed the structure and used it to house military records and to serve as an army medical museum. Among the exhibits were three cervical vertebrae from the body of John Wilkes Booth that showed the wound made by the bullet that killed him.

On June 9, 1893, the day the assassin's brother, Edwin Booth, was buried in Boston, all three floors in the former Ford's Theater collapsed, killing twenty-two clerks and injuring sixty-eight others. The building was again rebuilt and today stands as the Lincoln Museum. Among many objects displayed there are Booth's derringer, the sofa on which Major Rathbone and Clara Harris sat, and the blue Treasury Department flag that tripped Booth and caused him to break his leg. This flag has been marred twice. Souvenir hunters snipped a square piece from it, probably sometime shortly after the assassination. Another corner bears the mark of Booth's spur.

Footprints, outlined in black, mark the approximate place on the stage where Booth landed after leaping from the box. The tourist today can follow these footprints across the stage of yesteryear. Booth had been able to race along a backstage passageway and out a door into the alley, but his footprints now end against a wall. The stage door has been bricked up; there is a window in its place.

Following the path of Booth's flight from Ford's Theater through Maryland and Virginia to Garrett's barn is no easy task. Here his footprints, unlike those in the Lincoln Museum, have been obscured by time, though some traces still remain. The back alley with its half-twist to the left which leads out to F Street now serves as a loading zone for trucks that service the many stores and buildings in this busy downtown Washington block. Booth, when he worked at Ford's, stabled his horse in this alley. One of the buildings, the rear of which is on the alley, is now a burlesque house. The assassin, on reaching the alley the night of April 14, 1865, spurred his horse and clattered across the cobblestones and out onto F Street. He sped east around the Capitol, then down Pennsylvania Avenue.

The present sagging Anacostia (or Navy Yard) bridge appears to be a product of a bygone age, but it is not the same narrow, wooden structure that Booth used to cross into Maryland that night. Only by careful analysis of old road maps is it possible to trace Booth's route after crossing the bridge. Bulldozers have blotted out most of the old landmarks. A modern Sears shopping center now stands atop a hill, probably not far from the Bryantown road where Polk Gardiner saw the two conspirators gallop by in the night.

Route 301, a four-lane divided highway, today parallels much of Booth's route south. It passes near the town of Clinton. The United States Post Office gave the town this name not long after the assassination, erasing thereby the distasteful name of Surrattsville. The old name, however, still lingers in town as well as at a new section that calls itself Surratt's Gardens. Next to the Clinton post office the old Surratt home still stands; it has probably not had a coat of paint since the day John Lloyd gave Booth and Herold their weapons and whiskey. Farther down the highway is the village of T. B., named after a former Maryland legislator named Thomas Brooke, who, in the middle of the seventeenth century, carved his initials on a boundary stone to mark his property. Booth and Herold rode through T. B. after one o'clock in the morning. Afterward, residents alleged they had heard the fading echoes of the horses' hoofbeats.

Above what is now Waldorf, Maryland, Booth and Herold turned from their planned route to seek medical assistance at the house of Dr. Samuel A. Mudd. The Mudd house still lies deep in the woods, along a winding country highway called Gallant Green Road. To get there from Waldorf one must pass St. Peter's Church, where Mudd attended mass the day after Booth came to the doctor's house with a broken leg. One of Mudd's grandsons, Joseph B. Mudd, farms the doctor's tobacco fields. Above the living room fireplace hangs a faded picture of Dr. Mudd that was taken during his imprisonment in the Dry Tortugas.

South of Bryantown lies St. Mary's Church, where Dr. Mudd was buried. The church burned to the ground on December 16, 1963. Narrow roads turn from the church to Colonel Cox's house, which is still located at the crest of a tree-dotted hill. Booth and Herold spent a week hiding in the swamp nearby. The farm of Thomas A. Jones, on which huckleberries were cultivated, stands to the right of the road leading from Route 301 to Pope's Creek. Near there, Booth and Herold climbed into the boat provided by Jones to cross the Potomac into Virginia. Today a modern toll bridge ($1.00 per car) spans the Potomac.

One can follow US Highway 301 along much of the route John Wilkes Booth took through Virginia. Whereas he had to wait hours for the tide to rise so that the ferry could carry him across the Rappahannock, a bridge now permits automobile travelers to whisk across in minutes. The site of the Garrett home is five minutes from this bridge. The Garretts disliked the notoriety brought to them by the man who died in their blazing tobacco barn. They did, however, pry up several boards on the porch that were stained with Booth's blood and sell them. The Garretts lived in the house until the early 1930's, then abandoned it. About 1937 the brick chimneys were removed, the house collapsed, and brush overgrew the rubble. In time, the state of Virginia swept the debris away and converted the site into a roadside picnic grove. It seems ironic that the place where Booth breathed his last should be marked by little more than a picnic table and benches and receptacles for rubbish.

A thousand miles to the south, a different kind of marker honors the memory of Dr. Samuel A. Mudd. Legend, as well as the New York *Herald*, has clouded somewhat our picture of Fort Jefferson. Man-eating sharks and fierce barracuda were supposed to lurk in the Fort Jefferson moat. Evil guards tended these monsters to keep them voracious until they could feast on the flesh of a prisoner who dared to try to escape. In 1936 Warner Brothers portrayed, with some artistic license, Dr. Mudd's life on the island in a film, *The Prisoner of Shark Island*, with Warner Baxter portraying the physician. Sharks and barracuda did indeed frolic in the surrounding waters of the Gulf, but seldom did they come near the moat. The moat was designed to be a seawall as much as an obstacle to either attack or escape; it was too shallow and, usually, too polluted with garbage and sewage to give comfort to sharks. Instead of man-eating sharks, fierce turtles inhabited the moat. Enlisted men, bored with a steady diet of salt pork, frequently journeyed at night to the surrounding keys and waited for turtles to crawl out of the water and lay their eggs on the beach. Then, with a rush, the men would seize a turtle, flip it on its back, and hide to wait for the next one. Those turtles that were not consumed immediately were tagged for identification and dumped into the moat until needed by the cook. Of course, while snapping turtles can be vicious, a movie entitled *The Prisoner of* Turtle *Island* would scarcely have attracted attention at the box office.

Fort Jefferson reached its pinnacle of fame with the imprisonment of the Lincoln conspirators. In the fall of 1873, a hurricane swept across the Gulf and damaged the fort's sagging walls. Construction of the obsolete fortress ended the following year. The recurring yellow fever epidemics caused the army to abandon the mighty hulk. Thereafter, it served occasionally as a quarantine station and, in every war except the last, was quickly reoccupied to prevent it from falling into the hands of the enemy. In 1898, the battleship *Maine* sailed from Fort Jefferson for her rendezvous at Havana. During prohibition days, Fort Jefferson became a station on the rum-runner's route from Havana to Tampa. Recently, refugees have landed at the fort after escaping by boat from Castro's Cuba.

In 1935, Fort Jefferson became a national monument. But it is too inaccessible to rival Yellowstone or Gettysburg as a tourist attraction. Unless a visitor brings his own bedding he cannot comfortably remain overnight. For several years business groups in the Keys have discussed the possibility of establishing hotel accomodations and regular ferry service to the Tortugas, but to date, nothing has been accomplished. Things are done slowly in the tropics.

Conclusion to Expanded Edition
A Final Word

Descending a steep set of stairs after a tour of the Dr. Samuel A. Mudd House Museum near Waldorf, Maryland, I steadied myself briefly by grasping the banister, and it suddenly occurred to me that a broken-legged John Wilkes Booth might have done the same a century and a half before. After being examined by Dr. Mudd on a sofa still part of the Museum décor, Booth hobbled upstairs to sleep. Returning downstairs later that afternoon, certainly he would have grasped that same banister for support. My handprints were atop those of John Wilkes Booth.

I had come to the Mudd Museum as an end point in bringing *The Union vs. Dr. Mudd* back into print. My desire to reprint had begun with my visit to Fort Jefferson, as described in the prologue. And now after offering new readers the tale of the Maryland doctor who innocently or not set Booth's broken leg, it seemed fitting that I visit again Dr. Mudd's home to offer closure to the story.

Ironically, the home of Dr. Mudd, a man convicted of conspiracy to kill the President of the United States, has now become—according to Danny Fluhart—the most-visited historic site in Charles County, south of Washington, D.C.

Fluhart, president of the Dr. Samuel A. Mudd Society, served as guide for my wife, Rose, and I during our recent visit. "The Museum is self-supporting," Fluhart informed us. "We never have accepted federal grants." No surprise, considering the uneasy relationship the Mudd family has had with the federal government that sent their ancestor to prison. For years, Dr. Richard D. Mudd of Saginaw, Michigan (one of Dr. Mudd's thirty-three grandchildren), waged a heroic campaign to overturn the verdict of the military court. Richard Mudd served as one of my primary sources during the writing of *The Union vs. Dr. Mudd*. Even after publication of this book in 1964, he persevered with attempts to clear the family name.

Updating his efforts, Richard Mudd filed a petition with the Army Board for Correction of Military Records in 1990 to set aside Dr. Mudd's conviction. Although the Board agreed with the petition and recommended its implementation, Acting Assistant Secretary of the Army William D. Clark two years later declined to adopt the recommendations of the Board. After several appeals, Richard Mudd filed suit in U.S. District Court to review the decision and issue a Declaratory Judgment that Dr. Mudd was wrongly convicted. Federal Judge Paul L. Friedman dismissed the petitions but ordered the Secretary of the Army to reconsider the recommendation. In 2000, the Secretary determined that Sam Mudd was not wrongfully convicted. Continued appeals failed to obtain a reversal, and in February 2003, the Supreme Court declined to accept the case. Dr. Richard D. Mudd had passed away a year earlier at the age of 101. His son, Thomas Boarman Mudd, admits that the family probably will no longer seek exoneration for their famous (or infamous) ancestor.

Innocent or guilty, the case of the doctor who set Booth's broken leg continues to fascinate scholars and Civil War buffs. The Mudd Museum offers them and ordinary tourists a peek at one corner of the Lincoln Assassination. As Danny Fluhart walked us through the house on a tour he gives frequently to visitors, my attention was drawn to two items of furniture: a checkerboard table and a desk crafted by Dr. Mudd in prison, showing remarkable workmanship. What appraisal might they attract if ever shown on *Antiques Roadshow*? Priceless!

Many pictures and pieces of furniture were in the house while occupied by Dr. Mudd with more items from the same period acquired from donors and family members, many who still live in the neighborhood. Most impressive to me was the fact that Dr. Mudd's home stood atop a hill overlooking 218 acres of farmland that has resisted the efforts of developers to fill it with expensive homes. You can stand in the front yard and look in all directions and imagine yourself back in 1865.

The Mudd family has owned at least part of that property since 1694. The house visited by Booth apparently was built in 1830 and given to Dr. Mudd by his father shortly after Sam's marriage to Sarah Frances Dyer in 1857. Tobacco served as one of the main cash crops in Maryland in the mid-nineteenth century. Dr. Mudd's father may have owned as many as a hundred slaves at one time. Dr. Mudd owned a half dozen or more, lost to him in the aftermath of the Emancipation Proclamation, decreed by President Abraham Lincoln on January 1, 1863. Maryland remained in the Union, but most of its citizens certainly sympathized with the Confederates during the Civil War. That probably included Dr. Samuel A. Mudd, a fact that weighed heavily against him during the trial of the Lincoln conspirators.

The events surrounding the assassination of President Abraham Lincoln have inspired books almost too numerous to count. In preparing this reprint edition of *The Union vs. Dr. Mudd*, I read many most recently published. I would like to have read all, but according to William Hanchett, author of *The Lincoln Murder Conspiracies*, "the Library of Congress lists more cards after Lincoln's name than after that of any other historical figure except Jesus and William Shakespeare." That includes at least one mainstream biography that appeared a decade after mine, *The Riddle of Dr. Mudd*, by Samuel Carter III. Several members of the Mudd family have published books seeking to rehabilitate their ancestor's name: *The Fall and Redemption of Dr. Samuel A. Mudd*, by Robert Summers, a great-grandson, and *Dr. Samuel A. Mudd and the Lincoln Assassination* by John McHale Jr., the husband of great-granddaughter Mary Mudd McHale.

Dr. Mudd also appears as an important supporting character in books about John Wilkes Booth and the Lincoln Assassination. Some have painted Dr. Mudd as guiltier than the historical record seems to show. In *Blood on the Moon*, Edward Steers Jr. suggests that Dr. Mudd was an active participant in the conspiracy to kidnap, if not kill, Lincoln and that he might even have been a member of the Confederate network that transported spies and goods back and forth across the border. William A. Tidwell, in *Come Retribution*, says the same and also theorizes that Confederate President Jefferson Davis and General Robert E. Lee may have moved troops into the area of Virginia where

Booth might spirit a kidnapped Lincoln. While admiring the scholarship of both authors, I found too many of their theories based on circumstantial evidence and hearsay. Steers also published another book titled *His Name Is Still Mudd*, the title speaking for itself. Thomas Boarman Mudd refers to both authors and several others as "revisionist historians," but in fairness, they may be correct in suggesting that Dr. Mudd was guiltier than as currently portrayed.

The book that best combines historical scholarship with readability is Michael W. Kauffman's *American Brutus*, the biography of John Wilkes Booth. Kauffman takes a neutralist position concerning Dr. Mudd's guilt. Most popular among the Lincoln assassination books is *Manhunt: The 12-Day Chase for Lincoln's Killer* by James L. Swanson, identified on its cover as "New York Times Bestseller." Swanson achieved that level of sales by producing a work of creative nonfiction, including this description of the moment John Wilkes Booth arrived at Dr. Mudd's doorstep: "Their eyes locked in recognition and in an instant the doctor knew the identity of the man who lay prostrate before him." As of this writing, *Manhunt* reportedly is being made into a motion picture due to be released in 2009.

What do I believe when it comes to the guilt or innocence of Dr. Samuel A. Mudd? It is a simple question that requires an incredibly complex answer. I can't improve on the summary answer to this question on pages 210 to 213 in the first edition of *The Union vs. Dr. Mudd*.

In producing this second edition, I have eliminated the acknowledgments, since most of the individuals named and thanked have passed on. Two who remain live only a few miles from my home in Long Beach, Indiana: Richard E. Gosswiller suggested the title for this book; Marianne Burke, now his wife, helped type the manuscript.

In preparing the second edition, I had the help of Thomas Boarman Mudd, Dr. Mudd's great-grandson, and Mary Mudd McHale, Dr. Mudd's great-granddaughter. I had a pleasant chat with both at Mary's home the night before Danny Fluhart offered me the tour of the Dr. Samuel A. Mudd House Museum.

Because of Dr. Mudd's imprisonment at Fort Jefferson in the Dry Tortugas west of Key West, having the University Press of Florida agree to publish the reprint edition certainly proved fortuitous. Heather Romans, rights and permissions manager at the Press, provided the impetus to get this project moving. Eli Bortz, acquisitions editor, worked closely with me in bringing the book to market.

Finally, my wife, Rose, was with me during the initial writing, and we also visited Fort Jefferson and the Mudd Museum together. I mentioned three children in the acknowledgments to the first edition, and I now have nine grandchildren who hopefully can enjoy with their descendants the story of Dr. Samuel A. Mudd.

BIBLIOGRAPHY

ARNOLD, SAMUEL BLAND. *Defense and Prison Experiences of a Lincoln Conspirator.* Hattiesburg, Mississippi: The Book Farm, 1943.

BUCKINGHAM, J. E., SR. *Reminiscences and Souvenirs of the Assassination of Abraham Lincoln.* Washington: Press of Rufus H. Darby, 1894.

CLARKE, ASIA BOOTH. *The Unlocked Book.* New York: G. P. Putnam's Sons, 1938.

DEWITT, DAVID MILLER. *The Judicial Murder of Mary E. Surratt.* Baltimore: John Murphy & Co., 1895.

EISENSCHIML, OTTO. *In the Shadow of Lincoln's Death.* New York: Wilfred Funk, Inc., 1940.

―――――. *Why Was Lincoln Murdered?* Boston: Little, Brown and Company, 1937.

HARRIS, T. M. *Assassination of Lincoln.* Boston: American Citizen Co., 1892.

MOORE, GUY W. *The Case of Mrs. Surratt.* Norman, Oklahoma: University of Oklahoma Press, 1954.

MUDD, NETTIE. *The Life of Dr. Samuel A. Mudd.* Saginaw, Michigan: Privately republished (with minor additions) by Richard D. Mudd, 1962.

OLDROYD, OSBORNE H. *The Assassination of Abraham Lincoln.* Washington, D.C.: Privately published by O. H. Oldroyd, 1901.

PETERSON & BROTHERS, T. B. (ed.). *The Trial of the Alleged Assassins and Conspirators.* Philadelphia: T. B. Peterson & Brothers, 1865.

PITMAN, BENN. *The Assassination of President Lincoln and the*

Trial of the Conspirators. New York: Funk & Wagnalls Company, 1954.

Roscoe, Theodore. *The Web of Conspiracy.* Englewood Cliffs, N.J.: Prentice-Hall, Inc., 1960.

Townsend, George Alfred. *The Life, Crime, and Capture of John Wilkes Booth.* New York: Dick & Fitzgerald, 1865.

Watts, Judge R. A. *The Trial and Execution of the Lincoln Conspirators.* Lansing: Michigan History Magazine, 1922.

Wilson, Francis. *John Wilkes Booth.* New York: Houghton Mifflin Company, 1939.

UPDATED BIBLIOGRAPHY
Related books published since 1964

Carter, Samuel, III. *The Riddle of Dr. Mudd*. New York: G. P. Putnam's Sons, 1974.
Chamlee, Roy Z. *Lincoln's Assassins: A Complete Account of Their Capture, Trial, and Punishment*. Jefferson, N.C.: McFarland and Co., 1990.
Hanchett, William. *The Lincoln Murder Conspiracies*. Chicago: University of Illinois Press, 1986.
Jones, John Paul, ed. *Dr. Mudd and the Lincoln Assassination: The Case Reopened*. Conshohocken, Pa.: Combined Books, 1995.
Kauffman, Michael W. *American Brutus: John Wilkes Booth and the Lincoln Conspiracies*. New York: Random House, 2004.
McHale, John, Jr. *Dr. Samuel A. Mudd and the Lincoln Assassination*. Bowie, Md.: Heritage Books, 2000.
Steers, Edward, Jr. *Blood on the Moon*. Lexington, Ky.: University Press of Kentucky, 2001.
———. *His Name Is Still Mudd*. Gettysburg, Pa.: Thomas Publications, 1997.
Summers, Robert. *The Fall and Redemption of Dr. Samuel A. Mudd*. Self-published, lulu.com, Arlington, Va., 2007. Also available online (Dr. Mudd's great-grandson).
Swanson, James L. *Manhunt: The 12-Day Chase for Lincoln's Killer*. New York: Harper Perennial, 2007.
Swanson, James L., and Daniel R. Weinberg. *Lincoln's Assassins: Their Trial and Execution*. New York: HarperCollins, 2001.
Tidwell, William A. *Come Retribution*. Jackson: University Press of Mississippi, 1988.

Weckesser, Elden C. *His Name Was Mudd: The Life of Dr. Samuel A. Mudd, Who Treated the Fleeing John Wilkes Booth*. Jefferson, N.C.: McFarland and Co., 1991.

INDEX

ABD-EL-KADER, 166
Accokeek, Md., 8
Acknowledgments, ix, x
Adair, J. W., 191
Adrian, Mich., 80, 116
Africa, 175
Aiken, Frederick (Mary Surratt's atty.), 90
Albany Penitentiary, N.Y., 128, 131, 132, 139, 146
Alexandria, Egypt, 198
Algiers, Algeria, 166
Allegheny River, Pa., 31
Allen's Fresh, Md., 44
American, Baltimore, 134
Anacostia Bridge, D.C., 217 *(see Navy Yard bridge)*
Anacostia River, Pa., 75
Andrews, Maj. George P., 190
Appomattox, 37, 202
Argentina, 194
Arnold, Maj. Gen. Lewis G., 144
Arnold, Samuel Bland, viii, 15, 28, 31-35, 37, 71, 73, 74, 76, 80-82, 88, 90-93, 122, 125, 127-29, 131, 133, 145, 146-49, 151, 155, 156, 162, 172, 173, 179-82, 185, 190, 191, 193, 195, 197, 201, 203, 206
Aspenwald, 151
Assassination of Abraham Lincoln, The, vii
Assassination of President Lincoln and the Trial of the Conspirators, The, viii
Atlanta, Ga., 29

Atzerodt, George, 7, 32-33, 35, 43, 71, 75, 80, 81, 90, 95, 97, 112, 119, 125, 127, 128, 129, 134
Atzerodt, Richter, 75
Avon Creek, Md., 57

BADEN, Germany, 85
Baker, Lafayette (Secret Service Chief), 60, 75-76, 80, 149-51, 156
Baker, Lt. L. B., 60
Baltimore & Ohio Railroad Station, 56
Baltimore, Md., 19, 20, 30, 31, 34, 35, 37, 68, 73, 77, 105, 148, 201, 202, 206, 215
Baltimore Medical College, 19
Barnes, Surgeon Gen. Joseph K., 5
Barnum's Hotel, Baltimore, Md., 31, 32
Baxter (Grenfell's friend in Carlyle, Ill.), 170
Baxter, Warner (actor, portrayed Mudd in movie), 218
Bean, E. D. R., 9, 12
Beantown, Md., 9, 41
Bel Air, Md. (Booth's birthplace), 26, 27
Bell, John, 160
Bell Plaine, 60
Beauregard, Gen. Toutant de, 166
Ben Hur (A Tale of the Christ), 84, 135
Benier, Emil, 67, 68
Benning bridge, D.C., 36

229

INDEX

Bernard, Simon (outlined design for Ft. Jefferson), 142
Best, John, 3, 10
Bib, the survey steamer, 193
Billy Bowlegs, 28
Bingham, John A., 88, 115, 120-22, 125, 126
Bishop, Jim, vii, 18
Blandford Dr. J. H. (Dr. Mudd's brother-in-law), 202
Bloyce, Charles, 113, 114
Boarman's Reserve, Md. (Dr. Mudd's birthplace), 18
Bonaparte, Napoleon, 31, 142
Booth, Asia (J. W.'s sister), 28, 29, 30
Booth, Edwin (J. W.'s brother), 13, 27, 29, 30, 55, 70, 71, 216
Booth, John Wilkes, vii, viii, 4-17, 21-25, 26-38, 39-56, 57-64, 67-70, 72, 73, 74-76, 78, 79, 80, 82, 85, 89, 94-98, 101-04, 106-07, 110, 114-17, 118, 122, 123, 125, 128-29, 132-35, 197, 200-01, 203, 204, 207-13, 216-18
Booth, Joseph (J.W.'s brother), 27
Booth, Junius Brutus, Jr., (J. W.'s brother), 17, 27, 29, 67, 68, 70
Booth, Junius Brutus, Sr., (J. W.'s father), 27
Boston, Mass., 143, 144
Bowie, Walter, 105, 114
Bowling Green, 61, 63, 69
Bowman, Dr. William T., 22
Boyd (notorious guerrilla—Booth chose his name as alias during escape), 12, 46, 57
Bragg, Gen'l. Braxton, 168
Brent, Robert J. (Md. Congressman—Mudd wanted him for atty. but he refused), 89
Brents, the, 18

Bristow, England, 18
Brooke, Thomas (town of T.B. named after him), 217
Brookville, Ind., 84
Brown, John, 19, 30, 31, 85
Browning, Orville H. (Sec. of Interior), 135
Browning, Mrs. Orville H., 135
Bryant, William A., 58
Bryantown, Md. (where Dr. Mudd lived), 3, 5, 8, 9, 10, 11, 12, 13, 14, 15, 16, 17, 21, 23, 25, 45, 47, 48, 49, 53, 69, 104, 107, 110, 117, 120, 122, 207, 209, 211, 212, 217
Buchanan, Pres. James, 72, 88
Buckingham, J. E., 39
Bull Run, Battle of, 83
Bureau of Military Justice, 88
Burlington, Vt., 37
Burnett, Henry L. (Asst. Judge Advocate), 88, 89, 119, 171, 196
Burnett House, Cincinnati, O., 67
Burtle, 26

CAMERON, SIMON (Sec. of War in Lincoln's Cabinet), 72
Camp Douglas, 165, 168, 169, 170, 171
Canada, 23, 37, 78, 96, 168, 169, 197
Caribbean, the, 141
Carlyle, Ill., 170
Catonsville, Md., 28
Charles County, Md. (where Dr. Mudd lived), 16, 17, 21, 22, 41, 45, 94
Charleston, S.C., 88
Chase, Chief Justice Salmon P., 197
Chattanooga, Tenn., 71

INDEX

Chevrolet-Saginaw Gray Iron Foundry, 210
Chicago, Ill., 49, 83, 165, 168, 169, 170
Church of England, 166
Cincinnati Law School, 90
Cincinnati, O., 68, 89, 90, 165, 171
Civil War, vii, 21, 57, 71, 75, 84, 127, 141, 143, 145, 150, 165, ¨166, 167, 180, 196
Claggert, 54
Clampitt, John W. (Mary Surratt's atty.), 90
Clark, Henry A., 89
Clark, John Sleeper (Booth's brother-in-law), 28, 70
Clay, Clement C., 82
Clendenin, Lt. Col. David R., 83, 86
Cleveland Academy of Music, 31
Clinton, 217
Cobb, Silas T. (Sgt. on guard at Navy Yard bridge), 40, 41, 42
Colfax, Schuyler (Speaker of the House), 37
Colossus of Rhodes, 28, 29, 32
Comstock, Brevet Brig. Gen. Cyrus B., 83, 85, 86
Confederacy, the (Confederates), 7, 16, 21, 23, 33, 34, 46, 52, 59, 61, 63, 71, 75, 82, 90, 94, 114, 125, 130, 132, 145, 156, 158, 165, 166, 167, 168, 169, 179, 180
Confederate Veteran, The, 193
Conger, Lt. Col. Everton J. (in charge of army troops searching for assassins), 60, 61, 62, 64, 74
Congress, 82, 91, 158, 159, 179, 199, 200, 201, 214
Conover, Sanford, 130

Conrad, Christian, 160
Conspirators, vii, viii, 33, 35, 64, 92, 126, 139, 149, 171, 213, 219; arrest of, 73-79; assassination by, 4, 6, 39; plot of, 7, 15-16, 32-37; search for, 8-73; sentences of, 127-29; trial of, 82-126
Constitution of the United States, 93, 152, 188
Corbett, Boston (claimed shooting Booth), 64, 74
Cottingham, George (special detective), 44, 53
Court of Military Inquisition, The, 82
Cox, Colonel Samuel, 26, 51, 52, 56, 70, 132, 208, 211, 218
Cox, Samuel, Jr., 208, 209, 211
Cox, Walter S. (O'Laughlin's atty.), 90, 122
Crabbe, Lt. George W., 173
crackpot leads, 49, 54
Crimean War, 166, 193
Cuba, 145, 175, 176, 177 *(see also Havana)*

Dana, Asst. Sec. of War Charles A., 8
Dana, Lt. David D. (in charge of Federal cavalry troops searching for assassins), 8, 10, 11, 45, 49, 120
Davis, Conf. Pres. Jefferson, 15, 16, 73, 82, 88, 94, 125, 130, 158, 168
Davis, Mrs. Jefferson, 158
Davis, John F. (servant of Dr. Mudd's), 122
Day Lincoln Was Shot, The, vii
Declaration of Independence, 83
Deery, John, 26

INDEX

Defense and Prison Experiences of a Lincoln Conspirator, viii, 81
De Leon, Ponce, 140
Detroit, Mich., 49, 103
Devil's Island, 139
Dodd, Gen'l., 129, 133, 134
Doherty, Lt. Edward, 60
Donnelly, Sgt. Edward, 161, 162, 163
Doster, William E. (atty. for Paine and Atzerodt), 90, 119, 122, 130
Dramatic Oil Company, 31
Dred Scott decision, 91
Dry Tortugas, Florida Keys, Fla., 132, 133, 135, 139-42, 143, 144, 146, 147, 148, 149, 152, 154, 160, 165, 176, 181, 185, 189, 193, 197, 202, 204, 205, 206, 208, 209, 217, 219 (*see also* Fort Jefferson)
Dunn, James, 161, 162, 163, 164, 171, 173, 190, 193
Dutton, Capt. George W., 133, 134
Dyer, Jere (Mrs. Mudd's brother), 19, 112, 113, 116, 187, 199
Dyer, Sarah Frances (*see* Mrs. Mudd)
Dyer, Thomas O. (Mrs. Mudd's brother), 202

EASTERN Branch Bridge, 39
Edward, Dr. E. W., 170
Eglent, Elzee, 106
Egypt, 198
Eisenhower, Dwight D., 214
Eisenschiml, Otto (historian), viii, 55, 60
Ekin, Brevet Brig. Gen. James A., 86, 128
Ellsler, John L., 31

Elmira, N.Y., 197
Emancipation Proclamation, 20
England, 194, 198
Europe, 145
Evans, William A., 106, 107, 111, 112, 115, 123
Ewing, Hugh, 90
Ewing, Thomas, Jr. (Dr. Mudd's and Sam Arnold's atty.), 89-90, 91, 93, 97-98, 101, 103-04, 106, 110-14, 115, 117-19, 120, 122, 123-25, 126, 130, 131, 132, 133, 134, 135, 146, 153, 208, 211
Ewing, Thomas, Sr., 90

FARRELL, Francis R., 12
Finlay, Dr. Carlos, 175, 179
First Baptist Church, Washington, D.C., 215
Fitzpatrick, Honora, 106
Fletcher, John, 42
Florida, 140, 142, 143, 147
Florida, the gunboat, 132, 133, 134, 139, 146, 147
Florida Keys, 140, 142, 143, 219
Ford, John T., 70, 71, 199, 215
Ford's Atheneum, 215
Ford's Theater, 5, 6, 12, 15, 20, 33, 35, 37, 39, 40, 45, 49, 68, 81, 99, 100, 110, 125, 206, 215-16
Forrest, Edwin, 35
Fort Jefferson, viii, 132, 139-45, 146-47, 149, 150, 154, 155, 156-64, 165, 171-74, 175-86, 188, 189-90, 191, 193, 195, 203, 204, 205, 206, 207, 211, 213, 214, 218-19 (*see also* Dry Tortugas)
Fort Independence (Boston Harbor), 144

INDEX

Fort Monroe, 73, 149, 158
Fort Pulaski, 145
Fort Sumter, 10
Foster, Brig. Gen'l. Robert S., 83, 84, 85, 128
France, 142
Francisco de Assisi, the frigate, 176, 177
Franklin, Pa., 31
Frederick, Md., 18
Fredericksburg, Va., 59
French Revolution, 72

GAMBO Creek, 58
Garden Key, Fla. (on which Ft. Jefferson stood), 141
Gardiner, Benjamin, 121
Gardiner, George, 21, 22
Gardiner, Polk, 42, 43
Garibaldi, 166
Garrett, Richard H., 61, 62, 64, 70, 132, 216, 218
Garrett, Jack (son of Richard), 62
Gautier's Restaurant, Washington, D.C. (Booth called meeting of conspirators here), 35, 36
Gavacan, Simon (detective), 39, 50, 51, 103, 120
Geeseborough Point, 76
Georgetown College, Washington, D.C., 18
Georgian Bay, Canada, 169
German Opera Company, 35
Germany, 85
Gettysburg, Pa., 219
Grant, Gen. Ulysses S., 7, 37, 70, 72, 82, 86, 184, 202
Grant, Mrs. Ulysses S., 37
Great Britain, 142, 166, 168
Greenmount Cemetery, Baltimore, Md. (where Booth is buried) 201

Grenfell, Col. George St. Leger, 89, 145, 156, 164, 165-74, 182, 184, 190-94, 195, 196
Grover's Theater, 15, 35
Guinea Station, 62
Gwynn, Andrew, 106, 113, 114
Gwynn, Benjamin, 106, 112, 113, 114
Gwynn, George, 106

HAMILTON, Col. Charles, 147, 148, 150
Hamlet, 29, 30
Hancock, Maj. Gen'l. W. S., 129
Hardy, John, 12
Harper's Ferry, 19, 85
Harris, Brig. Gen'l. T. M., 83, 86, 91, 97, 107, 110, 126
Harris, Clara, 37, 216
Harris, Senator, 37
Harrison, Pres. William H., 90
Hartranft, Brevet Maj. Gen'l. John F., 80, 81, 116, 126, 129, 132
Havana, Cuba, 143, 175, 176, 191, 194, 219
Hawk, Harry, 6
Henston, 4
Herald, New York, viii, 131, 139, 140, 141, 203, 204, 218
Herold, David E., 4-11, 13-14, 32, 33, 35, 36, 41-45, 46, 48, 49, 51-52, 55, 56, 57-64, 73, 74, 75, 78, 80, 81, 85, 90, 101, 107, 115, 125, 127, 128, 129, 132, 133, 209, 210, 211, 212, 213, 218
Hicks, Thomas B., 20
Hill, Gen'l. Daniel H., 158, 159, 162, 172
Hines, Thomas H., 168, 169, 170, 171
Hoey, Detective, 54

INDEX

Holden, Dr. J., 172
Holroyd, Joseph, 191
Holt, Judge Advocate General Joseph, 87-88, 89, 93, 94, 96-97, 99, 100-07, 113, 115, 117-20, 121, 126, 127, 128, 130, 133, 146
Hood, Brig. Gen'l. John B., 24
Hookstown, Md., 31
Howard County, Md., 77
Howe, Brig. Gen'l. Albion P., 56, 83, 85
Hughes, Col. J. J., 58
Hunter, Maj. Gen'l. David, 56, 83, 84, 85, 91, 94, 99, 101, 107, 110, 116, 126, 128, 129, 130

ILLINOIS, 169
Indiana, 167
Indianapolis, Ind., 89, 196
Ingraham, Colonel, 68
Inquirer (Philadelphia), 109
Italy, 198

Jack Cade (play), 35
Jackson, George T., 192
Jefferson, Thomas, 142
Jennifers, the, 18
Jett, Willie S., 59, 60, 61, 62, 64, 69, 132
John S. Ide, the steamer, 60
Johns Hopkins hospital, 206
Johnson, Andrew, 7, 40, 72, 82, 83, 88, 95, 128, 129, 134, 146, 158, 159, 171, 186, 199, 200, 201, 202, 205, 208
Johnson, Bradly, 171, 190
Johnson's Cabinet, 82
Johnson, Reverdy, 91, 92, 97, 122
Jones, Robert R., 95
Jones, Thomas A., 52, 56, 57, 70, 132, 208, 218

KANSAS, 90
Kautz, Brevet Maj. Gen'l. August V., 83, 85, 128
Keene, Laura, 37
Kelly, Seaman Henry, 153, 154, 155
Kentucky, 165, 167
Key West, Fla., 140, 144, 150, 161, 164, 176, 180, 184, 185, 189, 191, 193, 203
Kirkwood House, 95, 96, 134

LAVERTY, Detective, 54
Leale, Dr. Charles, 6
Lee, John, 95
Lee, Gen'l. Robert E., 37, 166
Life of Dr. Samuel A. Mudd, The, viii
Lincoln, Pres. Abraham, vii, viii, 4, 6, 7, 15, 16, 20, 26, 29, 30, 31, 33, 34, 35, 36, 37, 38, 39, 40, 44, 45, 47, 53, 56, 57, 70, 72, 73, 74, 76, 77, 78, 82, 83, 85, 88, 89, 91, 100, 102, 104, 106, 109, 110, 117, 120, 121, 122, 125, 126, 127, 129, 130, 133, 134, 139, 152, 156, 165, 171, 186, 196, 197, 199, 200, 203, 206, 209, 211, 213
Lincoln, Mrs. Abraham, 6, 15, 37
Lincoln Museum, 216
Lincoln, Robert T. (President's son), 37, 70
Lincoln's Cabinet, 71, 72, 104, 105
Little Texas, Md., 78
Liverpool, England, 198
Lloyd, John, 23, 43, 44, 53, 68, 69, 84, 85, 132, 217
Lloyd, Mrs. John, 44
Lloyd, Joshua, 44, 49, 102, 103, 118, 120
Loggerhead Key, Fla., 191

INDEX

Lord Baltimore, 18
Louisville, Ky., 88, 149
Loutrel, 203
Lovett, First Lt. Alexander, 39, 40, 42, 43, 44, 45, 49, 50, 51, 53, 54, 55, 69, 100, 101, 102, 103, 120, 122, 212, 213
Lower Maryland, 7, 9, 10, 16, 24, 32, 50
Lucas, William, 58, 59

MACBETH, 29
Magic Flute, The (opera), 35
Maine, 85
Maine, the battleship, 219
Maryland, 10, 15, 18, 19, 20, 21, 30, 36, 39, 42, 46, 54, 55, 57, 62, 89, 90, 91, 94, 95, 98, 148, 197, 199, 202, 206, 208, 216, 217
Massachusetts, 158
Matchless, the schooner, 184
McAllister, Samuel, 115, 116
McClure's Magazine, 150
McConnell, Brevet Major C. C. (cruel commander at Fort Jefferson), 161, 162, 163, 164, 190, 191, 193, 194
McCulloch, Hugh, 82
McMullen, A. W., 193, 194
Mediterranean Sea, 198
Meers, Thomas Y., 31
Meigs, Capt. Montgomery (designed Fort Jefferson), 142, 143
Mende, Elsie Porter, 86
Merricks, the, 18
Mexican War, 84
Mexico, Gulf of, 132, 133, 140, 141, 142, 145, 154, 192, 193, 194
Michigan History Magazine, 80
Miles, Thomas, 35

Military Commission (which judged accused conspirators), 83-86
Milligan, Lambdin P. (his case used as precedent in Mudd's case), 89, 196-98, 213
Mississippi, 88
Missouri, 90
Mobile, Ala., 142
Montauk, the monitor, 75
Monticello, Ky., 85
Montreal, Canada, 33, 197
Moore, William, 9
Morgan, James E., 89
Morgan, Col. John, 85, 165, 166, 167, 168, 170
Morgan's Raiders 85, 165, 167, 168, 170
Morris, Clara, 27
Mosby's Command, 59
Mudd, Andrew Jerome (Dr. Sam Mudd's son), 19
Mudd, Dr. George D. (Dr. Sam Mudd's 2nd cousin), 48, 49, 50, 117, 118, 120, 121, 122, 212
Mudd Henry Lowe (Dr. Sam Mudd's father), 3, 11, 16, 17, 20, 48, 69
Mudd, Mrs. Henry Lowe, 189
Mudd, Jeremiah T. (a relative), 22
Mudd, Joseph B. (Dr. Sam Mudd's grandson), 217
Mudd, Lillian "Netti" Augusta (Dr. Sam Mudd's daughter and biographer), viii, 18, 19, 135, 189, 205, 206, 207
Mudd, Dr. Samuel Alexander (*listed chronologically*), vii, viii
  age, 3, 17, 99, 205, 207
  description of, 17, 18, 99, 204, 205, 206, 207, 213

236 INDEX

Mudd, Dr. Samuel Alexander—Cont.
as a child, 18
education, 18, 19
childhood sweetheart, 18
marriage, 19
children, 19
owned slaves, 20, 21
political sympathies, 20
house and farm, 3, 5, 19, 21, 204, 205, 206, 217
farm activities, 3, 4, 8, 9
arrival of Booth and Herold, 3, 4, 5, 8, 25, 39, 43, 45, 209
admits meeting Booth before, 12, 13
first meeting with Booth, 15, 16, 17, 21, 22, 34, 208, 209
second meeting with Booth, 22, 23, 24, 25
patronized Surratts' tavern, 23
involved as conspirator, 33, 35
delays informing authorities, 25, 48, 49, 212
questioned by authorities, 50, 54, 55
taken into custody, 56
Herold claims Mudd recommended them to Dr. Stewart, 58
at Old Capitol Prison, 64, 71, 77
farm damaged by soldiers, 68
first arrested, 69
Stanton responsible for his ordeals, 71, 83, 93, 132, 135, 149, 150, 165, 213
evidence compromising him, 78, 79
removed to Washington Penitentiary, 80, 81, 213
charge against conspirators, 82

Mudd, Dr. Samuel Alexander—Cont.
phrenological analysis of him, 86
inconsistencies and distortions in accounts of him, 8, 10, 13, 14, 21, 34, 35, 46, 47, 48, 50, 51, 55, 116, 117, 127, 209, 210, 211, 212
trial, 82-126
names his attorneys, 90
brutally treated in prison, 92
testimony regarding him, 94-107
defense by Ewing, 110-23, 211
defense summation, 123, 124
prosecution summation, 125, 126
sentences, 128, 129
questionable "justice" of trial, 130
treatment by military commission, 131
Ewing plans retrial, 131, 132
removed to Fort Jefferson, 132
plans escape from Fort Jefferson, 133, 153, 154, 213
denies "confessions," 134
wife visits Stanton, 134, 135
letters to wife, 71, 77, 135, 136, 152, 154, 155, 156, 164, 171, 177, 178, 181, 182, 183, 184, 186-89, 195, 196, 200
at Fort Jefferson 133-203
meets Col. Grenfell, 156
writes about Grenfell, 171
healer of yellow fever epidemic, 175-85, 203, 214
stricken and recovers from yellow fever, 185
soldiers petition for his release, 186, 200

INDEX

Mudd, Dr. Samuel Alexander— *Cont.*
case compared to Milligan's, 196, 197, 213
hopeful of pardon, 199
wife summoned to Washington to receive his pardon, 202, 203, 214
released from Fort Jefferson, 203
does yellow fever research for government, 206
returns to his home and practice, 206
elected to Maryland legislature, 206
statement to Sam Cox, Jr., 208, 209, 211
own account of events when arrested, 211, 212, 213
accounts of his death, 207, 208
grandson's study of his life, 210
Congress provides bronze memorial, 214
Ft. Jefferson national monument honors him, 219
Mudd, Mrs. Samuel Alexander, 3, 4, 8, 9, 11, 13, 14, 18-19, 22, 25, 46, 48, 68, 69, 71, 76, 105, 133, 134, 135, 146, 152, 154, 157, 158, 178, 183, 188, 202, 206, 210, 211, 212
Mudd, Dr. Richard (grandson of Dr. Sam Mudd), 210
Mudd, Thomas (family ancestor), 18
Muroc, Capt., 74
Murphy, Sgt., 159

NAPLES, Italy, 198
Narva, the steamer, 176, 177
Nassau, 168

National Hotel, Washington, D.C., 23, 97, 106, 107, 133
Navy Yard bridge, 8, 16, 39, 40, 41, 42, 73, 217 (*see also Anacostia Bridge*)
Newport, 44
Newportland, 44
New Hampshire, 143
New Orleans, La., 29, 145, 149, 175, 188, 202
Newton, Gen'l., 150
New York, 35, 131, 168, 185
New York City, N.Y., 143
Noriel, William, 191, 192
Norton, Marcus P., 106, 107, 111, 112, 115, 123

O'BEIRNE, Maj. J. R. (provost marshal of District of Columbia), 39, 40, 44, 54, 60
Octroon (play), 215
Ohio, 90, 167
Ohio Penitentiary, 168
O'Laughlin, Michael, 15, 28, 31-37, 71, 73, 80, 81, 82, 90, 95, 122, 125, 127, 128, 129, 131, 133, 145, 146, 147, 148, 155, 156, 157, 182-83, 185, 186, 197
Oldroyd, Osborn H. (historian), vii, 17, 18, 67, 77, 207, 208
Old Capitol Prison, Washington, D. C., 64, 68, 71, 77, 78, 85
Orr, James, 192
Our American Cousin (play), 6, 37

PAINE, Lewis, 7, 8, 32, 33, 42, 71, 73, 74, 75, 76, 80, 81, 90, 97, 115, 122, 125, 127, 128, 129
Peanuts John, 41
Pennsylvania, 158

238 INDEX

Pennsylvania House, Washington, D. C., 22, 24, 98, 107, 115, 116
Pensacola, Fla., 142, 194
Perry, Capt., 105, 114
Peterson, Miss (Dr. Mudd's governess), 18
Peterson, T.B. & Bros., 108, 109
Philadelphia, Pa., 78
Pike, Lt. Albert, 173
Pikesville, Md., 78
Pilate, Pontius, 135, 136
Piney Church, 9, 12, 25
Piscataway, 8
Pitman, Benn (court recorder), viii, 95, 102, 108, 109, 126
Pittsburgh, Pa., 72
Plowdens, the, 18
Poore, Ben Perley, 98, 99, 108, 109
Pope's Creek, 116
Port Conway, 59, 60, 63
Porter, Brevet Col. Horace, 72, 73, 83, 85, 86
Portland, Maine, 151
Port Royal, 59, 63, 64
Port Tobacco, 7, 32, 44, 54, 68, 95, 117
Potomac River, 7, 11, 16, 17, 32, 42, 45, 56, 57, 60, 74, 75, 116, 117, 132, 209
Powell, Lewis Paine (*see* Lewis Paine)
Prentiss, W. R., 150
Prince George County, Md., 68
Prisoner of Shark Island, The (film), 218

QUEEN, Dr. William, 16, 17, 22, 45
Quesenberry, Elizabeth R., 57, 58

RAPPAHANNOCK River, 59, 60, 63
Rathbone, Maj. Henry, 37, 41, 216
Reed, Maj. Walter, 175, 179
Reeve's church (*see* St. Peter's Church)
reward for capture of assassins, 49, 51, 60
Richards, A. C. (Supt. of Washington police), 43
Richmond House, 169, 170
Richmond, Va., 7, 11, 23, 24, 29, 30, 33, 34, 37, 52, 59, 70, 73, 85, 106, 134, 166, 168, 169, 171
Robespierre, 72
Robey, Franklin, 52
Robinson, Lt. Frederick, 172, 173, 174
Roby, Len, 9, 44
Roby, Rufus, 9, 44
Rockville, Md., 33, 34
Rollins, William, 60, 61, 63
Roscoe, Theodore (historian), viii, 60
Route 301, U.S. Highway, 217, 218
Ruggles, Lt., 59

SAGINAW, Mich., 210
St. Charles College, Howard County, Md., 77
St. Ignatius Church, Port Tobacco, Md., 68
St. John's College, Frederick, Md., 18
St. Louis, Mo., 90
St. Mary's Roman Catholic Church, Bryantown, Md., 15, 17, 21, 48, 207, 208
St. Mathew's Institute, Washington, D.C., 78
St. Peter's Church, Bryantown, Md., 48, 206, 217
St. Timothy's Hall, Catonsville, Md., 28

INDEX

Sand Key, Fla., 180
Saturday Evening Post, 143
Saugus, the monitor, 74, 75
Scott, the ship, 153, 154
Scott, General Winfield, 144
Secret Service, U.S., 75, 80, 149, 151
Sevastopol, U.S.S.R., 193
Seward, Sec. of State William H., 7, 42, 44, 53, 73, 82
Seymour, Samuel James, 38
Sheridan, Gen'l. Phillip H., 150
Sherman, Gen'l. William Tecumseh, 25, 90
Siberia, 139
Simms, Mary, 105-06, 112-114, 123, 131
Simms, Milo, 114
Smith, Harry (Dr. J. Sim Smith's son), 182
Smith, Dr. J Sim, 179, 180, 182
Smith, Mrs. J. Sim, 182
Soldier's Home (Lincoln's summer residence), 34, 36
South Carolina, 171
Southgate, Rev., 207
Spain, 141, 142
Spangler, Ned, 33, 35, 41, 75, 80, 81, 90, 122, 125, 127, 128, 129, 131, 133, 134, 145, 146, 147, 148, 155, 156, 178, 183, 185, 195, 199, 201, 203, 206
Speed, James, 82, 83
Springfield, Ill., 56, 83, 85
Stanton, Sec. of War Edwin McMasters, 8, 39, 60, 71-73, 76, 80, 82, 83, 93, 121, 132, 133, 134, 135, 147, 149, 156, 165, 168, 171, 192, 193, 199, 201, 213, 215
Steubenville, O., 72
Stevens, Rep. Thaddeus, 158

Stewart, Joseph B., 4
Stewart, Dr. R. H. (refused to treat Booth), 58, 132
Still Waters Run Deep (play), 36
Stone, Frederick (Dr. Mudd's and Herold's atty.), 90, 101, 102, 110, 111, 115, 122, 128, 208, 213
Stone, Dr. Robert K. (Lincoln's personal physician), 6
Stone, Maj. Valentine H., 174, 179, 180, 183, 184
Stone, Mrs. Valentine H., 183
Stuart, Gen'l. Jeb, 168
Stump, William, 38
Sumner, Senator Charles, 158
Sun, Baltimore, 38
Supreme Court, 90, 91, 92, 119, 131, 196, 197, 199, 213
Surratt, Anna, (John's sister), 73, 106
Surratt, John H., 8, 16, 23-24, 32-37, 43, 68, 73, 74, 75, 77, 78, 82, 84, 94, 95, 96, 97, 98, 105, 106, 107, 112, 113, 114, 115, 116, 125, 133, 134, 197-98, 199, 206, 217
Surratt, Mary (John's mother), 23, 33, 35, 42, 43, 53, 71, 73, 78, 80, 81, 82, 84, 85, 87, 90, 91, 95, 97, 98, 106, 112, 125, 127, 128, 129, 130, 132, 133, 197
Surratt's Gardens, 217
Surrattsville, 8, 43, 44, 78, 85, 97, 132, 217
Swann, Oscar, 26

TAYLOR, Zachary, 28, 90, 91
Tallahassee, Fla., 150
Tampa, Fla., 219
Tangier, Morocco, 166

T.B. (village), 44, 217
Tennessee, 105, 167, 199
Thomas, Dr. John C., 110, 111
Thomas, Dr. Edward, 185, 186
Thomas, Maj. James, Sr., 9
Thomas, Daniel J., 104, 105, 110, 111, 112, 115, 123, 130, 131
Thompson, John C. (introduced Dr. Mudd to Booth), 16, 17
Thornton, James, 61, 63
Thorpe, Lt. Frank (provost marshal at Ft. Jefferson), 190, 191
Times, New York, viii, 75, 96, 99, 104, 105, 107, 109, 110, 111, 112, 114, 115, 128, 130
Tompkins, Brevet Col. Charles S., 86, 128
Toronto, Canada, 169
Townsend, George Alfred, 44, 49, 93, 98
Trenton, N.J., 70
Tribune, New York, 208
Troy, Md., 117
Troy, N.Y., 106
Turner, Judge, 135
Tyler, 4
Tyser, 4
Tyson, 4

UNION, the (Unionists), 7, 10, 20, 46, 57, 70, 72, 84, 90, 105, 120, 165, 169, 170, 196, 212
United States Army, 69
United States Public Health Service, 206
University of Maryland, 19
Upper Cedar Point Neck, 116
Upper Marlboro, 43, 85

VAN REED, Lt. William, 157
Veteran's Reserve Corps, 39, 87

Virginia, 6, 15, 16, 45, 58, 60, 106, 132, 168, 216, 218 (*see also Richmond, Va.*)
Virginia Military Academy, 83
Visitation Convent, Frederick, Md., 18

WALDORF, Md., (present name of town where Dr. Mudd's house is located), 217
Wallace, Maj. Gen'l. Lew, 83, 84, 92, 99, 101, 107, 110, 126, 127, 128, 135
War Department, 12, 60, 71, 74, 78, 97, 98, 108, 147, 155, 200, 213, 215
Warner Brothers, 218
Washington Arsenal, 75, 80, 81, 86, 108, 130, 132, 201
Washington, D.C., 5, 12, 18, 20, 21, 22, 23, 24, 33, 34, 35, 36, 37, 42, 43, 44, 45, 49, 51, 52, 56, 68, 69, 70, 72, 73, 75, 76, 78, 82, 83, 85, 94, 96, 104, 106, 109, 115, 116, 125, 132, 133, 134, 135, 140, 143, 158, 168, 171, 193, 196, 197, 200, 202, 203, 205, 209, 213, 215, 216
Washington, Frank, 3, 4, 10
Watkins, Capt., 46
Watson, William J., 111
Watts, Judge R. A., 80, 81, 88, 116, 124, 127
Web of Conspiracy, The, viii
Welles, Gideon, 82, 88
Wells, Col. H. H., 55, 69, 84, 103, 104, 213
Wentworth, Maj. George E. 153, 154, 155, 156
West Point, 83, 85, 143, 166
White, Capt., 105, 114

INDEX

White House, The, 30, 53, 83, 85, 201, 202
Whitehurst, Dr. D. W., 180, 185
Why Was Lincoln Murdered?, viii
Wiechmann, Louis, 23-25, 43, 70, 77-79, 85, 94-98, 105, 115, 116, 123, 125, 132, 133, 197, 198
Williams, Detective William, 39, 40, 50, 51, 103, 120
Wilmer, Parson, 9, 25, 43, 49
Woodbury, Capt. Daniel Phineas, 143

Woodland, Henry, 60
Woodville, Md., 110
World, New York, viii, 44, 93, 98, 171, 172, 190
Wright, Lt. Horatio G., 143
Wyndham, Sir Charles, 27, 29

YELLOWSTONE National Park, 219

ZEKIAH Swamp, 9, 11, 25, 26, 56

Hal Higdon has been a professional writer for over four decades. He is a frequent contributor to *Runner's World* and is author of the bestseller *Marathon*. In 2003, the American Society of Journalists and Authors awarded him the Career Achievement Award. He is the author of thirty-four books, including *Leopold and Loeb: The Crime of the Century*.